MW01005735

They Love a Man in the Country

PEACHTREE PUBLISHERS, LTD.
ATLANTA ★ MEMPHIS

Published by
Peachtree Publishers, Ltd.
494 Armour Circle, NE
Atlanta, Georgia 30324

Manufactured in the United States of America

10 9 8 7 6 5 4 3 2 1

Design by Lisa Lytton-Smith

Library of Congress Cataloging in Publication Data

Bowles, Billy.
They love a man in the country : saints and sinners in the South/
Billy Bowles, Remer Tyson.
p. cm.
Includes index.
ISBN 0-934601-67-4:
1. Southern States—Politics and government—1865–1950.
2. Southern States—Politics and government—1951–
I. Tyson, Remer. II. Title.
F215.B69 1989
975'.04—dc19 89-30327
CIP

ISBN 0-934601-67-4

To Fred Travis of Tennessee,
Rex Thomas of Alabama,
and others who meet the deadlines
and love the rogues.

Contents

They Love a Man in the Country

Buzzard a la King

In Texas, the Harris County district attorney in Houston once rivaled the governor in power and influence. Texans still talk about a D.A.'s race just after World War I between Tom Branch and Tom Clark.

Branch was a country lawyer and legal scholar. He wore celluloid collars and galluses. Clark was a political hanger-on. They clashed in debate on a hot Saturday afternoon in Baytown, Texas.

Farmers cooled themselves with funeral home fans and the barbecue simmered off to the side as the candidates mounted a specially built platform.

Branch spoke first, then Clark, who saved a sucker punch for the end:

"I had promised myself I'd never mention this," Clark said, "but this job is so important I have to. I fought for my country in the war. But let me tell you what Tom Branch did. When the Army was fixing to get him, Tom Branch went out behind the barn and he took the axe and he cut off his trigger finger."

Turning to face his opponent, Clark thrust his own trigger finger into the air and cried out: "Show 'em your trigger finger, Tom Branch, show 'em your trigger finger!"

Everyone in the crowd knew that Branch had lost his index finger in a childhood accident. But he made a mistake. Instinctively, he clapped his hand over the stub, and the crowd saw him.

Rising for his rebuttal, Branch mopped away the sweat on his face and began slowly:

"Yes, it's true. When the Army came to get me I went out behind the barn, and like Tom Clark says, I took the axe and I cut off my trigger finger."

The crowd stirred.

"But let me tell you why I did it. You all knew my daddy. You know he fought in the War Between the States. You remember when he died. On his death bed he turned to me, his oldest boy, and he made me promise I would never leave my mama and my sisters and my brothers. So when the war came, I had a choice. I could go and fight for my country, or I could break the promise I made to my daddy on his death bed. I decided I had to keep my word. So I went out behind the barn and I took the axe and, like Tom Clark says, I cut off my trigger finger."

It was so quiet you could hear the barbecue sizzling.

"But let me tell you how Tom Clark got in the Army. When the Army came for him, they didn't find Tom Clark. His mother was so ashamed she told them where Tom Clark was hiding in the brush. They had to go out and get him. They took him by the collar and they drug him through the brambles. The marks of those brambles are still there."

Wheeling to face his opponent, Branch pointed the stub of his trigger finger and bellowed: "Show 'em your ass, Tom Clark, show 'em your ass!"

Tom Branch won the election.

And all over the South, Tom Branches won elections with their performances on the stump. It was an era when politics in the South was theater, before television ruined it, and a politician had to entertain you or he was a cooked goose. Issues didn't matter unless they concerned race.

Saul Friedman, who cut his newspapering teeth in Texas, told us about Tom Branch and Tom Clark just as we were setting out to gather material for this book. It was a venture we undertook for the same reason a farmer from Columbus County, North Carolina, said he ate a buzzard: "for the big of it."

But this is not a joke book or a collection of tall tales. Our stories are rooted in real events involving real people. Some were not politicians. Early on, we decided we could not ignore bootleggers, undertakers, newspaper reporters, lobbyists, mule traders and other saints and sinners. We have been faithful to the way the stories were told to us, but we can't vouch that they have not been improved upon in their many tellings. A story is like good whiskey and violins. It gets better with age.

We made three forays into the South in 1977, 1978 and 1979, traveling in a beat-up Volkswagen and sleeping on the ground. Those trips were stories in themselves. Some of the stories came from our many years of covering Southern politicians. Jobs that separated us by several thousand miles delayed the writing until 1987.

At the outset, our main concern was to find the people who lived these stories, or knew them well, before they died off. We weren't always lucky. Tom Bevier, a newspaper fugitive from Memphis, told us not to miss Judge Soggy Sweat in Corinth, Mississippi. When we arrived in Corinth we dialed directory assistance and the operator who answered told us: "He passed away last week." Others, including Marvin Griffin of Georgia and Jim Cummings of Tennessee, have died since we interviewed them. Big Jim Folsom of Alabama died while we were writing.

Our newspaper friends and old politicians, out of office and no longer having anything to hide, knew instantly what we were looking for. Often as not they leaped into their stories.

In recounting them, we have kept in mind George Wallace's description of Terry Sanford when the two former Southern governors were running for President in 1972. "He's a fine, high-type gentleman," Wallace said, "but he'll bore your ass off."

This is not a fine, high-type book.

II

I

Tennessee's Unholy Trinity

In the 1950s a trio of country lawyers from Middle Tennessee gained notoriety in the state capital at Nashville as the Unholy Trinity.

The three lawyer-legislators were Jim Cummings of Woodbury, I.D. Beasley of Carthage and Pete Haynes of Winchester.

A playful spirit and love of high jinks masked the seriousness of their work. Their modest aim was to run the state. Cummings once summed up their philosophy succinctly: raise the money in the cities and spend it in the country.

As a byproduct, Cummings saw to it that there were more people on the state payroll in his tiny Cannon County than in metropolitan Knoxville.

Beasley, a roly-poly bachelor who chewed on his cigars, brought so much state largesse to Smith County his grateful constituents and critics alike referred to him as an industry.

Haynes, a crack criminal lawyer who chewed tobacco and used a spittoon, amassed power summed up in his nickname.

Although he never held the office, his political friends addressed him as "governor."

This merry, mischevious country cabal held such a grasp on state government that Memphis, Tennessee's largest city, had to sue in federal court for relief. As a result, a 1962 United States Supreme Court decision changed the politics of the nation and set off rumblings throughout the world. The court decision established the constitutional principle of one-man, one-vote.

1

Mister Jim and Miss Linda

HIS VOICE PRECEDED his presence. Jim Cummings was talking on the telephone in the next room, but we could hear him as we conversed with his secretary, Linda Brown, in the waiting room of his law office on the square in Woodbury.

"He'll just talk, talk, talk, and he won't let you talk back to him," she told us.

We had driven 600 miles to see this little pot-bellied man who tormented city bosses and Tennessee governors for more years than any other man in history. He started his political career as a Cannon County Circuit Court clerk in 1914, campaigning for the office on horseback, and he rose no higher than a state legislator from rural Tennessee. But he and his wily confederates took on the city slickers from Nashville and Memphis and Knoxville and picked them clean, until the Supreme Court changed the rules of the game.

When we visited them on a warm April day in 1977, Linda Brown was secretary, caretaker and companion to the eighty-seven-year-old country lawyer. She was a friendly, outgoing woman, married to the local postmaster for thirty-two years. She acted as judge and jury for Cummings when he tried out his arguments before taking them to court. If he failed to convince her of his client's innocence, he plea bargained. She also helped him keep track of his whiskey.

"Mister Jim takes a nip every once in a while," she told us as we waited for him to get off the phone. "Not very often. But when he takes a nip it lasts for about two or three days. He comes in and says, 'Well, Miss Linda, let's you and me take a little ride. Hell, I got to go home.' I know right then we're heading for the beer place." The beer place, we would learn in due time, was where you bought bootleg whiskey.

Linda said that if she located a bottle for Mister Jim at the office, he would say, "Nooooo, I don't have to go home."

Mister Jim talked on the phone like he talked in his parlor, at the top of his lungs. George Barker, a reporter for the Nashville *Tennessean,* said that Cummings "speaks as if against the wind." His voice, high-pitched and piping, demanded you pay attention to it.

Linda said Mister Jim was talking on a wall phone installed next to his desk because he was always losing the desk phone under the debris.

"When I started working here we had a home telephone system," Linda informed us. "You just cranked the phone and told the operator you wanted to talk to George Brown. But a few years back we got a modern dialing system. Well, Mister Jim refuses to let me dial for him. And he constantly gets the wrong number, but he finds out who it is and has a long conversation."

Linda first came to Cummings' office to operate an insurance business, then an income-tax business, with Cummings' late wife, Hesta. Years later, when Hesta Cummings got sick and quit coming to the law office, Linda quit a $600-a-month job to work for Mister Jim full time.

She said that when she offered to join him, "He said, 'That will suit me 200 percent. Now I may not be able to pay you *hardly* as much, but I'll pay you every penny I can.' So I said, 'Okay,' and I resigned the job and came to work. Well, about a month later, I said, 'Mr. Jim, it's time for me to get paid. How much are you going to pay me?' He said, 'Well, I figured about $60 a week.' I said, 'Hell, I'm not going to work for that.' Well, I finally got him up to $75. Six days a week."

We were in luck with Miss Linda. She had none of the protective veneer of the big city secretary. Not only was she an accommodating Southern woman, she also took pride in this old man and saw nothing to be ashamed of.

She told us of a busy week in the office doing income tax returns.

"He stayed in my office might near all day long," she said, "and to every one of my income tax people he'd say, 'Honey, let me hold your hand while she does your income tax.' And he would hold her hand. One girl said, 'You know, this is the first time Mister Jim has ever paid any attention to me.' I said, 'He's drunk.'"

Judges asked Linda to accompany Mister Jim to the courtroom because he was always handing them the wrong papers. One day when he went to court alone to testify in a land case, she got worried about him because he was gone so long.

"Directly I went over there," she said, "and the judge was standing out in the hall taking a break. I said, 'Judge, what on earth is going on?' He said, 'Mister Jim has not hushed all day. His attorney got up and said, "State your—" and he didn't even get "name" out before Mister Jim started. Mister Jim said, "My name is Jim Cummings." His lawyer has never said another word.'"

Linda said her husband, George Brown, had just retired as postmaster, and she confided: "Course, I don't need to be working here, but I can't leave Mister Jim. He's lost without me. When I'm on vacation, they say he won't even come to the office."

We heard the phone being slammed into the wall receiver, and moments later James Harvey Cummings walked into the waiting room hitching up his britches under his belly.

"I been talking to a damn recording," he announced.

2

"We're in the Penitentiary"

Jim Cummings came out of his office just like Linda said he would, like a hurricane. It was hard to get in a word. The voice we had been hearing belonged to a small man wearing a bow tie, slender except for a bulge in his middle that made it difficult for him to keep his pants up. He exuded mirth and high spirits and a devilish nature. He had the kind of voice that would make a dog howl.

"Come in here, let me talk to you," he said, loud and shrill, ordering us into his law office. "Come in here! Come right in, and we'll get ahold of this and see what I can do to be helpful to you. I'm cooperative, I'll say that. I'll try to help you if I can."

As we walked into his small, cluttered law office, Linda seized the opportunity to break in: "I've been entertaining these people," she said. "I told them a story or two about your telephoning and your lawsuit. I'm going to 'fess up about that."

"About *what,* honey?"

She repeated her confession but left out the incriminating parts.

"Oh, that recording," Mister Jim said. "This pretty, sweet voice said—and I'm not hearing good, maybe—that I'd gotten the wrong number and to hang up. I said, 'Thank you.' To a damn recording."

"And I told them about Sam frequenting the house of ill repute," Linda said.

Cummings explained that Sam was a client arrested in a whorehouse raid. While cross-examining Sam, the prosecutor had asked, "On this night, were you frequenting this house?"

"No, sir," Sam replied. "'I was not frequenting. All I was doing was sitting down there strumming my guitar."

Miss Linda was enjoying herself. She was invaluable to us as prompter, reminding the eighty-seven year old raconteur of stories she had heard him tell for years. Even when she suggested them, she reacted to the stories as if she were hearing them for the first time.

"Who were the two guys who woke up in the penitentiary?" she prompted.

Mister Jim straightened up in his chair as if startled, his eyebrows rose and his face lit up.

"Oh, that was my *BROTHER!*" he roared. "And Barton Dement. Look over there: that picture."

He pointed to a wall filled with pictures:

"Barton Dement's over there, he and Governor Clement, right at the far end, RIGHT AT THE FAR END! Do you see a picture right at the bottom, in this corner. RIGHT THERE! THAT FELLA!"

Clarence Cummings and Barton Dement were well-known lawyers from Murfreesboro who served in the Tennessee Legislature.

"They went to Nashville," Mister Jim recalled with glee, "and in the course of their day's work, they got to drinking, fooling around, overindulged. And they had some friend who was a guard out at the penitentiary."

As the night went on, Mister Jim said, "the guard realized that he needed to do something for my brother and Barton Dement. They were overloaded. So he took them out there and bedded them down in his quarters at the state prison. They fell into a deep sleep, of course. And the next morning they woke up and looked out the window and hell! Damn! They looked and saw they were inside the walls. Convicts were walking around."

It was as if Mister Jim were looking through a crosshatch of bars out across the exercise yard to the high walls.

"One of them said to the other, 'Whur in the hell *are* we? WE'RE IN THE PENIT—THAT'S the pen.tentiary. We're in the *penitentiary.*' Barton says, 'Clarence'—that's my brother's name—'Do you remember being put in here?' And Clarence said, 'Hell, I don't even remember having a trial.'"

Mister Jim took delight in the story. When others tell it, he said, they often make him the victim instead of his brother Clarence.

"Somebody got the story out that it was me," Cummings said. "I've been asked twenty times. I said, 'Hell no, that was my brother. That wasn't me. I'd a remembered the trial.'"

Friends in the Legislature were astonished that Cummings always showed up early for work at the state Capitol after fabled carousing sessions along Printer's Alley, Nashville's night life district.

"He was always famous for the fact that he stayed out real late at night with some of his friends," Linda boasted, "but he was the very first one at the Legislature the next morning, bright and clean and just feeling fine, and the others were dragging around."

"I had the reputation of not partying around beyond my ability to carry on in the Legislature," Cummings said.

"You just had a good time," Linda said. "Tell them the reason you told me you lived at the Noel Hotel."

"Well, there were two or three reasons. The Alley—Printer's Alley—was down behind there and so you could stagger in and stagger out of your room, didn't have too far to go. That was one little factor. But I never was one to be ashamed to be seen in a bar. And I was never one to be ashamed to be seen standing on the street talking to a gambler, or maybe somebody that walked the street. So I lived down at the Noel Hotel, frankly, because it was near by the Alley."

Cummings was a legend in the Legislature but his fame was far greater along Printer's Alley. One day in the early 1960's, he appeared on *The Noon Show* on Nashville's WSM-TV, and the host, Judd Collins, spotted WSM colleague Teddy Bart coming down the hall.

Collins hollered out, "Come here, Teddy, I want you to meet a friend of mine. This is Jim Cummings, a member of the Legislature."

Bart, who also played piano and sang at the Rainbow Room on the Alley, obviously needed no introduction. He greeted Cummings like an old friend. "Hell," Bart said to Collins, "he was the leader of my applauding gang for several years. He always led the cheering for my songs at the club."

As he told us these stories, Cummings chain smoked filter tip cigarettes, puffing on them till the butts were so short he had to slide them to the side of his mouth to keep from scorching his nose. Yet he had fretted that his late wife was wrecking her health with cigarettes in her later years.

"One day I said, 'Miss Hesta, you know what I believe? I do a little drinking and smoking, and I believe that smoking hurts me worse than drinking.' She smoked but didn't drink. She told me, 'Well, I don't doubt it, but I'll remind you of one thing, smoking don't make you act quite as big a fool.' That wound up my lecture to her about smoking."

3

The Pluperfect Mimic

I.D. BEASLEY, LIKE Jim Cummings, was a short man, and nearly as wide as he was tall. If you were introduced to someone from Smith County, chances are he or his brother or his uncle or a cousin owed his job to I.D. And the county's state employes revered the little cigar-chewing rogue from Carthage.

One day, Governor Prentice Cooper, a little man himself, with a hair-trigger temper, was hurrying through Smith County when the state trooper chauffeuring his car slammed on the brakes at a roadblock. Standing in their way was an old man named Shaw, a state employee who, naturally, owed his job to I.D. Beasley.

The trooper got out and tried to persuade old Shaw to let the governor through, explaining that they were on important state business and running late. While they argued, the governor got out of the car and stormed up to the barricade.

"You don't know who I am," he thundered. "I'm Prentice Cooper, the governor of Tennessee."

Shaw replied, "I don't give a goddamn if you're I.D. Beasley, you're not going through here."

Beasley spent his life in hotel rooms, living in the Walton Hotel in Carthage and rooming with Cummings in Nashville when the Legislature was in session. They spent a lot of their time with lobbyists, who were always eager to spend money on them.

"I've got a golden goose," they would boast when a lobbyist invited one of them to dinner.

Legislators rarely want for free whiskey when lobbyists are on the loose. So when Nashville businessman Mack Brothers sent Cummings and Beasley a big, heavy box labelled "Peaches," they assumed it was whiskey and that the label was meant to throw off nosy prohibitionists.

They put the box on the chest of drawers in their hotel room and went to bed talking about what a fine man Mack Brothers was. But both always had trouble sleeping with a full bottle in the room.

"Jim," I. D. finally told Cummings, throwing back the covers. "I think I'm gonna take me a drink. I just need a drink."

Cummings walked over and joined I. D. as he pried open the crate and reached inside.

"Goddamn," I. D. exclaimed, "these are *peaches*."

Beasley's fun-loving nature covered up a shyness that limited his law practice mostly to out-of-court settlements. He never had a wife or a home or a car. He hitched rides with friends or rode buses. Once when he was late for a legislative session because he had overlooked the change to daylight savings time, he introduced a bill to outlaw daylight savings time in Tennessee.

Balding, overweight, carrying 230 pounds on a five-foot-three frame, he said he wouldn't have a woman foolish enough to marry him. But a Nashville widow with whom he had a long-standing relationship told *The Tennessean* that I. D.'s love of Carthage prevented their marriage: "He wouldn't leave Carthage, and I wouldn't leave Nashville. But don't let anyone tell you I. D. Beasley wasn't a good man, capable of love. He loved everybody, but he ate too much."

In return, people were devoted to Beasley. More than

thirty years after his death, Tennesseans remembered him fondly. There are probably more stories about I. D. Beasley than any other Tennessee figure.

No one was safe from I. D.'s pranks, not even Jim Cummings. I. D. sneaked a drugstore clerk into their hotel room one night while Cummings was asleep and had the boy stand over the bed, his mouth foaming with toothpaste. When I. D. let out a blood-curdling yell and switched on the lights, Cummings woke to see the face of a madman, wild-eyed and mouth afoam, inches from his own.

Bounding terrified from the bed, Cummings grabbed a chair and started shrieking, "Kill him! Kill him!"

A stranger in Carthage once asked directions to the office of District Attorney General Baxter Key, one of I. D.'s close friends and a World War I buddy. I. D. accommodated the stranger but warned him that Key was deaf and could hear only if you shouted directly into his ear at the top of your lungs. Key later said, "That was thirty years ago, and I can hear him yet."

"I. D. was smart as a tack and was fearless, absolutely fearless, both physically and morally," recalled Joe Hickerson, Pete Haynes' law partner in Winchester.

When they were in the Legislature, Haynes approached I. D. to inquire how he planned to vote on a bill. Incensed, I. D. told Haynes it was none of his business and he didn't want to be told how to vote.

"Why, I. D., I'm not telling you how to vote," an amused Haynes replied. "I just want to know how you're going to vote. I've got you sold both ways and I've got to give one guy his money back."

Beasley was a mimic with a flawless ear. That talent was an awesome weapon, whether he deployed it for practical jokes or in power politics.

Railroad lobbyist and former legislator Dave Givens of Nashville said, "I. D. Beasley could mimic anybody in the world. He could sit and talk to you three minutes and call your best friend and he'd swear it was you talking over the phone."

Beasley mimicked governors, whores, angry fathers, mistresses and even his own mother to amuse himself and his confederates, further their nefarious schemes, gain revenge and sometimes out of pure meanness.

I.D. enjoyed a long friendship with Cordell Hull, who also was from Carthage and who served in the United States House and Senate and later as Franklin Delano Roosevelt's Secretary of State, holding that office longer than any other man. In 1932, I.D. also began a long friendship with Jim Farley, chairman of the national Democratic Party and FDR's chief political operative.

Hull, then in the Senate, had sent Farley to Tennessee to drum up support for Roosevelt in the 1932 presidential race. Hull directed Farley to attend Mule Day in Columbia, Tennessee.

Farley returned to his hotel room in Nashville that night proud of himself for the enthusiasm he had whipped up for Roosevelt and the national Democratic Party. In the glow of his success at Mule Day he heard the phone ring.

A voice he recognized instantly as Hull's said, "You jackass. In one day you've undone my lifetime of work for the Democratic Party in Tennessee. The best thing you can do is leave the state of Tennessee at once."

Farley was destroyed. He told Tennessee Democrats in the room with him he was bewildered. He didn't know what he could possibly have done to so upset Hull, who had always been one of his champions.

"Hell, Jim, that couldn't have been Cord," one of the Democrats said. "It was that damn I.D. Beasley."

"I.D. who?" Farley asked.

Farley's companions soon located Beasley and brought him, a little sheepish, to Farley's room. I.D. repeated the Hull performance. That started their friendship. Farley became Postmaster General and one of the architects of FDR's New Deal. He looked out for his Tennessee buddy.

Jim Cummings told us he always attended Democratic conventions as an elected delegate and that I.D. always went along.

"But not as a delegate," Cummings said. "Farley appointed

him sergeant-at-arms and, hell, I.D. had more privileges than the delegates did. Damn, he'd go to all the places that the Secret Service would throw me out of. I.D. was in a preferred class."

One of Farley's favorite stories concerned the extreme caution of Cordell Hull. Farley and Hull were riding on a train through the green Tennessee mountain country, gazing out the window at the scenery.

"Judge," Farley remarked to Hull, "that's a fine flock of sheep on that mountainside, isn't it?"

"Yes, replied Hull. Sheep or goats, one. I can't tell from here whether it's sheep or goats."

"Well, they look like they've been sheared."

"Yes," Hull ventured, "on this side, it seems that they have."

The Unholy Trinity saw as one of its missions in life to protect the people of Tennessee from foolish legislation such as truck-weight limits and morality bills.

"There was a preacher in the Legislature, old man Ruffin from way down in west Tennessee, religious gentleman, who wanted all sorts of legislation to establish morals," Jim Cummings told us. "He introduced every kind of damn bill you can think of. One was to require that all hotels keep a night cop on every floor to keep improper and, uh, uh, uh, things from going on in the hotel. Had several bills along that line. Everybody hated him for it. Hell, nobody wanted that kind of damn legislation."

Cummings said Ruffin lived in the Clark Hotel, a rooming house between the Capitol and the Hermitage Hotel where Cummings, Beasley and Pete Haynes were staying.

"Old Ruffin would go to the penitentiary every Sunday and preach to the convicts, good old man," Cummings said. "Old Miss Clark ran the hotel. She was a hard-as-nails and mean-as-hell old lady."

But Preacher Ruffin was her pride and joy. She called on him to say the blessing at the boarding house table.

One Sunday morning, the Unholy Trinity watched from their hotel as Ruffin left the rooming house headed for the penitentiary. They waited a short while, then I. D. telephoned the rooming house and asked in a sultry woman's voice, "Is Representative Ruffin there?"

"No, he's not here," snapped Miss Clark.

"I wanted to speak to him."

"Well, he's not here."

"When do you expect him back?"

"He'll be back after awhile."

Cummings said that I. D. hung up the phone.

"We all took another drink, and fooled around, and directly I. D. called back in the same woman's voice," Cummings said.

I. D. again got Miss Clark on the phone:

"Is Representative Ruffin there?"

"NO!" Miss Clark said. "He's not here. He's out at the—WHO IS THIS?"

I. D. gave her the name of a well-known Nashville prostitute and said, "I'm one of his girlfriends. He asked me to call."

That was too much for Miss Clark:

"I want you whores to quit calling here for old Ruffin. He claims to be a preacher and goes out to the prison and preaches all day to those convicts and comes back here and you whores call him."

"Well," I. D. said in the sultry voice, "he's a friend of mine and he asked me to call."

"I'm going to put that old bastard out of my rooming house."

Cummings said he and his co-conspirators watched Ruffin return from the penitentiary about noon and waited expectantly:

"We saw him coming out carrying his two damn valises."

Beasley once spent an evening on the telephone and threw the next day's legislative session into chaos, with senators and representatives accusing one another of broken promises and double dealing. George Barker of *The Tennessean* wrote that Beasley sat watching the spectacle with a poker face, "the only evidence of his suppressed mirth a stomach abounce with silent laughter."

Another time, speaking in the voice of Governor Hill McAlister, Beasley woke a legislator at one o'clock in the morning and summoned him to an urgent meeting at the mansion. Arriving in a cold winter rain, the lawmaker pounded on McAlister's door, waking an irritated governor.

"What in the world do you want?" McAlister demanded.

The perplexed legislator said, "Well, you called me."

"I didn't call you," the governor said. "That's that I.D. Beasley called you."

When Austin Peay was governor, Beasley tricked another legislator into voting against a bill after pledging to the governor he would support it.

"But governor," the legislator protested to the angry Peay, "you called me and told me to vote no."

Peay recognized what had happened.

"They'll have the fire made for I.D. Beasley before he gets to hell," Peay said.

Former state Senator Bill Baird said that Beasley terrorized local officials all over Tennessee by calling them on the phone and imitating state legislators who had the power to abolish their jobs.

"I.D. would call the superintendent of schools," Baird told us one morning in his Nashville office, "and he'd say, 'Well, I finally caught on to you. All this time you've been making like you were my friend. You're not my friend. You've never been my friend. You've fought me all the time and I've caught up with you and I've got the dead wood on you. I just want to tell you that I've introduced a bill abolishing your office.' The next morning at daylight the superintendent would be down here knocking on his representative's door trying to explain to him that he'd been for him all the time and trying to talk him out of introducing that bill. The representative wouldn't know what it was all about."

Baird told us he witnessed another prank that I.D. pulled on a state legislator and a pretty young woman on his payroll at the Capitol. The woman had a distinctly eastern European accent. Almost every afternoon, she visited her boss in his Nashville hotel room down the hall from the suite that Beasley shared with Jim Cummings. One day, about twenty minutes after the legislator let the girl into his room, I.D. called. In a distinctly eastern European accent, he asked if his daughter was down there.

Baird said the legislator replied nervously, "No, she's up at the Capitol. I haven't seen her. We're having a committee meeting down here."

Thirty minutes later, I.D. called again in a voice imitating the hotel desk clerk. He told the legislator that a man with a strange accent, mad as a hornet, was on his way up to the room. The clerk apologized that he couldn't stop the man because he had a search warrant and there was a deputy sheriff with him.

"We all had the door open, and it didn't seem like a second before she came running out of that room," Baird said. "She had a slip on. She come running out of that damn room in her bare feet with her shoes in her hand, running down the hall trying to get to the elevator. Old man Cox, who roomed down the hall, stopped her and called her into his room so she could put her clothes on."

Not even Beasley's mother escaped his practical jokes. After his death, she told an interviewer, "He would call the grocery man with an order and pretend he was me. He would say the most awful things."

Beasley died alone in his Carthage hotel room of a heart attack. Friends found a batch of prescribed medicine for a heart ailment that I.D. had never mentioned to them.

4

The Governor

FOR A COUNTRY lawyer, Pete Haynes moved in fancy circles. He hunted ducks with Associate Justice William O. Douglas of the United States Supreme Court, played cards on ocean cruises with bridge grand master Charles Goren and rode a camel in Egypt.

Haynes acted as front man for the Unholy Trinity. Jim Cummings operated as parliamentarian. I.D. Beasley performed as court jester.

The tobacco-chewing Haynes served five terms as speaker of either the Tennessee House of Representatives or Senate when a speaker held life or death power over legislation. He appointed committee chairmen and decided which legislation would come to a vote.

Furthermore, Haynes was a skillful forger. That talent came in handy when the trio needed a vote or two to prevail on a bill in the Legislature. They would draft a note on a personal memo pad they had stolen from the governor's office and send one of the opposing legislators scurrying down to see the governor.

"When a crucial vote would be about to come up we would resort to tactics you can't brag about," Cummings told us. "When the roll was about to be called Pete would go over to the sergeant-at-arms with a note signed by Governor Ellington or Clement or Peay or whatever saying, 'Would you please come down to my office. It's urgent.' He'd get that, and here he'd go running down to the governor's office. He dared not ignore the governor's office. He'd get down there and, hell, the governor's office would be crowded and it would take him ten, fifteen, twenty minutes to get in and find out the governor didn't want to see him. He would rush back and the bill would already have been passed and the motion to reconsider gone to the table and he'd have lost out on the bill."

The late Governor Buford Ellington once said, "If those three decided to kill you on a particular bill, they could kill you. It was as simple as that. . . . When they wanted something, they got it, by hook or crook. . . . Whenever Jim or I.D. or Pete came to my office, the first thing I would do was hide my personal memo pads."

Haynes' father, a well-to-do farmer and merchant in Franklin County, called him Pete because that sounded tougher than his real name, Walter. Haynes passed up a chance to join his father in business. Instead, Haynes studied law and became a successful criminal lawyer. In his first death penalty case, he lost his client to the executioner. But in more than 400 other capital cases he never lost another to death row. He turned down several offers from big-city law firms because he liked it in Winchester, the county seat two miles from Decherd, where he was born.

He used his ample theatrical abilities and quick wit with uncanny success whether presiding over the Tennessee Senate or pleading for the life of a client before a jury. He was a heavy-set six-footer who wore a scowl, but he had a knack of reading his audience. To help his clients he was known to limp a little or to shed tears. He won acquittal for an elderly client by weeping before the jury: "Are you going to send this gentleman with snows of many winters on his head to the cold walls of the penitentiary as he walks down the sad aisles of time?"

In another case, when he was defending an old friend and checkers partner, Haynes called his client to the witness stand.

"For the court record," Haynes said to his friend, "please state your name."

The witness looked startled.

"Please give us your name," Haynes repeated.

Puzzled, the man told Haynes his name.

"What do you do for a living?" Haynes asked.

His old friend bolted from the witness chair, enraged: "Pete Haynes, you've been in my store, and I've come to your office and we've been friends for forty years. But now that I'm in trouble you want to stand here and pretend you don't know me!"

At another trial, Haynes and his co-counsel, Pat Lynch of Winchester, were trying to discredit a young woman's reputation. While cross-examining her, Lynch angered the woman by questioning her virginity. Later, as the witness left the stand, she walked past Haynes and Lynch at the counsel table.

"You damn son of a bitch," she muttered to Lynch.

He turned to Haynes and said, "Did you hear what she called me? I'm a good mind to report her to the court. I'm an officer of this court."

"You'd better keep your seat," Haynes advised. "They might prove it on you."

By tradition, if a bill affected the affairs of only one county, the Tennessee Legislature enacted it automatically as a courtesy to that county's legislator. It also was a tradition for the new legislator to take advantage of this courtesy to throw his enemies out of office back home. Those jobs then went to the legislator's friends.

An east Tennessee mountaineer got elected and set out for Nashville to fulfill the tradition by abolishing his county's road board. Before the Legislature could vote on his proposal, the county road board members appealed to Pete Haynes to save their jobs.

As speaker of the House, Haynes' greatest power was to decide when bills would be called up for a vote, the exception being bills such as the mountaineer's that applied to only one county. Nevertheless, Haynes sought to block the mountaineer's bill by trying to befuddle the old man, timid and scared as he got up before the House for the first time. Haynes asked him about the enacting clause, the caption of the bill, its constitutionality.

Finally the old mountaineer told him, "Mr. Haynes, I don't know airy thing you're talking about, but I do know one thing. These here fellows, they fi't me from one end of the county to the other, and they said I was so ignorant that if I got elected I couldn't find the Capitol building. Well, I just want to show them I made it."

The House roared with laughter and Haynes gavelled the bill through.

The Unholy Trinity had its finest hour fighting Edward Hull Crump of Memphis, one of the nation's legendary political bosses. In statewide politics, Crump controlled the congressional delegation and hand-picked governors and United States senators. He ran Memphis like Henry VIII, imperially doffing his broad-brim planter's hat to passersby as he took the summer air on downtown strolls.

Crump could deliver votes to his candidates like he owned the city, which, politically speaking, he did. In 1934, Gordon Browning, a six-term congressman, ran against Crump's man for governor and lost because he got only 5,444 votes in Memphis and Shelby County. Trying again in 1936, Browning had the foresight to get Crump's endorsement and piled up his winning margin in Memphis and Shelby, where he got 59,874 votes.

Like the Unholy Trinity, Crump was a country boy. He left the farm in Mississippi when he was fourteen years old and headed for Memphis, arriving with twenty-five cents in his pocket. He ran that up to a fortune with his insurance business, largest in the South, and ended up owning a Coca-Cola franchise and bottling plants in upper New York State and plantations in Mississippi. The Coca-Cola tie-in was appropriate. With his red nose, pink cheeks and white hair in his old age, Crump looked like Santa Claus in the old Coca-Cola ads.

He was first known as the "Red Snapper," for his flaming red hair, then as Boss Crump. To his face, though, everyone but his wife and chief political operative, Frank (Roxie) Rice, called him "Mister" Crump. He was elected to office twenty-five times without a defeat, including four times as mayor and twice to Congress, but he really disdained holding elective office himself. At the height of his power, Crump often held no office at all, except czar. His real power lay in his ability to get others elected, which he did 118 times.

Crump didn't smoke, drink or cuss, but he had a mean streak as wide as the muddy Mississippi where it rolls past Memphis. Poor old Walter Chandler, Crump's man in the Memphis mayor's chair, had a high squeaky voice and couldn't carry a tune. To entertain visitors to his office, Crump would call Chandler on the telephone and ask him to sing the National Anthem, then play the mayor's pitiful rendition aloud over the intercom and laugh with his guests.

But Crump's chief weapon of cruelty was a poison pen that he applied in newspaper ads denouncing his opponents.

In 1948, six years before his death, Crump was starting to lose his political grip but not his will to fight. After electing Browning in 1936, Crump had a falling out with him and opposed Browning in the 1948 governor's race. Browning won the election, but did not escape the scorpion sting of Crump's customary full-page ad in the Memphis *Press-Scimitar*.

"I have said before," Crump wrote, "and I repeat it now, that in the art galleries of Paris there are twenty-seven pictures of Judas Iscariot—none look alike but all resemble Gordon Browning; that neither his head, heart nor hand can be trusted; that he would milk his neighbor's cow through a crack in the fence; that, of the two hundred and six bones in his body there isn't one that is genuine; that his heart has beaten over two billion times without a single sincere beat."

But even when Crump was riding the crest of his political power in the early 1930s, he was no match for the Unholy Trinity. The best known political story in Tennessee is what they did to Crump and his Nashville generalissimo, Roxie Rice, in 1933.

The two Memphis politicians were so confident of electing their man, Jim Corn, as speaker of the Tennessee House of Representatives, Crump went off to relax at Hot Springs, Arkansas, where he liked to play the horses, and Rice took in the Rose Bowl in California.

The three country legislators didn't take off long for the holidays. Instead, they assembled to plot how to defeat Boss Crump's man and elect Haynes as speaker.

"Mister Crump thought they just had it all sewed up and went off to the races," said Cummings, still relishing the memory when we interviewed him in 1977. "But we were in Nashville working at it diligently, and we were in striking distance of electing Pete."

They were at the Hermitage Hotel down the hill from the state Capitol when they calculated that Haynes would win if they could turn around one vote. Sitting around Haynes' hotel room scheming, they began to focus on a blind legislator from Chattanooga, D.M. Coleman, a Crump man known affectionately as "Coley."

"He was a piano tuner and a hell of a good man as ever lived on earth," Cummings told us, as he warmed to the story. "He came to the Legislature strictly to stand in with the powers that be and get appointed secretary to the Commission for the Blind that paid him a salary of three or four hundred dollars a year. He made it a point to be on the winning side if there was any way in hell to do it. He'd just as soon see his coffin coming as to be on the losing side."

They saw an opportunity to use I.D. Beasley's special talent at mimicry.

Cummings recalled: "I.D. said, 'I believe I'll call up Coley.'"

Fooling Coleman was an acid test for I.D., Cummings said.

"Blind men know things that you don't know how they know them," Cummings said. "They know them better than you do. But I.D. could speak just like Mister Rice. So I.D. called up Coley."

Cummings assumed the voices of his old friend I.D. and Crump's man, Coleman, as he recounted that long-ago telephone conversation:

"'Hello, Coley,'—I.D. didn't even have to tell him it was Frank Rice, it was so damn perfect.

"'Well, I'm glad you called me, Mister Rice. What's the situation?'

"I.D. said, 'Coley, I just called you to tell you, you've always been our friend and we got along. You know we've been for Jim Corn. But Coley, I just wanted to call you up and tell you that this Pete Haynes has got this thing won, and I just wanted to call you in advance so you could get in on the ground floor.'"

Cummings' belly shook and he wheezed with laughter at his story. He switched into Coleman's voice:

"'Aaaaaalll right, much obliged, Mister Rice. I've just been thinking about what to do.'"

But I.D. wasn't perfect, Cummings said. Before he hung up the phone, I.D. said in Frank Rice's voice, "Now you come by my room when you get to Nashville Sunday."

I.D. knew instantly he had made a mistake. If Coleman tried to visit Rice before the vote for speaker the next Monday morning he would find out that Crump's lieutenant had been in California and had not called him. But I.D. knew how he would deal with that later.

Cummings said, "Hell, the goddamn telephone wires hadn't gotten cold till the telephone rang in Pete's room."

Cummings switched again into Coleman's voice: "'Hello, Pete, this is Coley. I've just been thinking about what to do and I wanted to call you up and tell you I'm for you for speaker.'"

On Sunday afternoon, I.D. stationed himself at the elevator of the Hermitage Hotel, where Frank Rice kept a suite of rooms from which he ran Boss Crump's Nashville operation. Spotting Coleman as he arrived in the hotel lobby, I.D. strolled up to him:

"Well, Mister Coleman, I.D. Beasley."

"How you doing, I.D.?"

"Fine, Mister Coleman, where you headed?"

"I'm on my way up to Frank Rice's room. He told me to come by when I got here."

"Oh, yeah, yeah," I.D. told Coleman, "I've just been up there. He's got a petition to legalize the sale of whiskey and he wants you to sign it."

Supporting a whiskey bill in that prohibition era would have been the kiss of death for a legislator from Chattanooga.

"Weeelll," Coleman told I.D., "I don't believe I'll go up there right now."

On Monday morning, Coleman cast the vote that made Pete Haynes speaker for the 1933 session.

More than thirty years later, the victory over the Crump machine came back to haunt Pete Haynes when he went on a junket to the Florida Gulf with Governor Buford Ellington and other members of the Legislature. As they sunned themselves on the beach, an admirer of Boss Crump angered Haynes by rattling on about his admiration for the late Memphis political czar. Haynes finally suggested he shut up.

That night, Ellington planted a walkie-talkie under Haynes' bed and waited until Haynes went to sleep. Then, speaking into a walkie-talkie, Ellington said in a ghostly voice that woke the legislator: *Pete Haynes, Pete Haynes, this is Ed Crump. Why did you double-cross me in '33? Why did you double-cross me in '33?*

Haynes asked the lobbyist rooming with him: "Did you hear that?"

In on the prank, the lobbyist said he hadn't heard anything and told Haynes to go back to sleep.

Ellington waited, then woke Haynes again: *Pete Haynes, why did you double-cross me in '33?*

Again the lobbyist played deaf. He suggested that Haynes was drunk.

The governor woke Haynes a third time: *Why did you double-cross me in '33, Pete Haynes? Why did you—.*

Haynes sat up in bed and yelled, "You son of a bitch, I'll tell you something. I double-crossed you three times. You just found out about it in '33."

5

"We Just Got Fiercer and Tougher"

THE FRAMED PICTURES covering a wall of Jim Cummings' law office in Woodbury told a slice of Tennessee's history.

"That's my grandfather," Cummings said, directing our attention to one of the portraits. "My great-grandfather over there settled in this country and was a member of the constitutional convention that wrote the Tennessee constitution of 1870. That's his picture right there. There's my pretty wife. You'll have to brag on her. Here's Governor Clement. That's Governor Ellington. That's on my seventy-seventh birthday. They gave me a big party."

Among the framed items on the wall was a photograph of the nation's thirty-second president inscribed: "To my friend, James H. Cummings, from Franklin D. Roosevelt."

A piece of philosophy on the wall read: "Live so that when you die even the undertaker will be sorry."

Cummings served in the Tennessee General Assembly for thirty-six years, longer than anyone else in history. He retired in the middle of a term in 1971 without ever having lost an election. He credited that to his credo: "I went amongst the people." A long line of family members, dating back to Cummings' great-grandfather, served in the Legislature.

"Somebody from our family has been in the Tennessee Legislature a good part of the time since they got it," Cummings told us. "My people came here and cut the canebrakes off this country, built a log cabin at the head of the hollow, Cummings Hollow. I grew up here, and I've been here for generations."

As a legislator, not to mention a legend, Cummings was entitled to special license plates for his car. But he rejected such vanity plates.

"I wouldn't have the damn things," he said. "On my way back and forth to Nashville and other places, occasionally I would stop at places of ill repute, the least of which was bootleggers. When I was in places of questionable conduct, carrying on, I didn't want anybody passing and saying, 'Well, I saw your car at so and so last night. I never would have one of those damn things."

Cummings told us he learned that lesson early.

"When I was a boy," he said, "there was a young man that lived in our community that had a spotted horse. There wasn't many back then—now, they're common—but circus-type horses. Spotted. Dalmatians are the dogs, aren't they? I forget what you call the horses, spotted horses, but he had a spotted horse. We all traveled horseback in those days, you know, or we walked, a'courtin' or whatever we were doing, moral or immoral. And he had this spotted horse, and everybody knew every damn place he stopped. Wherever they saw this spotted horse tied, they said, 'Marion, we know where you were last night.' So I got an early lesson in my life not to be identified by your mode of conveyance."

When he first entered politics running for Circuit Court clerk, Cummings canvassed the hills and valleys of Cannon County on horseback, asking the farmers who had known his family for generations to vote for him. They shared their meager meals with him and offered him a bed at nighttime.

"I took 'em up damn quick when they asked me to go and spend the night with them," Cummings recalled.

Over the decades, one memorable night had stuck with him.

"There was a merchant who had a country store and was an undertaker," he said. "The man kept coffins, and if a death occurred in a family, people would gather and dig his grave and carry him in a horse-drawn vehicle and put him away. So this man said, 'Why don't you spend the night?' And I said, 'Yes, I'll do that very thing.'"

After supper, he said, the undertaker showed him his room, "the damn bedroom where he kept his coffins stored," Cummings recalled. "I was about twenty-two years old. All those damn coffins were piled up high and there was a bed right in the middle of them. Imagine me spending the night amongst all those coffins. But I was so damn tired I finally went to sleep."

Cummings told us about another night he spent with a friend that summer.

"Money was the scarcest thing, no money at all. Didn't have to spend any. No gasoline."

Cummings said his friend suggested that they go to church about a half mile away, advising: "It'll be good for you, mix a little religion and politics together."

"So we went down there," Cummings said, "and it was just one *big* room. There was fine preaching. Brother Stacy was up in his pulpit. We sang a few songs. I was sitting back there looking pious as I could be. Then Brother Stacy said, 'Now we're going to take up a little collection.' So they carried a little table and set it right out in the middle of that big room, and everybody was to come up and make their contribution right on the table."

More than a half century later, as Cummings told the story, he chuckled at his predicament at that small country church.

"I got to thinking, goddamn, I had just one big silver dollar in my pocket," Cummings recalled. "I hated like hell to give it up. But I knew if I went up there and took any change back, somebody would say, hell, I bet he took more change than he put down. So I just finally bellied up to the situation and went up and flipped that big silver dollar down so everybody heard it."

Slamming his palm hard on the desk in his law office he demonstrated how he had slapped down his last dollar on that collection table.

"That's one dollar that the Lord got off me that I begrudged, 'cause that was the last damn dollar I had. I was running for an office that paid eight hundred dollars a year."

It was a dollar well spent. Cummings won that election and every election he entered thereafter.

By the time we interviewed him in April 1977, his name had been enshrined on a state highway, a wing of a legislative building and a plaza across from the Capitol in Nashville, a Cannon County park and a women's dormitory at Middle Tennessee State University at Murfreesboro.

When university officials dedicated the dormitory, they invited Cummings, then in his mid-eighties, to visit the young women who lived there. Cummings said he told the officials, "It reminds me of the girl of the night who happened to get the wrong room number. She knocked on this fella's door—he was some fella that looked about like me—and she said: 'Pardon me, I knocked on the wrong door.' He said to her, 'No, young lady, you haven't knocked on the wrong door. You're just twenty years too late.'"

Cummings told us about another knock on a door when master mimic I.D. Beasley was still alive, and they shared a room at the Andrew Jackson Hotel near the state Capitol.

"My voice has always been a little high-pitched," Cummings said. "Some fellas in a room next to us mistook our voices for women. They knocked on the wall three times. I.D. knocked back three times. They knocked three times again. I.D. knocked three more times. So in a minute or two, our phone rang. They said to I.D., 'We're just spending the night here and we're from New York. How about you girls coming over and having a drink with us.'

"Oh, I.D. caught on right quick. He talked just like a woman, 'We can't. We're from out-of-town ourselves. We're not familiar with doings around hotels here.' Finally, I.D. said, 'You just come over to our room.' So in a minute or so here they came, knocked on the door. I.D. and I went to the door. I.D. said, 'What in the goddamn hell are you doing here? Are you the ones bothering our wives?'"

The men fled back to their rooms for their bags.

"When we looked down the hall, they were running," Cummings said, "negotiating the curve at the corner to go down to the elevator. Goddamn, they were striking fire with fire."

In his law practice, Cummings defended a Cannon County man accused of killing his wife by plowing her to death. The state prosecutor charged the man with homicide, contending that he forced his wife to pull a plow in the field and that she suffered a miscarriage and died.

"It was just a little old light, hand-made plow that this man and his family would pull to work their garden," Cummings told us. "So that got into evidence, and damn, it went like wildfire. The press services got it, and they went out there and found a damn great big horse plow, a number-twenty Oliver plow, on the man's farm, and enterprising news people took photographs of that. It left the impression that the man was hitching his wife and children to that big old horse plow. It got the widest publicity in the world."

Cummings won an acquittal. He said he was able to prove that an abortion, rather than overwork, had caused the woman's death.

In another case, Cummings got a man convicted of murder so he could go free. Cummings' client, a Warren County bootlegger, had been charged with first-degree murder after his business partner disappeared and his skeleton turned up in the bottom of a well many years later.

Cummings argued that the bootlegger might be guilty of second-degree murder but not first-degree murder, because there was no evidence of premeditation. The jury agreed and convicted the bootlegger of second-degree murder.

Cummings knew what the jury didn't. The statute of limitations had run out on second-degree murder after ten years. Cummings' client went free.

When we saw Cummings, his legislative career was over, his law practice had just about wound down, and he was confronting old age and death. He told us about a conversation he had on a visit with I.D. Beasley's brother, a retired county judge Cummings' age:

"I said to him, 'I'm still practicing law. I'm busy all the time myself. I just wondered what in the hell you do all day.' He said, 'Oh, I'm busy all day, Jim. I spend half my time trying to think of somebody's name and the other half going to the urinal. I never have a dull moment.'"

Cummings was in a reflective mood, returning to his childhood. "We lived about three miles from the school and we walked, carried our lunch, molasses in a little bucket and a bottle of milk. In the fall of the year, of course, they had to dismiss school for two or three weeks to pick peas and things like that. In the winter, damn whooping cough or the measles set in, epidemic, and they'd be just whooping and hanging their heads out the window, heaving and coughing. Everybody drank out of the same dipper, and it went from one to another. If itch got prevalent, everybody had it in school. If lice was on one's head, hell, before school was over everybody had lice."

Cummings' whole demeanor had changed as he turned to the serious purpose of his life:

"I came to know, at least it became my philosophy, and I carry it to this day and carried it through my entire legislative career, that people in rural, sparsely settled, non-affluent communities didn't have a fair chance in the race of life as compared with people who lived in the centers of wealth and population, who tripped to school down sidewalks or had buses to come for them, who had the best teachers, who had vaccinations against chicken pox and other diseases that interrupted or destroyed school terms in rural communities about half the time.

"People raised in the rural communities just didn't have a fair chance in the race of life. But come time to go to the war, they were big, strong-backed, weak-minded boys that made good soldiers. That's about the only time they participated equally with anybody else in government. And I made up my mind that I was going to devote my life to undertaking to correct, as far as I could, or at least modify, that inequity. And that's been the history of my life. I've made many a trade or voted for many a person's bill I didn't like in order to get support to help give more funds for health and education in rural communities. That's how Pete Haynes and I.D. Beasley and I became such fast friends. We all came from the same background and had the same interest."

Other legislators came and went, but Cummings, Haynes and Beasley returned to Tennessee's General Assembly year in and year out. Usually, two of them were in the House of Representatives and one was in the Senate, assuring them continuity of power in the Legislature.

Without the collaboration of the three country lawyers, a Tennessee governor couldn't get a bill through the Legislature. And the power of their rural bloc increased even more with the death of Memphis' Boss Crump in 1954 and the decline of his Shelby County political machine.

Crump's successors, pressed by increasing demands of a growing urban population, sued in federal court out of desperation. Acting in the Memphis lawsuit, *Baker v. Carr*, the Supreme Court handed down its one-man, one-vote decision.

"That meant the Tennessee Legislature fell into the hands of the centers of population and wealth, and our fight became more and more difficult," Cummings told us. "We were behind the eight-ball badly. But that didn't stop us a damn bit. We laid right in there and stayed with them, just got fiercer and tougher, and we fought, and my two colleagues died, one after the other."

Cummings cut one more deal, though. In exchange for his support of Governor Buford Ellington's plan to redistrict the Tennessee Legislature in compliance with *Baker v. Carr*, Cummings breezed through two more elections without a challenge from a serious opponent. He quit on his own terms in 1971.

"I had never been defeated for public office in my life,"

Cummings said, "and my observation is if you stay around long enough and ride a damn mule close enough to the mountain you'll finally get thrown. I wanted to get off that damn mule before I got thrown."

As we got up to leave, it was late in the day. The sun was going down on Cummings Hollow.

In the center of Woodbury stood the solid Cannon County Courthouse, dominating the little Tennessee town. Around the square there was no sign of the homogenization of America's small towns. No chain drug store, no chain hardware store, no pizza parlor, no Golden Arches. In Woodbury, folks still ate hamburgers at Haley's Cafe and Pool Room and plate lunches of fresh squash, okra and blackeyed peas seasoned with fatback at the Woodbury Cafeteria, where a sign out front advertised "Eats." They shopped at Webb's Grocery and the IGA. They bought RC Colas in twelve-ounce bottles dispensed from two faded vending machines standing in front of the IGA. The machines didn't tell the price of an RC, but everyone in Woodbury knew it cost a quarter.

Mister Jim and Linda Brown came outside to see us off.

We stepped out of the little building that Cummings erected in 1936 as a place to practice law. As we stood on the sidewalk saying goodbyes, the irrepressible Miss Linda told us, "If y'all want to have a beer tonight, it's on the left just before you get to the park. Bills."

"How late does it stay open?"

"Oh, he stays open to all hours, Bill does." Miss Linda explained. "He bootlegs whiskey from the house back there behind the store."

Mister Jim chimed in: "They're not restricted in practice to the statutes on the subject."

Standing there in the fading sunlight of this small town, Cummings looked frail. That thought had never come to us as he robustly talked away a morning and afternoon, taking us back to a different time. Suddenly, we had a sense of something coming to an end. Cummings was a man whose neighbors knew him, no matter what his mode of conveyance, and knew what they were getting when they sent him to Nashville to represent them. His kind was already being replaced. Voters were turning to politicians with Palm Beach tans, blow-dried hair and the voices of anchor men. It is a new breed the voters know only as an image on a television screen or as a stranger trying to slip a slick campaign brochure in their hands at a shopping mall while hovering aides, nervous about staying on schedule, keep glancing at their wristwatches.

As we parted, Mister Jim told us, "One of these days, the good Lord will bring you back through Woodbury for something. So stop. We've enjoyed it so damn much I hope something good will come out of it."

Miss Linda took him by the arm to steady him as they walked away, literally into the Tennessee sunset.

II

II

Gene and Marvin and The Georgia Wool Hat Boys

WOOL HAT BOYS LIVING in the branchheads decided Georgia politics from the end of Reconstruction until the coming of one-man, one-vote in 1962. These southern white men, after the Civil War, had returned home to find they had to do their own plowing, hoeing and picking. Their slaves had left. So the Confederate veterans put their hands to plowhandles and hoes and bent their backs over rows of cotton.

But they stubbornly refused to wear the cool, wide-brim straw field hats favored by their former slaves. Instead, the white farmers wore sweaty, narrow-brim wool hats. And as they bent to labor, the boiling Southern sun turned their necks red.

These Rednecks lived in the rural isolation of the branchheads. These are spots far back in the woods where water seeps out of the ground to form the smallest of Southern streams—a branch. Several branches flow together to form a creek, which joins other creeks to make a river.

When Republicans pulled federal troops out of the South in

the late 1870s, it opened the door for well-to-do local and state politicians flying the Democratic Party banner.

These politicians often represented the interests of plantation owners and big business at the expense of the poverty-stricken rural whites. But in the thickets of Georgia's piney-woods politics, these politicians were masters at masquerading as friends of the wool hat boys from the branchheads, appealing to their pride, their fears, their economic interests and their racism.

Eugene Talmadge—and after him, Marvin Griffin—were performers in a class by themselves on the Georgia stump. Talmadge rode the crest of the wave. Griffin caught it at the tail end of the era, as rural dominance was ending in the South.

That came about when the United States Supreme Court started handing down decisions on civil rights that made blacks a new political force, and on the one-man, one-vote principle that shifted power from the country to the city.

By then, most of the offspring of the early Rednecks had moved to town.

6

Black Widows and Red Galluses

OLD GENE TALMADGE billed himself as a dirt farmer from Sugar Creek in Telfair County, but he was a college-educated, land-rich aristocrat. He went off to the University of Georgia from the Cedars, the family plantation near Forsyth, Georgia, named for the matched cedar trees that lined the approach to the columned manor house. Talmadge pledged to Sigma Nu social fraternity and graduated from the university law school. He could trace his family in America back ten generations to an Englishman named Thomas Talmadge who emigrated in 1631.

Once old Gene got into politics, he created an image the wool hat boys could identify with. He arrived for courthouse square rallies in worn-out cars, pushed by a gang of supporters, ostensibly because he didn't have enough money to buy gas to get into town. He would get out of the car in a rumpled suit, his unruly black hair lying lank across his forehead. Once on the speaking platform and working the crowd into a lather with his fist-pounding rhetoric, he would shuck his coat and reveal his trademark, a pair of flame red galluses holding up his britches. He cultivated the image of "the wild man from Sugar Creek."

Roy Harris of Augusta, a lawyer, head of the White Citizens Council of America and one-time state political kingmaker, was sometimes a supporter and other times an opponent of old Gene. Harris told us, "All this being a big countryman, that was a pose with Gene. Of course he cultivated it all his life."

But in the 1942 race for governor of Georgia, the posing led to a loss of the most painful sort for old Gene.

"He used to like to open his campaigns in Moultrie, Georgia," Harris said. "He had a big barbecue down there. So, that was right when he was boasting about being a countryman, and he said he always liked to get in the middle of the woods to let nature have its course. A bunch of them were going down to Moultrie that morning, and they got in there some place close to Tifton. Gene made them stop to let him get out in the pine thicket, said he had to take a crap. He had the reputation of having a big, long one. And he got out there with that tallywacker of his switching around in the wiregrass, and a black widow spider bit him right on the end of it. He said it like to have killed him.

"When he got down in Moultrie, in the middle of his speech, he got so weak he had to quit and told them he was sick and asked Hellbent Edwards of Valdosta to take over and make his speech. Hellbent finished for him. Trying to show how big a countryman he was put Gene in contact with a black widow spider and cost him the election."

Harris' man in the 1942 race, Ellis Arnall, won the governor's office. Old Gene later told his political nemesis, *Atlanta Constitution* Editor Ralph McGill, that Arnall would not have beaten him "if that black widow hadn't bitten me on the balls."

But Georgia's white dirt farmers swallowed old Gene's countryman act hook, line and sinker. It made them feel good about themselves in Depression times when there wasn't much else to laugh about. As secretary of agriculture in 1930, before he became governor, Talmadge was accused by a Georgia Senate committee of using state money illegally to try to beat the hog markets in Chicago. He responded defiantly, telling Georgia farmers, "Yeah, I stole, but I stole for you."

So loyal were some of old Gene's supporters that they followed him from town to town to see his performances. Some would climb trees, perch on big live oak limbs overhanging the crowd and cheer him on:

"Tell 'em about it, Gene! Give 'em hell!"

And old Gene would wave his hand and reply, "I'm a'comin' to it, boys."

One family, the Haggards, was among the most loyal. Its members were called the tree-hanging Haggards.

Marvin Griffin, who commanded fierce loyalty himself when he was governor, told us about another strong supporter of old Gene in Berrien County, deep in south Georgia.

"Gene came down there in 1940 when he was running for governor, in Nashville, on a Saturday afternoon, to make a speech," Griffin told us. "One of the first ones that came up to him at the Confederate monument there on the square was George Rowan. Gene said, 'George, how you been getting along? George, I want you to help me beat this crowd. I don't just mean in Berrien County. George, ain't you got a pickup truck?' George said, 'Yeah.' Gene says, 'I want you to get in that pickup truck and cover all the counties that adjoin Berrien. And George, you look a little seedy. You got a job?' George said, 'No.'"

In 1940, the Depression still had a grip on south Georgia, Griffin said.

"Nobody had a job much," Griffin said, "except what you could scratch out of the ground. Gene said, 'George, when I get elected and get back in the governor's office in January, you come up there and I'll give you a job. You look like you need one.'

"Of course, George got out there and about wore out the rest of that pickup truck, tacking up signs and handing out handbills when Gene was going to speak in that section. Gene was elected. The day he was to take office, George was one of the ones who would get to the cafe at about five o'clock in the morning to drink coffee. A fellow said, 'George, you going to Atlanta today?' He said, 'No, Gene's got plenty to do today. He's going to be inaugurated today. He ain't got no time to mess with me about no job. I'm going to give him time to get his feet on the ground, and then I'm going up there to see him.' The fellow said, 'We heard him promise you the job. We heard him. If I were you, I'd go up there and get me a good job.'

"He waited about a week or ten days, and he come up there about five o'clock all dressed up and said, 'I'm going to Atlanta today to see Gene.' The truck broke down about Barnesville, but he got it fixed with some baling wire and stuff and made it in to the Capitol. There was a thousand folks milling around in there, wanting to see Gene about a job. George waited about half the day, and finally he got in.

"George said, 'Well, governor, I reckon you know what I came up here to see you about. You promised me a job if I helped you and you got elected, and I damn sure holp you.' Gene said, 'I know you did, George, I know you did. But I ain't got no job. I just, dammit, told you a lie. I ain't got a job. I just lied to you. That's all.' Gene had run out of patience by that time. George said, 'All right.'

"So he got in his truck and he come on home. The next morning, he was up there drinking coffee with the fellows. One of them said, 'You go to Atlanta yesterday, George?' George said, 'Yep.' Said, 'You see Gene?' George said, 'Yeah, saw him.' The fellow said, 'You get the job?' George said, 'No, didn't get the job, but I'll tell you one damn thing. Gene Talmadge will damn sure tell you the truth.'"

Rowan voted for old Gene as long as he lived, Griffin said.

Griffin went right into another Talmadge story. Old Gene was staging a rally in Gwinnett County next door to Richard B. Russell's home town of Winder in their 1936 race for the United States Senate.

"They were going to hold a rally over in Lawrenceville," Griffin said. "That was getting in Dick's territory, but Gwinnett County was always pretty stout for old man Gene. He set a speech down there one morning at eleven o'clock, and the Talmadge crowd was out there whipping up the damn bunch, shelling the woods to get a big crowd for Gene, to make a good showing, you know. They wanted folks of that county to know he could draw a big crowd.

"Well, the Russell folks had the same idea. They got to whispering around there and got up at least a thousand folks who were staunch Dick Russell people, and they put a pair of red suspenders on every damn one of them. They got just as close to the daggone platform as they could get. At a given signal, some fellow blowing a whistle or something, they hollered, 'We can't go with you this time, Gene! We've gone with you far enough!' With that, all of them red suspenders came off at the same time, and they flung them toward the speaker's platform. They looked like red snow."

The Russell people had alerted the press, and the Atlanta newspapers published front-page photos of the red galluses showering down on old Gene, Griffin said.

"That helped break old man Gene's back during that campaign," he said. "He lost to Russell in 1936 and to Walter George in 1938. Old Gene said, 'We've got to have the two best United States senators. I know, because I've been beat by both of them.'"

Griffin thought old Gene may have been cheated out of the 1938 United States Senate race against George, a prestigious Washington figure in national and international affairs who was chairman of the Senate Foreign Relations Committee for many years.

"I voted for Walter George in '38, but I ain't so sure old man Gene didn't win that race," Griffin told us. "You know the Talmadge crowd had a premature celebration, but they finally counted him out in Laurens County and two or three more counties, and George just did win. I've had some folks who were in on the deal to tell me they counted old Gene out, one from Laurens County particularly. I won't call his name, but he told me, 'I think you ought to know that Gene Talmadge really carried Laurens County, but we just couldn't afford to have him in the United States Senate.'"

"Why not?"

"They thought the prestige—they thought Senator George was not only a national but an international figure," Griffin replied. "He was a good old man. He was a corporation man, and of course if you believe in the free enterprise system, there is a place for the corporation. Sometimes it's one rabbit and one cow, fifty-fifty. One fellow puts in the rabbit for the barbecue and the other fellow puts in the cow."

In 1947, the Gene Talmadge era came to an end, and three men claimed to be governor of Georgia at the same time. They were Ellis Arnall, the outgoing governor; M.E. Thompson, lieutenant governor-elect; and Herman Talmadge, son of old Gene.

Drunken fistfights erupted in the state Capitol, the dead rose from the grave and voted alphabetically in Talmadge's home county, and Arnall arrived at the Capitol to find his desk in a lobby and the locks changed on the doors to the governor's office.

Arnall went back to the governor's mansion to hold a press conference and found Herman Talmadge and his family had occupied it.

Old Gene Talmadge's death set off the ruckus. He had run second in the popular vote to Marietta lawyer James Carmichael in the 1946 Democratic primary but won the nomination with a majority of county unit votes. Winning the Democratic nomination was the same as winning the election.

After the primary, Talmadge's family learned he was terminally ill and feared he would not live till January to be sworn in. Political friends quietly spread the word to write in Herman's name on the general election ballot.

Republicans did not field a candidate for the general election, but the Talmadge forces miscalculated. Herman finished third among write-in candidates, getting 617 votes to 669 for Carmichael and 667 for a north Georgia tombstone salesman.

When the Talmadge forces discovered their miscalculation, they reported that seventy-seven more votes for Herman had been found mistakenly filed in an envelope containing returns for lieutenant governor. These votes, mostly from Talmadge's home base of Telfair County, gave Herman 694 votes and the lead.

After Gene Talmadge died on December 21, 1946, lieutenant governor-elect Thompson contended he should succeed Arnall in January. Arnall and Georgia attorney general Eugene Cook agreed. But the Talmadge-dominated Legislature, on January 15, elected Herman.

Although his term had ended, Arnall refused to leave the governor's office until courts declared a successor. Thompson took his claim to the office to court. Herman Talmadge took over the governor's office and mansion by force.

Meanwhile, George Goodwin of *The Atlanta Journal* was in Telfair County tracing the seventy-seven Talmadge votes and found that in the Helena precinct, thirty-four people, some of them dead, had voted alphabetically. Among the thirty-four, those still living had moved away or failed to vote.

Griffin told us that in the chaos at the state Capitol, "I was the only fellow that got paid."

When the ruckus began, Griffin was Arnall's adjutant general in command of the Georgia National Guard. When it ended, he held the same job in the Herman Talmadge administration. His chief contribution, he said, was to protect the tattered silk Confederate flags, riddled with bullet holes, on display in the reception area of the governor's office.

When the Talmadge forces stormed the governor's office to begin their coup against Arnall, Griffin mounted a table and pleaded with them not to damage the flags.

"Goddamn the flags!" someone yelled.

Griffin said that made him mad as hell.

"I said, 'Hell, the *First Georgia Volunteers*? . . . You lay your hand on one of them old Confederate flags, and I'll knock you on your ass."

Nobody touched a flag.

Sixty-three days after Herman's coup, the Georgia Supreme Court declared the governorship belonged legally to

Thompson. Herman gave up the governor's office and mansion, but won election in 1948 to fill the last two years of his father's unexpired term. Elected lieutenant governor that year was Marvin Griffin.

7

The Thang That Got 'em Elected

MARVIN GRIFFIN, THE last champion of Georgia's wool hat boys, was one of the great stump speakers and an apostle of racial segregation and white rural politics.

But he tempered his views with telling country humor and never exhibited the meanness of other Southern seg politicians. In fact, a close friend and political co-conspirator of Griffin's was Atlanta Mayor William B. Hartsfield, who gained a national reputation in the 1950s as a leading Southern moderate on the race question.

"The newspapers would get after me for some stand I took, but I knew that the majority of folks in Georgia believed like I did," Griffin said when we visited him at his home in Bainbridge in the spring of 1977. "Then, I could afford to squall and raise hell because I had the majority on my side. I'd get to talking about what those fellows were trying to do to us. I'd put the onus on them as hard as I could. Of course, the next day they'd skin my ass like a blackjack. But that's all part of the game."

When Griffin was Georgia's governor from 1955 to 1959, an

unusually large number of state officials in his administration were indicted and convicted of corruption. The *Reader's Digest* said, "Never in Georgia's history had so many stolen so much."

But Griffin escaped indictment and boasted that he was the only governor in Georgia's history given a clean bill of health by a grand jury.

Griffin served only one term as governor, but he came from a political family and spent his life in politics.

"Politics is like killing rats," he said. "It's all day and all night."

He also gave the best definition anyone has come up with for the Georgia Legislature: "It's like three truckloads of bean pickers in the field without a foreman."

Griffin demonstrated his phrase-making genius and his prescience when he watched the 1960 presidential debates between Richard M. Nixon and John F. Kennedy. "Nixon," he said, "has the face of the accused."

The secret to Griffin's skill as a story teller was a simple one: "You have to put the saucer of milk down to where the cats can get to it."

In 1934, not long after he graduated from the Citadel in Charleston, South Carolina, Griffin won election at the age of twenty-seven to his late father's seat in the Georgia Legislature. He served as the powerful executive secretary to Governor E. D. Rivers in 1940. After four years of Army duty in World War II, in which he rose to the rank of lieutenant colonel, Griffin returned to politics as state adjutant general and was elected in 1948 and 1950 as Georgia's lieutenant governor.

After he left the governor's office, Griffin continued as a force in Georgia politics as publisher of the Bainbridge *Post-Searchlight*, the home town newspaper he inherited from his father. His front-page column was published in many other Georgia newspapers, and his reports from a fictional rustic character, Willie Highgrass, were widely quoted. Griffin kept a painting on the wall behind his desk showing the surrender at Appomattox, except that in Griffin's version Grant is surrendering to Lee.

Griffin has died since we spent the night with him and his wife, Laura Jane, in 1977. But he was full of vigor then. He showed us around Bainbridge, a wealthy town of 10,000 people with stately live oaks strung with grey-beard Spanish moss in extreme southwest Georgia, near the Florida border.

Although Bainbridge is a hundred miles from the Gulf of Mexico, Griffin made it an inland port when he was governor. He also started an import-export business while he was governor, importing rum from Fulgencio Batista's Cuba.

News that their governor was in the liquor business shocked Georgia's Bible Belt legislators. When a Georgia Senate investigating committee asked the governor if he was hauling rum from Cuba, Griffin replied, "I hope so!"

Griffin was standing in his yard waiting for us when we arrived. He was sixty-nine years old, a tall, broad-shouldered man with a face that reminded you a little of a friendly redbone hound. Right away he told us the sun was over the yardarm and it was time to strike a blow for liberty, which in his parlance meant having a knock of bourbon.

In the kitchen, he brought out a bottle of Evan Williams Kentucky bourbon and told us how he got into politics reluctantly in 1934, when his father died after serving in the Georgia Legislature for about twenty years. One of his father's friends, John M. Simmons, encouraged Griffin to run for the seat.

"I said, 'Man, I've been gone from here,'" Griffin recalled. "He said, 'They ain't going to elect *you* nohow. They're just going to vote for you on your pa's account. You don't think that, by God, they're going to elect you, per se, do you?' In fact, he said, 'I'll pay your entrance fee.' He did, and I served that term. That's the only term I served in the Legislature until I got to be president of the Senate as lieutenant governor."

Griffin represented a different kind of voter from his friend Bill Hartsfield, the Atlanta mayor. Until one-man, one-vote became the law, Georgia's county unit system favored rural areas so heavily that a vote in Echols County, with a population of 2,494, counted sixty-three times as much as a vote in Fulton County, which had 473,572 people. A candidate winning a majority of the vote in Echols county received two unit votes in the Democratic primary, where nomination was tantamount to election in those days of one-party politics. A candidate winning Fulton County, where Atlanta is located, received only six unit votes.

Georgia had 159 counties, all but six of them rural. Gene Talmadge used to campaign for governor in the 1930s by telling country crowds he didn't want any votes from a county that had streetcars.

"Old Bill Hartsfield and I, we were good personal friends," Griffin said. "He was against the county unit system, and he was for integration, and he was for this and he was for that, and he was for the big metropolitan area. Bill was for the *thang* that got him elected. And I knew that. Why, I knew damn well if I came out on a platform of that kind I wouldn't get to first base. I had the Crackers, the branchheads and the boondocks to contend with. That damn shore wasn't their philosophy.

"We'd get together in the campaign, and I'd say, 'Bill, you ain't come out and give me any hell lately.' I said, 'You know, it helps both of us. It would tighten things up for you in Atlanta, and you knocking hell out of me will tighten them up for me out in the state.' I said, 'Go ahead and get on me good and hard so I can pay you back in my next speech, and I'll jell a bunch of them out in the rural areas for me. It will improve both our positions. You ain't running for governor.'

"And we'd do it. And he'd call me and say, 'You're going to read about that speech I made to a civic club in Griffin, Georgia. I was down there today, and I tore you up.' And I said, 'Good, good, good. What did you say?' And he'd begin to tell me some of it. I said, 'Fine. Hell, that's good stuff.' I said, 'Naturally it'll be in the papers for me to read.' He said, 'Oh, yeah.' I said, 'Well, I'll tell you, I'm speaking at Lawrenceville, or Buford one, tomorrow. And you read the papers.'"

From 1948 to 1954, when Griffin was lieutenant governor and president of the Georgia Senate, he enjoyed the same adversarial relationship with the dean of state senators, Everett Millican of Atlanta.

"Everett and myself always knew what the damn score was," Griffin told us. "He'd say, 'I'm going to read the newspapers and ignore you this morning when you give us that off-the-cuff speech you were telling me about.' He said, 'I couldn't get re-elected to the Senate in Atlanta if I listened and clapped to that damn thing.' I said, 'I know. That's the thing to do, Everett. This is for state consumption. It ain't for you.'"

Griffin's speeches for state consumption dealt with race and got him elected governor in 1954, the same year the United States Supreme Court ordered integration of public schools in *Brown v. Board of Education of Topeka, Kansas*. Announcing his candidacy earlier that year, Griffin said, "I take my stand with the white people."

After he was elected, Griffin said, Millican came to see him at the state Capitol.

Griffin recalled their conversation:

"He said, 'You know they say it's silly for me even to think about it, but I'd like to be president pro tem of the Senate, just for the prestige of it, if there's any. I'm the oldest senator in point of service. I've been here fourteen years.' I said, 'Why in hell don't you run? By God, I'll keep the country boys off of you. You keep the city boys off of you. I don't see any damn reason why you couldn't be pro tem.'"

Georgia governors of that day were so powerful they handpicked officers of the Legislature.

"Shore enough," Griffin said, "a fellow from Dawson come in and said, 'Look a'here, I understand Everett Millican is going to run for president pro tem. Hell, he's no friend of yours.' I said, 'Now, wait just a damn minute. The man has been in the Senate for fourteen years. We've got to get along with these folks in Atlanta. Let's butter them up a little bit here to start with and elect old Everett president pro tem. By God, it ain't gonna hurt any.' The fellow from Dawson was planning on running himself, see. I said, 'I've done promised Everett I'd help him.' You know how it is, ain't nobody going to jump a new governor. Nobody's crazy enough in politics to shoot Santa Claus. So Everett didn't have any opposition."

There was a tradition in some Georgia counties for election officials not to report their returns until they knew who was going to be the next governor. Then they would make sure their county ended up in the winner's column. Fannin County in north Georgia was one of these, Griffin said. He told us about his experience with Fannin County officials in the 1954 governor's race. It involved him and his brother, Cheney Griffin, who would later be one of the Griffin administration officials indicted for corruption.

"I told my crowd, there's three fellows in Fannin County that made the rounds to all the gubernatorial headquarters," Griffin said. "Those were money folks, you know. They wanted $1,000 for carrying the county. They'd take a thousand from every damn candidate if they could get it, put it in their pockets and then count the votes like they wanted to. They'd take the ballots across to a fellow's corn crib, and they'd give the candidates what they wanted to give 'em. They just fixed things. I didn't give them a damn dime."

Griffin said Fannin County election officials guessed wrong in the 1954 governor's race and reported early that he had finished in last place in the county.

"Fannin reported that Tom Linder got 685, M.E. Thompson got 513 or something like that," Griffin said, "and it got on down there to me and I didn't get enough to wad a shotgun shell. They had gone over there to the corn crib and really fixed me up."

Later that election night, Griffin said, when it became clear that he was going to be elected governor, Fannin County's Democratic leader, Hoke Willis, called up Griffin's headquarters in Atlanta. Willis got Cheney Griffin on the phone. Holding his hand over the mouthpiece, Cheney informed his brother that Willis wanted to put Fannin County in the Griffin column.

"I told him, 'Hell no,'" Griffin said. "'It's bad enough to have to buy a fellow, but if he won't stay bought, he ain't worth fooling with. Tell 'em they missed the damn boat.' Cheney didn't tell 'em that. Cheney said, 'Oh, no! Don't put your county in our column. That wouldn't be honest.'

"He hung up the phone, and I said to Cheney, 'If we'd been tied in county-unit votes, what would you have told them?' He said, 'Hell, I'd have told them to put it in there. Be honest, but put it in there.'"

Griffin said dealing with local political leaders was not always so tricky. Uncle Booger Jim McCranie, the political boss of the little middle Georgia town of Rhine, could be counted on to do what he told you he would do, Griffin said.

"He was my friend," Griffin said. "He was the justice of the peace and counted the votes in the Rhine box. When I ran for governor the second time, they had all the precinct leaders in Dodge County at a meeting. They asked one of them, said, 'Joe, how is the governor going to do in your district?' He said, 'We're going to vote about a hundred and forty. We've got about two hundred and fifty registered, but we ain't going to get but about a hundred and forty to the polls. The governor's going to get somewhere twixt ninety and a hundred. The rest of it will be scattered.'

"They got down to Uncle Booger Jim McCranie, and they said, 'Uncle Booger Jim, how many votes is the governor going to get in your district?' He says, 'How many votes is he going to get? How many votes do I know to give him till I find out how many he do need?'"

Griffin laughed. "I said, 'Uncle Booger Jim, you got it right.'"

Griffin's time had passed by 1962, when he ran for governor against Carl Sanders, an Augusta lawyer who represented urban Richmond County as a state senator. But Griffin still drew huge crowds to his rallies at county courthouses from Rabun Gap to Tybee Light. In the tradition of Georgia stump politics, he fed them chipped pork barbecue and delighted them with country wit.

Attacking Sanders's performance in the state Senate, Griffin told crowds, "He hasn't got a record big enough for a tomtit to light on."

But Sanders, a younger, handsomer, slicker looking politician, came off much better on television than Griffin, and he swamped the sage of the branchheads on election day. Griffin's friends were shocked when he lost, because his crowds had been larger than ever toward the end of the campaign. They asked him what happened.

"A lot of people ate my barbecue that didn't vote for me," Griffin said.

Sanders became Georgia's first governor from a six-unit county—the ones with streetcars. He served only the one term, partly because his opponents latched onto a nickname hung on him by Griffin. In his race against Griffin, Sanders had distributed cufflinks in the shape of the state to promote himself, and Griffin branded him "Cufflinks Carl." To the boys in the branchheads, that nickname carried the connotation of the effete city slicker.

The best known story about Griffin, and the one he most enjoyed telling, concerned a battle in the Legislature over road bonds in 1958 when he was a lame duck governor, with less than a year left in office. Since he couldn't succeed himself under Georgia law, legislators already were choosing up sides for the next governor's race.

Building rural roads and letting city voters foot most of the bill was a good way to get the wool hat vote in Georgia. One of Griffin's first acts as governor had been to create a Rural Roads Authority and sell $100 million worth of bonds to build farm to market roads.

"Your roads are so bad," he would tell the farm boys, "your milk will curdle before you get it to market. Out there in the mud and sand, you've been paying gasoline taxes for forty years, and you ain't got a road by your house."

As he started his last year in office, most of the $100 million had been spent, and Griffin was under pressure from rural legislators to issue $100 million more in road bonds.

Corruption in the Griffin administration had been centered on the road contracts, however, and it had become good politics, especially among urban legislators, to attack efforts to pour more money into rural roads.

Besides, Griffin knew that the man who was an odds-on favorite to succeed him, Lieutenant Governor Ernest Vandiver, would want the credit for himself if there was to be any political gain in building more rural roads.

"I had rumblings that they'd probably fight it," Griffin told us. "I said to myself, 'Well, I haven't lost one in the Legislature yet. But if I do lose that one, ain't that a pretty good one to leave with the string hanging out if you're going to run again?'"

So he told his gang to go ahead and draw up their bill to issue the bonds, but to make it $50 million instead of $100 million.

The opposition rose up, just as he had expected, and the Griffin forces in the House of Representatives found themselves just short of the votes they needed to pass the bond bill.

"It took 103 votes in the House," Griffin said, "and I don't think we got but ninety-eight. It was nip and tuck, and they spent some money and they bulldozed some people."

That's where George Bagby came in.

"He's a little bitty fellow," Griffin told us. "You know George Bagby, from Paulding County. George and myself, we were the best of friends. I was elected governor, and for three years he voted for every administration measure I had on the floor of the House and made a lot of speeches for this one and that one."

But with a lame duck in the governor's office, Griffin's opponents knew his old friend from Paulding County was ripe for picking.

"They went and got old George Bagby," Griffin told us. "They said to him, 'You supported Griffin.' He said, 'That's right.' They said, 'You know, next January this time, where you gonna be? He won't be in office. The porters won't even speak to him loud when he's out of office. Tell you what, George, we got to beat this rural roads increased capitalization, and the city boys can't beat it. We got to have some good, old-style country boys speaking against this thing. If you'll help us beat that, we'll make you speaker pro tem next January when the new governor—Vandiver—comes into office.'

"Well, they took old George up on the mountain, and they showed him the green pastures, and it looked like the land of Canaan to him. Milk and honey."

Griffin said his own crowd also was "putting thumbprints on folks," trying to get the bill passed, and they asked him to talk to Bagby. He refused.

"I said, 'You have to remember one thing,'" he recalled. "'George is sort of looking out for himself. They done promised him something in the next administration. I'll be deader than Hogan's goat come next January when I come out of office. Let's don't fuss at him too damn hard.'

"Well, old George, he had to deliver. And he gets up in the House, and he says, 'My colleagues, I know what I have to say here on this floor today is going to enrage the governor. You know I've got a brother named John Bagby that's a license examiner out at Villa Rica, on the State Patrol. John was by my house and ate dinner with me last Sunday. I told my brother John that in good conscience I couldn't support this bill. I had to be against it, and the present governor would probably fire him from his job. But I told my brother: *John, that's all right. I've got a ham in the smokehouse, I've got meal in the barrel, and I've got a hoecake on the stove. We can take care of our own.'*"

"Well, I read that damn speech. I looked at it in *The Atlanta Constitution*. I believe it was on the front page the next morning. Of course, George had gone home for the weekend. It was Friday. So I called my secretary. I said, 'Come in here, Miss Maggie. Get me Colonel Peck Dominey on the telephone.'

"Now, in the first place, I didn't know George had a brother named John, and I didn't know John worked for the State Patrol as a license examiner out at the Villa Rica office until he told me, see.

"So I called Peck Dominey. I said, 'Colonel, have you got a man working for you at Villa Rica as a license examiner by the name of John Bagby?' He said, 'Now, boss, your brother Cheney told me to put him on.' I said, 'That's all right. George Bagby's a state representative, and this fellow is his brother. He supported everything my administration asked him to support until yestiddy. Now, George had a right to put John Bagby on the payroll in a job somewhere. Most representatives do get their brothers on if they're going to have to take care of them. But what time have you got?' He said, 'I got nine-fifteen.' I said, 'I want John Bagby fired and gone by nine-thirty. Can't disappoint a fellow.'

"And I said, 'Miss Maggie, take this telegram:

Honorable George Bagby
Representative, Paulding County
Dallas, Georgia

Dear George,

Get that ham out of the smokehouse,
get that meal out of the barrel,
keep that hoecake on the stove,
'cause John's coming home.'"

Griffin said his secretary protested.

"She said, 'My God, boss, you ain't going to send that to a state representative.' I said, 'I damn shore am. He bear-baited me. He just defied me to the extent he thought I wouldn't fire John. He just punched and gouged me.' I said, 'Miss Maggie, remember this: If you tell your friends you're going to do something, get up—if it's two o'clock in the morning and its snowing and raining and hailing or sleeting—and by God, get it done or get caught trying to get it done if you promised it to them. And treat your enemies the same way. Don't disappoint them, or they will never have any respect for you.'

"So we fired John."

Before Griffin left office, George Bagby ran for Congress, and one day he showed up at the governor's office.

"He come in," Griffin said. "You know, he's short and little and grinning to beat hell. I said, 'Sit down, George. What in the world's on your mind?' He said, 'Now, first, let me tell you, I got your telegram. And I took it and put it in my pocket and I went up the street and every fellow I'd meet, I'd stop and say, 'Look here, look here at what that damn fool governor sent me.' And he said the fellow would read it, then he'd start laughing and holding on to a pole.

"I said, 'What in the hell did you expect?' And he said, 'I showed it to about seven people, and they broke out laughing, and I figured it wasn't getting me much political mileage, so I put the damn telegram back in my pocket.'"

Bagby had come to seek Griffin's help in getting the political endorsement of an influential judge, Jefferson Lee Davis. Bagby said his remarks about Griffin during the road bonds fight had angered Davis.

"George said, 'I know you ain't mad at me, *are you?*'" Griffin said. "I said, 'Hell no.' He said, 'Well, Jeff Davis thinks you are. If you'd call him, I believe he'd support me, and he's got a raft of friends.'"

Griffin said he picked up the phone and called Judge Davis to tell him it was all right to support Bagby for Congress. The judge backed Bagby, but he lost anyway.

At a rally in Cartersville during his 1962 governor's race against Sanders, Griffin ran into John Bagby, the license examiner he had fired.

"The courthouse lawn was loaded," Griffin recalled. "I got through speaking, and by God, there stood John Bagby. I didn't know whether he had come to shoot me or what. So I decided the best offense was the best defense. All those overalled farmers and everybody's shaking hands. When I got down to the bottom of the steps, I said in a real loud voice, 'John, I don't reckon it would be kosher for me to ask you for your support and your vote?' He said, 'Hell, governor, I'm fer you. You didn't cost me my job. George did. I'm fer you. You do what you say you'll do. You couldn't do nothing else after George said what he did in the Legislature.'

"Of course, those Crackers standing around watching got to laughing. I said, 'I just want to ask you one thing, John, and I appreciate your support, and I want you to know I do. I just want to ask you, did old George have a ham in the smokehouse?' He said, 'Naw, it was sowbelly.'"

The George Bagby story illustrated a rule of Griffin's: "I believe in keeping politics honest. And the best way to keep it straight is to fire those who guessed wrong."

Griffin told us he had another rule in politics: "By God, there's going to come a time when you have to fish or cut bait."

He said such a time came when he was running for re-election as lieutenant governor in 1950.

"Anytime you didn't have a scheduled engagement somewhere, you'd just get in the car and drive fifty or sixty miles from Atlanta and politick," Griffin told us. "This particular afternoon, I didn't have much to do, there wasn't anybody in the office, so I took off to Fayette County."

His driver was Pete Wheeler, later state director of veterans' affairs.

"I said, 'Let's take a little jaunt down to Luthersville. Let's go,' and we took off," Griffin said. "I saw all these pickup trucks out there, and I said, 'Pete, pull in there. By God, there's a damn oasis.' Pete pulled up in there. I walked in the front door, and there was a fellow there. You can't be nice all the time, for sometime the public won't let you. You've got to shine your tail like a diamond every now and then.

"Well, I walked in this place, and this was before it was popular to have long hair, and this fellow's hair run all the way back down his collar. And he was about six-feet-three. He had me by about three inches. He was a tall, slim, damn fellow. As I walked in the door, all these cattle farmers were sitting there drinking themselves a soda water or a beer. And of course, when I walked in the front door, they all quit talking.

"Well, this fellow was sweeping out the front of the place with a broom. He stopped when I walked in. I walked up to him, and I said, 'Marvin Griffin is my name. I'm lieutenant governor, and I came by to see you and pay my respects and ask you for your help to get re-elected.' I stuck out my hand. He was one of those wiseacres. He said, 'I don't shake hands with any crooked politician.'

"All them farmers and cattlemen were looking at me. I said, 'Mister, you know, I came in here with good intentions. I want to tell you something, and then I'll leave by the same door I came in.' He said, 'That's the thing to do.' He was feeling pretty smart. I said, 'My daddy is dead and gone, but he told me one thing, he said don't ever start a row on another man's property, because you're in the wrong for being there in the first place. Now, I'm not going to start a row with you. This is your place, and I respect your place of business.' But I said, 'Twenty feet right in front of your place there is the public road. The right of way in the public road belongs to the people of Georgia. Now, you get the hell out there. I'm going to wear your ass out against the ground if I can, if the Lord will let me.'"

Griffin said he spun around and walked out to the road and turned to face the door.

"All them farmers got up, and they come to the door, see. They set down their drinks and come up there to watch, and I was standing out there. Of course, I saw he wasn't coming out, so I put on a little show. I'm glad that tall son of a bitch didn't come out there. I'd have had to whip him or die trying, you know. It had come to fish or cut bait. So I just walked up and down.

"I said, 'This is public property. It don't belong to you, and you insulted me. Now come on out here. Now, that's all I have to say.' He said, 'Oh, can't you take a joke?' I said, 'I can from a friend, but mister, I never saw you before.' He said, 'Well, I didn't mean anything by that.' With that, I said, 'All right. I ain't going to stir up anything.'

"But here come the farmers out of there. They said, 'It's about time somebody give that son of a bitch his comeuppance. Gimme me some of them cards. We're going to pass them out. We've got a real lieutenant governor. Give me some.' Me and Pete passed them out. There must have been twenty-five farmers, and they took fifty to a hundred cards apiece. Them Crackers were like me.

"I kept up with it. We damn sure carried that district."

Usually, though, Griffin needed only his wit. One afternoon in 1950, when he was running for lieutenant governor on the ticket with Herman Talmadge, he stopped to hand out matches at a little cafe in Doraville where Ford assembly line workers were drinking beer.

"Every stool had a fellow sitting on it drinking beer," Griffin said. "But the fellow on the end closest to the door—when I came in I made a hasty glance—he had six empties in front of him."

Griffin made sure he had shaken every hand in the place before he reached that stool.

"I'm glad I did," he said. "I'd tell them all, 'This is Marvin Griffin, your lieutenant governor, and I'm running for re-election, and y'all hired me two years ago for a two-year term, but I don't want you to fire me Tuesday week.'"

Then he reached the man on the last stool.

"When I got to him, I said, 'Howdy do, I'm Marvin Griffin, your lieutenant governor. You hired me two years ago. Now I'm running for a full term.'

"He blinked at me a couple of times, and he said, 'Mac, have a beer.' I said, 'No, I'm not a hypocrite, but I'm stopping in to see a lot of ladies going on my rounds to Atlanta, and I don't want to have them smell beer on my breath.' I said, 'Come play time, and the sun down, I'll take about *that* much bourbon with you in a wash pot, about three fingers, a mule's ear in a wash pot.'

"He looked at me, and he said, 'Mac, you seem like an all right guy to me. I'm going to vote for you.'

"Then he thought, and he said, 'But I'll tell you two sons of bitches I ain't going to vote for.' And the whole place got quiet. And I said, 'Who is that, buddy?' I ought to have had better sense than to have asked him. He said, 'I ain't going to vote for that Herman Talmadge or Marvin Griffin.' I said, 'You'd better screen 'em close, old buddy.' In the meantime, I stuffed that package of matches down his pocket, and that bunch, I just left them a'whooping and a'hollering."

III

The Folsoms: Standing Tall in Alabama

JIM FOLSOM PURSUED an old Southern will-o'-the-wisp. It destroyed him politically.

Against enormous odds in Alabama during the 1940s and 1950s, Folsom sought to forge a political coalition of poor whites and blacks.

His election twice as governor of the Birthplace of the Confederacy stands as testimony to Folsom's political abilities.

But the rising white resistance to the civil rights movement rolled over Folsom's spirited personality and political cunning.

And Folsom helped his foes more than they had a right to expect. He managed public affairs badly. He put his trust in some of the wrong people. He drank too much.

Through it all, his sister Ruby stood with him in public and private affairs.

Folsom, though, left an enduring legacy: He was right, and George Wallace was wrong.

8

"Going Places, Hell, I'm Places Now"

Big Jim Folsom loved drinking bourbon whiskey and kissing pretty women. But above all, he loved a show.

At a governors conference when Folsom was governor of Alabama in the 1950s, the Navy took the visiting dignitaries on a cruise aboard an aircraft carrier off the Virginia Coast to demonstrate how fast and skillfully it could launch airplanes. Folsom was the last to arrive, delaying the carrier's departure. The other governors, their wives, their aides and an array of gold-braided admirals and officious Pentagon brass were waiting when a taxicab wheeled up to the gangplank. The six-foot-eight, 250-pound Folsom unfolded from the back seat of the taxicab and stepped out holding an iced tea glass brimming with bourbon.

Folsom and Louisiana Governor Earl Long really wanted to see the carrier's engine room, but they remained with the other governors and the military brass when they assembled to watch the planes catapult off the deck in rapid succession. Folsom still held his iced tea glass, refilled with bourbon.

The crowd watched horrified as one of the planes hurtled

off the deck and crashed into the Atlantic. The pilot ejected and dropped into the ocean. Folsom's booming voice broke the silence.

"If that ain't a show I'll kiss your ass."

When we asked him about the story, Folsom laughed and said, "Well, that's right. I thought I said, 'A damn good show.' Well, it's the truth. Yeah, I guess I did say that. It took, didn't it?"

In his prime, running for governor in 1946 as "the little man's big friend," Folsom was a towering, handsome, outgoing man, exuding power. They called him Big Track.

Folsom wore a size fifteen and a half shoe. A born showman, masterful on the political stump, Big Jim championed the poor whites of rural and small-town Alabama, and they loved him for it. At the same time, he spoke out for the rights of Alabama's disenfranchised blacks when most other Southern politicians were getting elected as white supremacists. Folsom whipped the corporate "Big Mules" of Birmingham and the political bosses from the old slave-rich, cotton-growing counties of the black belt in south Alabama, the coalition that had held power since shortly after the turn of the century. In 1946, Folsom won the governor's office with the biggest majority in Alabama history.

Ineligible to succeed himself four years later, he easily won a second term as governor in 1954 despite a barrage of news stories about corruption in his first administration.

Life magazine reporter Paul E. Deutschman interviewed Big Jim in a hotel room in Mobile in September 1947, his first year as governor. Jim's brother-in-law, Ross Clark, an insurance man and honorary colonel in the Alabama militia, told Deutschman, "He's a big man, one of the greatest humanitarians since Lincoln and FDR. He's going places."

"Going places, hell," Folsom snorted, "I'm places now."

But when we visited him at his home in Cullman on an April Sunday afternoon in 1979, Big Jim had been down on his luck for more than fifteen years and was embittered at lawyers, blaming them for eliminating his pension. He was seventy years old, blind, nearly deaf, had an artificial heart valve, and the hopeless campaigns he was waging for governor every four years had become a sad joke. Yet James Elisha Folsom kept his dignity, and through the years, he remained a beacon for Alabama liberals and others opposed to George Wallace's segregation politics.

In 1974, editor Ray Jenkins and political reporter Claude Duncan of *The Alabama Journal* drove up from Montgomery to the Cullman County Courthouse where Big Jim was kicking off yet another governor's race against George Wallace. Jim's wife, Jamelle, was at his side.

"And there was, of course, Roland Johnson, clutching his battered guitar case and looking rather sad," Jenkins wrote. "He was the last survivor of the now-disassembled band, the original Strawberry Pickers, that Jim had carried around to entertain the folks while he discussed the issues. . . . 'I don't know why we don't have more people,' Jim began, 'we put an ad in the paper. But we'll have a rally. Roland, play a song.'"

Duncan told us he and Jenkins went by the Folsoms' house.

"Jamelle fixed 7-Up," Duncan said, "no booze at all. We talked to him. It got pretty obvious that Ray and I were admiring him, or humoring him, one or the other, or a little of both. As we were leaving, Jamelle thinks we were friends and all, takes my hand, and she says, 'Now y'all help out when you get back to write your story, and we'll let you in on the pie.'"

We arrived at Folsom's house five years and another governor's race later. Paint was peeling from the big, rambling, rundown house, small trees were growing from the second-story gutters, and the only telephone in the house was a pay phone on the wall in the living room.

Folsom's twenty-year-old daughter, Layla, greeted us at the back door, the only door anyone used in the busy comings and goings at the Folsom house.

"Are you the youngest daughter?"

"No," Layla replied, "we have a nine-year-old little one running around."

As we entered the house, Layla introduced us to a young man who cautioned us not to mistake him for a Folsom just because he was six-feet-five. All the Folsoms are tall. Big Jim's father was six-foot-six, his maternal grandfather six-foot-eight. Layla introduced the young man as P.D. Mynatt of Birmingham, her boyfriend.

She showed us around the house while we waited for Big Jim and Jamelle to come downstairs.

"This used to be a gorgeous house," Layla told us. "It really used to be nice."

"How old is it?"

"Gosh, it's over ninety years old, I know," she replied. "If pa could see, maybe he could realize what needs to be done. But it's hard for us to make him understand what needs to be done. Not seeing, he can't understand." Layla said they once had several telephones, upstairs and downstairs, but her father had replaced them with the pay phone about six years earlier. He said he did it because the children were running up high phone bills.

"We all knew it was him, though," Layla said.

We moved into the kitchen, and Layla introduced us to a next-door neighbor, Barbara Farrar, who had dropped in and was sitting at the table.

Layla and P.D. were telling us about Cullman and Cullman County. They said only a handful of blacks lived in the county and none in the city of Cullman. The county's only blacks resided in "the colony," a tiny settlement also known as Arkadelphia. Until a couple of years earlier, P.D. said, visitors to Cullman were greeted by a sign at the city limits that said, "Nigger, don't let the sun set on your head."

"At the city limits," he said, "like, you know, 'Welcome to Cullman.'"

"Isn't that terrible?" Layla said.

"No," Barbara Farrar said.

"I think it is," Layla said.

"I think they made a point," P.D. said.

We asked Layla what it was like being one of the nine children of Big Jim Folsom.

"It's nice," she said. "I love him very much, but it has been strange. A lot of strange things have happened."

"What besides the pay phone in the living room?"

"People ask me all the time, 'Are you any relation to Big Jim?' I say, 'Yes.' And they say, 'Oh, he must be your grandfather.' And I say, 'No, he's my father.' I really get embarrassed about it, to be with him, and they say, 'Is this your granddaughter?' He loves it. Melody catches it all the time. She's nine."

Fathering children at an advanced age ran in the family. Jim's grandfather, John Hodge Dunnavant, was seventy-four when he fathered Jim's mother, Eulala Cornelia Dunnavant.

Layla said Big Jim was disappointed he had so few children.

"He always believed in keeping his wives barefoot and pregnant," she said. "That's what he tells us is the way he kept mama."

"She didn't have any shoes?"

"I don't think he would let her wear them." She laughed.

As Big Jim and Jamelle walked down the stairs, Layla warned us that her father was on a tear against lawyers: "It was his one issue in the last campaign."

Big Jim was still a huge presence, even stumbling his way in with a cane. He looked older than we had expected, and his weight had edged up to two-sixty. After the introductions, he asked Jamelle to check our credentials.

"Yeah, they've got their credentials, Jim," she said in a loud voice to her husband. Then in a soft aside to us, she said, "Oh, Lord, since Jim can't see, that's what makes him suspicious. He just two years ago lost his sight. Mostly, he's blind, so, you know, it makes you—I guess it makes him not trust. So don't feel . . ." Her voice trailed off.

Jamelle, married to Big Jim since 1948 and mother of seven of his children, was a plump, brown-haired woman almost short enough to stand under her husband's extended arm. When they met in 1946, she was an excited eighteen year old girl, and he was a thirty-seven-year-old widower running for governor. He first saw her in a crowded store where he was shaking hands in her hometown of Berry, Alabama. He spoke at a rally, then took her to a drugstore for a Coca-Cola.

Big Jim's first wife, Sarah Carnley Folsom, died in 1944,

leaving him with two small daughters. She was from Elba, Jim's hometown. Folsom soon earned a reputation as a hard-drinking ladies' man. His trademark on the campaign trail was kissing pretty girls. They called him Kissin' Jim.

As a bachelor governor for two years, Big Jim's First Lady in the governor's mansion was his sister Ruby, cut from the same cloth. At the mansion, Big Jim called "special sessions," his term for poker games that his cronies were good at and he wasn't. Whiskey flowed. Folsom called it "the necessities of life."

One of the cronies who was later indicted for perjury, Roy Drinkard of Cullman, told us about life in the mansion. He said things got so rowdy that Jim's and Ruby's sister Thelma moved into the mansion to pass a reform bill.

"Thelma is a good old staunch Baptist," said Drinkard, an undertaker and land developer who was acquitted of a charge that he lied when he denied taking a $1,500 payoff to arrange a convict's pardon during the Folsom administration. "Thelma is the conscience of the family who took mama's and daddy's place after they died. She got tired of how Ruby and Jim were behaving in the governor's mansion, and she went down there to straighten things out.

"A bunch of Jim's cronies came up at five o'clock in the afternoon. They would just pile in there and eat and drink and while the night away, and he wouldn't be able to work the next day. Thelma met them on the front porch with a broom. She told them, 'Y'all not coming in here.' They said, 'What do you mean? Jim invited us in.' She said, 'No, James don't want you. James has had a change of heart.' She called him James. They said, 'What do you mean, he's had a change of heart?' She told them, 'James has turned away from whiskey and women, and he's taken up prayer and the Bible.' She turned 'em away. That lasted about one night."

In the 1946 campaign, Big Jim was well on his way to earning the reputation that brought Thelma to the mansion. His massiveness, good looks and abundant energy electrified young Alabama girls such as Jamelle Moore and her friends. They attended a Folsom rally one afternoon in Berry, where Jamelle got her first look at Big Jim.

"I had four really pretty girlfriends, and they were all standing there giggling," Jamelle said. "And when Jim started speaking, he looked over there and winked at me and, oh boy, that really excited me. Here's this giant of a man coming to town running for governor. I remember he said, 'You sure are smart folks here in this town, 'cause you got such good looking children.' And then we all really giggled, you know, four young girls about Layla's age. When he got through speaking, boy, he headed right toward me, shaking hands. He was coming straight toward me, and he looked so huge, and I had never seen anybody like Jim. Six-foot-eight!"

That night, after a rally at the Fayette County Courthouse, Big Jim sent aide Bill Lyerly to Jamelle's house to pick her up to go with him to a campaign cocktail party at the home of a local doctor. Jamelle said her mother didn't want her to go, because Folsom was twenty years older than she was. But her father, Mel Moore, was Folsom's county campaign manager.

"Dad said, 'Let baby go,'" Jamelle recalled.

"When we got there," Jamelle said, "all these women were at the front door. There must have been twenty beautiful girls lined up on each side to kiss Jim. The doctor had planned it that way."

"I was kissing 'em all on the forehead," Folsom told us.

"He'd just go through there and peck them on the cheek or forehead," Jamelle said, "but I thought, 'Good Lord, what a man.' When we got inside, of course Jim had a drink. They asked me what I wanted, and I said, 'Well to tell you the truth, I love chocolate milk. I guess you don't have one.' Jim looked over and said, 'Hell, Doc, if she wants a chocolate milk, go back there and shake her up a milkshake.'"

We asked what happened after the rally.

"Well, hell," Folsom said, "now you done quit talking and gone to meddling."

Big Jim came to politics naturally. His father was Joshua

Marion Folsom, a wire-pulling courthouse politician named for General Francis Marion, the South Carolina Swamp Fox of the American Revolution. Big Jim's grandfather Dunnavant freed his two families of slaves in 1850 and spoke against the Civil War but lost four of his sons in the fighting.

"He spoke against the war," Big Jim told us, "but I guess those boys were drafted. I don't know what it was. Anyway, they went on, and Grandpa Dunnavant was so hard against it, well hell, they took off against those boys, and, hell, they had 'em up there in the front lines and they were dead before they got started good. That was how rough it was."

Big Jim was born October 9, 1908, the fifth of seven Folsom children, on a south Alabama farm on the Pea River outside Elba, the seat of Coffee County. Nearby, at Enterprise, Coffee County farmers erected the world's only statue of the boll weevil, built in tribute to the little bug that crawled up out of Mexico and ravaged Southern cotton crops. It forced them to start growing peanuts and other crops more profitable and easier on the back than cotton.

Joshua Folsom was deputy sheriff, county commissioner and tax collector at Elba. Joshua's brother, Moses (Doc) Folsom, was sheriff. They headed one courthouse faction, and Judge J.A. Carnley headed another. In 1893, Doc Folsom was assassinated after he refused to hang a black man he believed innocent, Big Jim told us.

"He didn't want to hang him," Folsom said. "And so he went to the governor and asked him to pardon him, but the governor wouldn't do it. They tell me the state sent a special hanging man. They got mad about that. He was going to his home up in the county, halfway between Elba and New Brockton. They waylaid him and shot him. I've been by there a lot of times."

Prohibition killed Big Jim's father in 1919. Big Jim told us that his father was the first man in Alabama to die of poison moonshine whiskey after the Volstead Act was ratified.

"I was a kid, and we were down there close to the Gulf," Folsom said. "We had been, since the Civil War, going down there and getting fish. During the Civil War, we went down there to get salt and fish. Boil out salt. And this old custom was to go down there in the spring and fall, fishing. Pa went down there right after they passed Prohibition. Pa had stayed back to cook while they went out fishing. A fellow sold him poison whiskey, and he took several drinks. He lay around about three weeks and died from it."

Big Jim grew up under a strict Baptist mother, but his father's death put him into politics. His first race was on the wet ticket to elect delegates to a state convention to repeal the Volstead Act in the summer of 1933.

"My mama was a big dry, but she was against poison whiskey," Folsom told us.

He lost that race, his first of four straight election defeats, but he was in politics for life. Blind, halt and deaf, he ran for governor for the ninth and last time in 1982, five years before his death on November 21, 1987. Big Jim's maverick tutor in politics and history was his uncle John Dunnavant. In the Democratic South, his Uncle John was first a Republican, then a Populist, and eventually a leader of the Tax League. John was suspected of leading an Elba Tea Party, stealing and destroying Coffee County tax records in protest of high taxes.

Big Jim consolidated the Elba courthouse factions by marrying Judge Carnley's daughter, Sarah, in 1936. The judge was an outspoken Populist who influenced his young son-in-law. Carnley was an admirer of Andrew Jackson and passed that admiration on to Folsom, who named his second son Andrew Jackson Folsom and named his first daughter Rachel Folsom, after Old Hickory's wife.

When George Wallace named a junior college in north Alabama after John C. Calhoun, the secessionist senator from South Carolina, Folsom roared angrily, "John C. Calhoun! Why, Andrew Jackson threatened to horsewhip him if he tried to carry out a rebellion."

Folsom also was influenced by another uncle.

"I want to live to be like Uncle Bill," he told us. "They told him he was going to drink himself to death. Well, he did. He lived to be a hundred and one. He was pa's brother-in-law.

Uncle Bill died not long ago. He had a bunch of kids, about ten kids that he was trying to raise. The river got out of its banks, and two young farmers down there came running up to him the next morning and said, 'Uncle Bill, Uncle Bill! The river is out over the corn and it's going to kill our corn crop, our peanut crop and everything else.' He was on the front porch asleep. He turned over and said, 'Let 'er slosh, let 'er slosh,' and went back to sleep. So he lived to be a hundred and one."

We asked Big Jim how he happened to run for governor. He told us he had known he would be a governor—maybe in California if not Alabama—since he was a young merchant seaman. He went to sea after dropping out of Howard College in Birmingham in 1929, at age twenty, and traveled to seventeen countries in three years. After he became governor, he told a *Life* magazine reporter he had his first beer at his first port, Genoa, Italy. One of his best known quotes as Alabama's chief executive was, "The only thing better than beer for breakfast is whiskey."

"I got off the ship in New York, and the bread lines were four blocks long," Big Jim told us. "My money had run out, and I was having a hard time getting another ship. I saw an advertisement that wanted men over six feet tall at the Paramount Theater there."

Big Jim said his job was hawking tickets to passers-by, but he really was practicing to be governor.

"My brother, Bob Folsom, was in the Navy," Big Jim said, "and he and a boy named Gilmore came down the street on their way over to the first automatic pilot school for ships. I was out there practicing public speaking, and my brother came by and said, 'What in the hell are you doing here?' I said, 'Well, I'm practicing public speaking. I'm going to run for governor.' He said, 'You're crazy as hell.'"

After Franklin Delano Roosevelt's election as president, Folsom returned to Alabama in 1933, went to work for Depression relief agencies and lost four straight elections and withdrew from a fifth over the next eleven years. He ran two congressional races in his home area against entrenched FDR New Dealer

Henry B. Steagall, chairman of the House Banking and Currency Committee. That got his name known in south Alabama, even though he lost. Then he moved to Cullman in north Alabama and went into the burial insurance business with his brother-in-law, Ross Clark, married to Thelma Folsom. Policy holders paid premiums their entire lives to cover their burial costs.

"I lived up there at Guntersville for two years, administered the WPA over there, and got acquainted with people all over north Alabama selling insurance," Folsom told us. "That's the way I got up here. But it fell right in the slot for me to be governor. I got out and peddled insurance six years."

Big Jim lived in Mrs. Floyd Shannon's rooming house when he first got to Cullman. Lecil Gray, a powerful probate judge from Walker County, southwest of Cullman, told us, "Jim looked around over the state to see where the oldest congressman was, that might be the first vacancy, and he moved up to Cullman, in that district." Gray said Kenneth Griffith induced Folsom to run instead for governor in 1942 against two well-known south Alabama politicians, Bibb Graves and Chauncey Sparks.

Griffith, a Cullman lawyer, was the son of Circuit Judge Aquilla (Quill) Griffith and later became a judge himself. Big Jim told us about that meeting with Kenneth Griffith in a Cullman office building.

"There's a clothing store over there, upstairs from Kenneth Griffith's office, where we all hung out a lot," Folsom said. "They were cussing about all the candidates were from down yonder. They didn't like Sparks. They liked Graves. They didn't like the other fellows, didn't know any of them. Graves was the only one, and Graves had it sewed up. I was standing over there, and Griffith called me up to his office.

"He wasn't judge then. His daddy was judge. And he was pretty heavy on that bottle, anyway, all his life. He didn't have a hell of a lot of law practice. He called me up there and was setting down on the table. I never had met him. I'd shook hands with him, but I didn't know him. And we sat down, and he had a bottle setting there—Pogue's Old Time Deluxe, one pint. It was bourbon, Kentucky bourbon, straight whiskey. He asked me to have a drink, and so I poured a little in a glass. I don't know whether I put in a little Coca-Cola with it or not—he had Coca-Cola there—or whether we drunk it straight and then followed it with Coca-Cola. But I took the drink, and then we got to talking about this and that and the other.

"He was mad as hell. He had managed Sparks' campaign before. He'd been on Sparks' committee, and they left him off, and he was mad as hell. He'd had half that bottle; it was about half full. Finally he said to me, 'By God, why don't you run for governor?' Hell, that's all I wanted. I said, 'Let me have that damn bottle and take a drink or two and I'll talk to you about it.' And we talked and talked about it, how north Alabama had been left out. I said, 'Let me go to that damn store over yonder and get me a full pint of that damn stuff and come back and we'll talk some more about that.'

"And we got a damn full pint. There's a lot of elections, a lot of damn qualifying, been done over a drink. And by the time we got halfway in that second pint, why, hell, we were already—hell, we was in the runoff then. There wasn't no question. Hell, we was already in the runoff.

"I said, 'We'll qualify in the morning. We'll go to the bank.' We didn't have, neither one of us, enough money. Qualifying took a hundred and twenty dollars. Time we was through, why, I walked him down the steps, got him home, and I went home. Well, hell, the next morning I was ready, I was there, I was banging on his door. I got there about six-thirty. I was walking up and down the hall when Griffith got to the office. I said, 'Lawyer, what were we talking about last night?' We went in and talked about it. We went over there to the bank that morning and asked at the bank if they would accept our loan. The bank told me if I would sign the note for it, why they would let me have it, a hundred and twenty dollars."

Big Jim said front-runner Bibb Graves, a two-term governor, was seventy years old and that he died eight days after the qualifying deadline.

"That left the race between me and Sparks," Folsom said.

"Another candidate, Chris Sherlock, had the money. I didn't have any, and he was giving my friends a thousand dollars a week. A fellow was driving me over the state, and I was just speaking on street corners. Their pot was giving us a thousand dollars a week. That got us over the state."

"Why were they giving you a thousand dollars a week?"

"They wanted to be sure there would be a runoff after Bibb Graves died. Sherlock thought he would be in the runoff, see. And they gave me money to keep on the road to be sure there would be a runoff."

Sparks got a majority of the vote in the Democratic primary and won the election without a runoff. But the campaign had been a big victory for Folsom. A governor of Alabama could not succeed himself, and Big Jim had finished second. That put him in line for the governor's office four years later.

9

Putting the Suit On Big Jim

BIG JIM WAS IN LINE to be governor, but he had a problem. America was at war, and he had to get the suit on.

It took string-pulling courthouse politics reaching all the way to the Pentagon to make the six-foot eight-inch Folsom America's tallest warrior of World War II. Briefly.

William Bradford Huie, who was born and raised twenty miles up the road from Cullman in Hartselle, Alabama, had a hand in the maneuver. At the time, Huie was in the small-town newspaper publishing business. Later, he wrote several fiction and non-fiction best sellers, including *The Revolt of Mamie Stover, The Execution of Private Slovik, The Americanization of Emily, The Klansman,* and *Did the FBI Kill Martin Luther King?* A lesser known Huie book was *A New Life to Live*, the story of a young man who claimed to be Big Jim's illegitimate son.

Huie has died since we interviewed him in April 1979 at his beautiful home set back among the hardwoods in Hartselle. He met us at the door, a smiling, sixty-eight-year-old man with a military manner, bald and wearing a knit turtleneck under an open-neck shirt. He received us warmly and took us to see his office where he said he began writing every morning at five o'clock. A Siamese cat slept in the in-box on his writing desk. Then we went out on the open patio to talk. Huie told us before we turned on our tape recorder that he would have to interrupt the interview at 11:30 A.M. because he had lunch every day with his ninety-year-old mother, who lived down the street from him. As we talked, Huie sipped from a large glass half filled with scotch on ice.

Huie told us that his books had sold thirty million copies and that six of them had been made into motion pictures. But he told us, "Now, I don't want to write a story that can't be turned into a television film." He explained that only about eighteen million people see a movie and that 121 million people saw the two TV showings of *The Execution of Private Slovik.*

Only as we were leaving did Huie tell us how they put the suit on Big Jim. He told the story straight through, hardly pausing for a fact or date or name. It was an admirable performance by an accomplished story-teller.

"Hell, I even owned a piece of Folsom," Huie told us.

"What do you mean, you owned a piece of him?"

"In Alabama, politics is a gamble. A man who can run comes along and looks like a man you can elect as governor, see, and you put up money for him and thereby you get a piece of him, you buy a piece of him, and then when he becomes governor you expect to multiply that anywhere from ten to fifty times. That's the way the game is played. And there are all sorts of ways you expect to get that money back. You put up ten thousand dollars, and the bastard's a long shot and everything, and if he comes in, by God, you don't expect to work much the rest of your life. And so that's the way it goes. Wallace. Old George Wallace created more millionaires and every damn thing else."

"How much did you buy into Folsom?"

"I bought into Folsom unwittingly," Huie replied, "because it happened this way. My younger, my only, brother, when he got out of the University of Alabama in 1936, wanted to go into the printing business, the weekly newspaper business. So we did. We had a printing plant and three weekly newspapers printed up at Cullman. In a county seat, you represented one political faction or the other, because what you wanted was legal advertising so that when your gang was in there you handled the printing contracts, all the record books, every damn thing else. You got all the printing contracts and took a rakeoff off them, you kick back, and your competitors didn't get any legal advertising while your gang was in the courthouse.

"If you didn't belong to any faction, you never got anything. So you had to set up your newspaper in support of one faction or another. So our paper was set up in 1936 as the supporter of the Yellow Dog Democrats. A Yellow Dog Democrat, you know, is a man who would vote for a yellow dog before he'd vote for a Republican. So we belonged to the old Yellow Dog faction—the Bibb Graves faction.

"Anyway, Folsom was selling burial insurance in Cullman. That's another racket that grew up in Alabama, sold for a quarter. Big Jim was a burial insurance salesman in Cullman. And our gang, in that time, God, they had had Graves! They had had him twice! The parole racket was very big then, still is in Alabama. And so, God, they'd gotten rich out of Graves. They'd had Graves for eight years. Now they're all oiled up to make Graves governor again in 1942. They are going to get rich.

"Oh, the war's going on, so hell, we just got it made, except one thing happened. After it got too late for anybody else to qualify, Graves died. Hell, Graves had been odds-on to become governor. And the second man's going to win, no way to beat the second man. So, there are about sixteen other guys running for advertising in the governor's race. And what you do in that case, you go out here and you pick a long shot, you back him, and you get all the other Graves gangs who made money out of Graves in every other city and county in Alabama, and you all line up behind this long shot.

"You try to put him in a runoff with the guy who's going to win. And while you lose—in those days the governor could not succeed himself directly—your man gets the publicity. And then if you keep him in the limelight, and he doesn't make any mistakes in the next four years, he's automatically governor four years later.

"So our gang, without anywhere to go in 1942 with Graves dead, they look down, and they see Big Jim Folsom. Six feet, eight inches tall, goddamn, he's their man! He looks like a governor. They're going to make a governor out of him. I'll never forget. Hell, they go down there and they get Folsom and they run him against a guy named Chauncey Sparks, who's going to win. But they get in there. And Sparks, of course, wins. But goddamn, Folsom damn near overtakes him. He damn near becomes governor.

"Okay, it's now 1943, no way Folsom can be prevented from being governor in 1946. Hell, we even get the suit on him, in the military, you see. Always, it's called 'the suit.' In Alabama politics, you see, it was very valuable. Also, before you run for governor, you needed a card in the hero's union. That meant you needed to be a member of the American Legion.

"Here's what happened: Our gang puts Folsom in the race. And what I'm involved in—because I'm a substantial owner of the business, my brother Jack is running it and everything—we not only support Folsom, we do all his goddamn printing. So at the end of the campaign, why the Folsom for governor people owe us seven or eight thousand dollars for printing that has been done for Folsom. So in 1943, my brother has to go in the Navy, and I'm getting ready to go in the Navy. We don't have anybody to run the business, so it's got to be sold. It is being sold to a circuit judge in Cullman County who is head of the old Yellow Dog Democrat faction who had picked up at least eight farms in the parole racket, getting boys who had cut somebody on the churchyard, taking the farm to get the boy out of prison.

"But anyhow, I'm sitting down there with the judge, and we're going over the accounts receivable, because we're selling him this business, with our debts, to see what our debts are worth. So I go down there, and hell, here's seven thousand dollars owed to this business by the Folsom for Governor Committee. This is after the race, early in 1943. So I said, 'Judge, goddamn, I guess we can just charge that off to experience, don't we?' He turned around to me and—he had a habit of slapping you on the knee. . . ."

Huie slapped his knee to demonstrate.

"He said, 'Bill, that's the best seven thousand dollars you ever spent in your life, boy. You own seven thousand dollars worth of Folsom. God, Folsom is the next governor of Alabama. No way, boy. He's got to win. He can't lose. If we'd spent five thousand more, we'd have elected him governor in 1942. Hell, he's got the power of the unknown tongue. Hell, these country people think he's Jesus. You never heard anything like it. Now, listen, you've never met him. I've got to take you out here and show him to you before you leave town, because we've got things to do. That's the best money you ever spent. You're going to get that back fifty-fold.

"And so we go down and get in the car, and we drive out there. Folsom had been out mowing the yard or something. He was sitting on the floor, on the porch, just had on a pair of overalls, barefooted, sweating. So the judge and I got out and we walked in. I'd never met him. Folsom had never met me, but he knew my brother very well. We look alike. So we went in to talk, and old Big Jim said, 'Bill, I can be governor. But I've got to get the suit on.'

"He had been to every form of the military, and they had all turned him down because they had one rule in the Second World War. If you were more than six-feet-six, none of them would take you because they didn't have anything for you to wear and no place to sleep or anything else. He had been rejected by everybody. No branch of the service would take him. He said, 'Hell, I'm six-eight in my bar' feet. They won't take me. I got to get the suit on! Look what Stassen's doing. Look what Lyndon Johnson's doing. They're all getting the suit on, running around, and hell, I've got to run for governor in 1946. I can't win unless I get the suit. Get the suit on me and I can't lose.'

"Well, I laughed, and I said, 'Hell, we ought to figure out a way to get the suit on you, Jim.'

"At any rate, just two adds to that. His wife had died, and he had two daughters. As we drove away, old Judge Griffith turned to me and he said, 'Now, Bill, you won't believe it, but that's the next governor of Alabama.'

"I said, 'Surely not, judge.'

"He said, 'Goddammit, Bill. You just don't know what he can do to these country people. He's going to be the greatest popular figure, most popular political figure in the history of this state. We've got to get the suit on him. Lister's got to help us.'"

We interrupted him to ask: Who's Lister?

"That's Lister Hill," Huie said. "Hill had always played the military racket, and even in the House, he'd gotten Maxwell Field built when he represented the Montgomery district in Congress. And then, of course, he was number two behind Dick Russell on the Senate Armed Services Committee. So he was very powerful with the Pentagon. So, the judge said, 'Now, you're going back to Washington. You go see Lister, because Lister's got to help us get the suit on Big Jim. We also, as soon as we can get the suit on him, we got to photograph him and make some mattes, and we've got to send them out to all the country newspapers and everything so they can run pictures showing how old Big Jim is out there on the ramparts carrying on for democracy.' And the judge said, 'Now, we got to have a little money to send them mattes out. You're already hooked for seven thousand dollars. Another five hundred ain't going to hurt you. Come on up to my office.'

"We went up there, and he called another four or five rascals, all of whom owned pieces of Folsom, and we all had to come in with another five hundred bucks apiece to pay for those mattes, assuming we're going to get the suit on Folsom, you see.

"Well, I'm in Washington the next three or four days, and I go up to Lister Hill's office. I've known him a long time, and we got over in the corner, and I said, 'By the way, senator. . . .' Now that same gang had carried water for Lister Hill for years, see. And all during the war, war plants anywhere around, all they had to do was have a little scribbled note from the judge or somebody else to go to any of these war plants to get a job. And

I said to the senator, 'Now, you know some good buddies of yours down in Alabama carried a lot of water for you. And they got somebody down there they want to make governor. Big Jim.'

"Hill said, 'Yeah, I heard about him, I heard about him.' I said, 'Well, you're going to hear a lot more about him. Besides, senator, they've elected you to put the suit on him.' I had been given Big Jim's numbers and sizes, everything. I pulled them out. 'Oh,' Hill said, 'you know I can't do that, Bill.' I said, 'Oh, of course you can't, senator. I know you ain't got no input in the Pentagon, but we've got to get the suit on Big Jim, and he's six-eight, by God, in his bare feet, and we've got to have him in military uniform so we can photograph him to send out them mattes.' He said, 'You know I can't do it.' I said, 'Well, I know you can't do it.'

"About two weeks later, Folsom gets a notice from over here at Fort McClellan to report for induction into the Army. So he goes over there. Now, they don't want him. Hell, they got nothing for him. But they go on there and put a suit on him, and they photograph him, and we send out the mattes. Matter of fact, he didn't do a damn thing. He just continues to politick around. Nobody wanted him. They didn't have any place for him. They'd been ordered to put the suit on him and induct Private Folsom. You could go down here at Cullman County, in the probate office, and you could find in there that six months later, Private Folsom was released from the Army 'at his own request.' In other words, soon as some son of a bitch would agree to it, they turned him loose. In 1946, he campaigns, of course, as a G.I. He was lucky in that his brother got killed in the Philippines. His brother made the supreme sacrifice."

Big Jim later became commander of an Alabama American Legion post—head of his own hero's union.

10

A Damn Nine-foot Coffin

BEFORE HE WENT upstairs for the night, Big Jim insisted that we spend the night in a spare downstairs bedroom. Although we had a car parked in Folsom's back yard, Big Jim also insisted on calling over Boots Maddox, his part-time chauffeur and a former Cullman taxicab driver. Folsom put us in Boots' charge. He instructed Boots to take us out to dinner, bring us back, show us our bedroom and stay over himself so he could take us to breakfast the next morning.

And before he went upstairs, Big Jim motioned to the living room and told us, "I've got a pay station in there, if they'll move the coat off so you can use it. A pay station. That's the only one we got, too, boys."

Layla, Big Jim's twenty-year-old daughter, had warned us that her father got up early, and sometimes used to walk through the house at four o'clock in the morning waking everybody by clanging a cow bell. He was late the next morning. It wasn't till about 5:30 A.M. that he came down the stairs roaring, "We're gonna lose the crop! We're gonna lose the crop!"

When he got to the kitchen he was still yelling:

"All right, come on. Hell, you two can't do a day's work lying in bed all day. We're going down to the truck stop. Y'all ready?"

"We're ready if you are. How are you feeling this morning?"

"I'm better than y'all are. I got a good night's sleep. When I get dressed, I'm all right."

Big Jim was dressed and ready. He had on a blue dress shirt, buttoned at the neck, no tie, and a grey suit with faint red pinstripes.

When we got outside, Boots was waiting beside Folsom's brand new, dark-blue Ford LTD, with a green state of Alabama license plate, number S–5. We got in the car and headed out for Jack's Truck Stop.

"You knew the sink's stopped up, didn't you?" Folsom asked us, referring to the bathroom next to the room where we had slept.

"Yes, we found that out."

As we rode, Folsom started railing at lawyers and judges. He had struck that theme repeatedly since we arrived the previous day. Big Jim had entwined his personal anger over the loss of his $29,000 annual state pension with several lifelong beliefs, including one-man, one-vote and a conviction that lawyers should not be allowed to collect legal fees while serving in the Legislature. He called them "two-pocket son of a bitches."

Compounding Folsom's bitterness was the memory that the day he went blind he learned the Alabama Supreme Court had ruled his pension was unconstitutional. Jack Folsom had told us that his father was under a lot of pressure when the pension issue was before the courts. The day of the final court hearing, as Big Jim was preparing to go to court, blood vessels in his eyes burst. He entered a hospital and missed the hearing.

Jack recalled that the next morning, August 8, 1976, Big Jim's doctor came in and said, "Governor, I hate to tell you this, but you're blind."

Ten minutes after he got that news, an Associated Press

reporter called for Big Jim's comment on the court ruling that took his pension away.

"Them goddamn two-pocket son of a bitches down there," Big Jim told us, "they want the courts, the chief justice, to be the king and each lawyer to be a prince. And that's all the law they want."

We were riding to the restaurant in a state car. The year after Folsom lost his pension, the Alabama Legislature passed a bill making him a special counsel to the governor with an annual salary of $18,000. After meeting with Forrest (Fob) James, Jr. late in the 1978 governor's race, Folsom withdrew as a candidate and threw his support to James, who was elected. Governor James rewarded him with use of the state car and a driver to chauffeur him around.

"So I don't have the money I used to have," said Big Jim, ranting on about lawyers and judges as we rode. "But it don't make no damn difference, no way. One advantage I've got on them, when them son of a bitches die they've got just a little old six-foot coffin, and by God, I'll have a damn nine-foot coffin, you understand? I got 'em beat. I'll have 'em beat when I die."

About that time we rolled up in front of Jack's Truck Stop, owned by Mr. and Mrs. Jack Allred. We could tell it was a good place to eat. The lot was filled with eighteen-wheelers that had pulled off a four-lane highway Big Jim completed to Cullman as he was leaving the governor's office in January 1959. Work on the truck stop had begun before the highway was opened up to traffic. Big Jim was a breakfast regular and their favorite customer.

"Here's the governor," said a waitress in slacks with a bouffant hair-do.

"Hello, Big Jim," said another waitress.

"Hello here!" Big Jim called out to them.

As soon as we were seated and the waitress started pouring coffee, Big Jim said, "Boots?"

"Yessir, I'm right here with you, one-sixty, and one-thirty-three."

Boots had gone immediately to the juke box.

"That's right," Folsom said.

A record fell, and Freddie Fender's high tenor voice shrilled the opening lyrics of *Vaya Con Dios*, selection 133 on the juke box. Minutes later, number 160 played. It was *Somewhere My Love* by Ray Conniff, the other Folsom favorite.

Mrs. Jack Allred came over to our table to banter with Folsom about grandchildren. She was a pretty, blonde woman who looked to be in her late thirties but had a new grandchild, her fourth, born to her thirty-six-year-old daughter. Mrs. Allred asked us, "Did Big Jim tell you we keep *Somewhere My Love* on the jukebox always?"

"You've kept it on there for him?"

"Because of him, because they played it at his wedding. He's so sweet. He made us such a good governor."

"What's that, grandma?" Folsom asked loudly.

"I said you made us the best governor we ever had," Mrs. Allred told him.

"Now, what about that," said Big Jim, pleased. "This four-lane concrete road came right here."

"We haven't had any good roads since you left office," she told him.

"Come right here so we could build this cafe so I could come down here and meet my truck driving friends," Big Jim said.

"That's right," she told us. "He threw the scales in the river."

"I threw the scales in the river and wouldn't let 'em weigh 'em," Folsom said.

"They love him," Mrs. Allred told us. "The truck drivers love him."

Folsom was drinking his scalding coffee in great slurps. We asked him to tell us about throwing the truck scales in the river.

"During the war, they had been running to seventy thousand pounds and a hundred thousand pounds," Folsom said, "but the state cut the weight limit to about thirty-eight thousand. These boys had been used to a hundred thousand, seventy-five thousand, and they were my friends. Not only that, the railroads had been raping the state since 1850, and they're still doing it. And these boys were struggling for a living.

"I come in, I just ordered the weight business stopped. It stopped for four years. The fellow that followed me, hell, he put the damn weighing back in and had them trucks lined up two or three miles, being weighed on portable scales on a little old side road over there. And those little old truckers said, 'By God, wait'll Jim gets back in there. Them damn scales will be throwed away.'

"And shore enough, I got back in there, I throwed the damn scales away, just carried them out on the bridge and throwed them in the damn river."

Big Jim was skilled at using symbolism to consolidate support behind him. Campaigning for one-man, one-vote in 1954, ten years before the Supreme Court ruled on the issue, he used two pieces of galvanized pipe to make his point. Holding up a piece of one-inch pipe before a Walker County crowd, Big Jim told them, "That's Walker County. And Walker County has one representative. That's the amount of water you draw in your Legislature, with your governor, with your Highway Department, and on your Pardon Board. But look at this, this is a three-inch pipe, and it represents Dallas County. Now, Dallas County is about the same size and population as Walker County, but Dallas County has three times as many representatives as Walker County."

Then he held both pieces of pipe up high for the Walker County audience to see.

"Now," he said, "watch this three-inch pipe swallow this one-inch pipe."

In 1946, the centerpiece of Big Jim's successful campaign for governor was a long-handled shuck mop and a big cedar suds bucket. In those days, poor country people cleaned their floors with mops made of corn shucks that they dipped into soapy water in a suds bucket. Big Jim made his shuck mop and suds bucket a powerful symbol to the country people. Speaking from a flatbed trailer in the towns and branchheads of rural counties, he would walk up and down scrubbing with the mop and telling voters that was how he planned to clean out the Capitol from the basement to the dome when he got to Montgomery as governor. He told them he was going to open all the windows.

"I'm not going to stop scrubbing until I get a clean, green breeze from the north and everything smells nice and pretty again," he told crowds that got bigger and bigger as he campaigned all across the state in 1946.

After he got more votes that year than anyone in Alabama history, someone asked Big Jim what was a green breeze.

"Hell, I don't know," he said, "but they voted for it."

The suds bucket solved Big Jim's biggest problem going into the 1946 governor's race: money. His friend and supporter, one-time Probate Judge Lecil Gray of Walker County, told us Folsom was so broke in 1946 he was leaning toward running for Congress in the Seventh District against Representative Carter Manasco.

"I had been off to the war," Gray told us, "and I saw Jim sitting over there in the Jeff Davis Hotel, and he was trying to decide on the last day for qualification whether to run for Congress or governor. He had a lot of pushing from congressional people to get him in the governor's race. He was actually pushed into the governor's race by the Manasco people to get him out of the congressional race.

"Strangely enough, and this would probably embarrass Jim, people made him up some money if he'd run for governor. And Jim wrote his check when he qualified for governor. And by God, the check bounced. They took the money out of the bank as soon as they got him qualified for governor and left the poor son of a bitch without the money to qualify."

After he went out and borrowed the money to pay the qualifying fee for governor, Big Jim hit the road with the Strawberry Pickers, a crew of country singers, pickers, fiddlers and bass thumpers he recruited with a newspaper ad. Clyde McClintock played fiddle. Clifford White from south of Garden City played guitar. Red Hudson of Hanceville sang and strummed guitar. Hobart Key from the Cullman route performed on bass and fiddle and his brother James on bass and guitar. And the leader, Roland Johnson, split his time between Class AA professional baseball and helping Folsom draw a crowd as lead singer and guitar player.

An occasional Strawberry Picker when Folsom held rallies around Montgomery was a mournful singer named Hank Williams, a scrawny, hollow-eyed local boy on his way to the country music Hall of Fame.

The suds bucket paid their way around the state. Big Jim would start his speech and bring out his shuck mop and suds bucket. Then he would tell Roland and the boys to play a tune and have someone start passing the suds bucket through the crowd.

"He'd tell them, 'Pass the bucket,'" Roland Johnson told us. "'Boys, y'all put in the suds, and we'll do the cleaning. We'll do the mopping at that state Capitol down there. We're going to open up them windows and let a cool breeze from the north come through that Capitol. We're going to clean it up.' We passed the suds bucket the first time in Athens, Alabama, and then we left there and stopped at the Elkmont River west of Hartselle and counted the money. And there was thirty-seven dollars and some few cents in the bucket.

"We went on to Tuscumbia, passed the bucket again. It was fifty-something dollars we got there. And Jim turned around and said to us, 'Boys, you're looking at the next governor.'"

After making the first tour of the 1946 campaign through north Alabama, Johnson said, "We left and went south, down through what is known as the black belt in Alabama, down Highway 5 through Centreville and Marion, over to Demopolis, Camden and Jackson and on into Mobile.

"Now the people down in the black belt, they didn't care too much for Jim. They hadn't been putting money in the suds bucket. In fact, we didn't have enough money to pay out of the Battle House Hotel. The next morning, they sent the ballyhoo man out. You know, the ballyhoo man in politics is the man with a loud-speaker who drums up crowds or parades in the town. They sent him out to Bay Minette.

"We went to Bay Minette and passed the suds bucket over there, and people put in, which Jim never did forget. That's in Baldwin County. After the speaking, we eat. Then we went to Foley, toured all the towns in Baldwin County, on the Gulf, went back to the Battle House and spent the night, paid our bill, and went back to Cullman."

Former judge M. Gresham Hale, later a lobbyist for the Alabama Department of Mental Health, told us in Montgomery, "Big Jim used a lot of good psychology. He would go around with his suds bucket, you know, wearing a pair of overalls with a patch or two on them, and folks would drop a quarter or half a dollar in that suds bucket, and they automatically had a stake in that campaign. And they'd go to work for him. That's the best psychology any man ever used."

Another piece of psychology Folsom used grew out of his conviction that there are more sinners out there than saints. His reputation as a hard-drinking ladies' man frequently got his name in Alabama newspaper headlines. When that happened, he would begin his speeches by pleading guilty to all charges. If the sin was serious, he would enlarge on it, making a joke of it.

"They're accusing old Jim of having one woman pregnant down here," he told a huge campaign audience in downtown Mobile. "It's a damn political lie. I got four of 'em that way."

When he told us that in the restaurant, he chuckled.

"And the next town we went to, they didn't ask a damn thing about it," he said. "Stopped that real quick."

In Bible Belt Alabama, Big Jim's reputation as a womanizer was fueled by his habit of kissing girls in his 1946 campaign, lining them up at his rallies and grabbing them as they passed by on the street.

Life magazine ran pictures that showed him dancing with actress June Haver and eighteen-year-old Virginia Warren, daughter of Earl Warren, then governor of California and later chief justice of the United States Supreme Court.

Shortly after Folsom was elected governor, his enemies tried to amend the state constitution to allow the Legislature to call itself into special session without his approval. Friends warned him that his opponents were going to try to discredit him by trapping him with a prostitute or starting the rumor he was consorting with one. He told us how he defused the threat. He said he told a Washington County campaign audience all about it:

"A circuit judge warned me, 'They're going to trap you. They're going to trap you with a pretty woman. They're going to trap you just as sure as hell.' I studied it over, and I said, 'Well, judge, do you mean they'll use one of the best looking girls that ever walked the streets of Montgomery?' He said, 'Yes sir, governor, they're going to send off to New York for her, bring her in here, put her in a fine automobile and fine clothes. They're going to have you meet her and you're going to fall into their trap.' I said, 'Judge, you mean she's built like this?' He said, 'That's right.' I said, 'All up and down and every whichaway?' He said, 'The most perfect figure you ever saw in your life.' I said, 'Judge, you've just got to go back and tell 'em that if they set that kind of trap, and if they bait it with that kind of bait, they're going to catch old Big Jim every time, every time.'"

He beat the amendment.

In the 1954 campaign, when he won a second term, his opponents accused him of stealing during his first four years as governor. Again, his defense was to confess on the stump: "Of course I stole. If you get anything from those people down there you got to steal it. But I gave it back to you."

Confession was a device Folsom used often. He told us he was only trying to deflect criticism about his drinking when he quipped that the only thing better than beer for breakfast was whisky.

"Of course I never drank any beer or whiskey or anything on the stump," he told us. "Except late in the afternoon for a bracer."

And when he was criticized for inviting black Congressman Adam Clayton Powell of New York to the Alabama governor's mansion for a drink of scotch, Folsom said, "I'd never give him scotch. It was real whiskey."

Big Jim explained his rationale for confessing in public when accused:

"Ain't no use of denying it if they're accusing you of something. Always enlarge on it, especially if it ain't so. You go to denying something, they'll say, hell, he's guilty."

We asked, what if you are guilty?

"Well hell," he said, "I'm not going to talk about that."

But Folsom sometimes dismissed accusations as mud-slinging. Toward the end of his 1954 campaign, when the charges of corruption against him were piling up, Big Jim began telling the throngs: "You're going to hear a lot more things about old Jim. They're going to sling a lot more mud. But don't worry about that mud. Back when I was a kid, my mama and daddy used to take us to church on Sunday, and I'd wear a white shirt. One day, we were playing out there at the church, and a little boy slung some mud on my white shirt. Mama told me, 'Don't rub it off. Let it dry. It will fall off by itself.'"

He repeatedly assured supporters in 1954 that everything was going to be all right:

"Boys, it's going to cloud up, but it ain't going to rain."

He won, piling up more votes than all six of his opponents combined.

Just before dawn on inauguration day, Montgomery was drenched by a cloudburst.

"But so help me God," Big Jim told us, "just as I got up there to be sworn in, the sun broke out for the first time that day. I looked up, and I said, 'Folks, it clouded up, but it never did rain.'"

At seventy years old, Folsom was still defiant. While we talked, he drank several cups of coffee, strictly against his doctor's orders, and ate two orders of buttered toast and greasy bacon, his false teeth clicking as he chewed.

As we got up to leave the restaurant, waitresses fussed over Big Jim, and Mrs. Allred told us our breakfasts were on the house.

We returned to Folsom's house and found John Guthrie waiting for us, along with Jack Folsom, Jim's son. Big Jim introduced Guthrie as a coal dealer and former state legislator who once tried to kill Folsom programs but had since become a good friend.

Guthrie also was Jim Folsom, Jr.'s father-in-law. Big Jim had invited Guthrie over to tell us about memorable moments in the Folsom years. Right off, we noticed an amusing habit. Guthrie rarely completed a sentence.

We transcribed verbatim a portion our taped conversation with Guthrie about Big Jim and Judge Kenneth Griffith, the man who talked Folsom into running for governor the first time:

"But judge knew, you know, he was really—'cause judge never was defeated himself, when he run for judge. Judge—Jim appointed him probate judge, which that was a good—back then it paid forty—you know, forty thousand dollars a year, fees and all that, you see. So judge appointed him—I mean, Jim appointed him. He was his legal adviser, so he appointed him a judge. And judge come in, and judge never was defeated, and he run for circuit judge, then he retired, you know. Then he—now if he was living where he could just sit down and he could just—but he, you know—dead. But Jim is actually, Big Jim is the only man that I can remember—now Bibb Graves was, you know, was, he was kindly the people's governor, but that's the only one Alabama's ever really had. All the roads—there's more signatures on the roads, of Jim's, his signature, I found it after I was in the Legislature, than any other, than any man, any governor, I guess, in history. And he, he never, he never, well, he just didn't—and he first endorsed Harry Truman, when nobody else, you know, when they was all down on Harry, you know. . . ."

But some of Guthrie's rhetoric was worth the struggle to transcribe it. Like when he told us about going to Dallas to attend the Cotton Ginners Association convention.

"At this time, we had a lot of cotton in Alabama," Guthrie said. "Soybeans, now. But anyway, so I went out, in Dallas—so I flew out, and I'm bad—when I drank, I drank, don't I, Jack? I get on one every once in awhile, and so I was out there, you know, went out, and so when I got—I got pretty loaded, and I got off the plane. Well, I was registering in Joe Fleming's name, because he had a suite—the rooms for us, see, and there wasn't—and so, this guy was hard of hearing. And the lobby was full, practically. Men and a few women. So the guy kept—he asked me the second—you know, about—and I said where I was from, see. And I'd done registered. And I thought he could—he was trying—and so I said, 'I'm from the state where the governor can stand flat-footed and screw a mare mule.' Well, when I said that, the damn guy over in the—you know—said, 'Heeeeyyy! Alabama!'"

11

"I Stood for Something"

BETWEEN 1933 AND 1982, Big Jim Folsom ran in twenty elections ranging from delegate to attend a Prohibition repeal convention to president. He won only three times: once as a delegate to the 1944 Democratic National Convention in Chicago, where he voted a Franklin Roosevelt-Henry Wallace ticket, and twice to serve as Alabama governor.

While governor in 1948, he announced for president, but he couldn't win a seat as delegate from his own state to attend the convention where the Democratic party picked the nominee. Running for one of the four at-large seats to attend the convention in Philadelphia, he finished tenth in a twenty-man field.

In his second term as governor in 1956, Folsom's own state party rejected him as a national committeeman. And after he had served two terms as governor, voters turned him down for the state Public Service Commission.

His own nephew beat him in one race. In 1972, Fred Folsom, a George Wallace supporter that year, defeated Big Jim for delegate to the Democratic National Convention in Miami. Folsom lost six races for governor and one for the United States Senate.

"I didn't win many times," Big Jim told us. "Yeah, I did. I won *every* time. I stood for something. I stood for something. Yeah, I did. I stood for something."

The remarkable thing about Folsom's election record wasn't that he won so seldom but that he won at all.

Big Jim was totting up his wins and losses for us: "How many is that? National committeeman in 1956? Lost that one. That's seven. Lost, yeah, hell yeah. Yeah. Anybody that wouldn't hang a Negro, anybody that wouldn't hang a black man every other speech would get beat at that time."

One of the few years Folsom didn't run for anything was in 1960. He sat out a race for the Democratic National Convention that nominated John Kennedy for president.

"They were still hanging black folks, and there was no use to," Big Jim said. "In the black belt, those fellows eat and breathe and sleep with the black folks and run for governor and get elected. Now, those people down there, those black folks in south Alabama, didn't get blue eyed from looking at the moon and they didn't get half white from spilling Clorox on them."

Big Jim said there was a lot of "night integration" going on.

Folsom complained that the white politicians from the black belt—so named for the color of its soil—spewed racism all over the state.

"They come right up here to the courthouse and holler 'nigger' three times, and go to the next courthouse and holler 'nigger' three times, and the next one, and the next one up here, and these hillbillies just go crazy as a damn nutsyboon."

Big Jim had lost count of his wins and losses by the time he reached 1964, when he badly needed a job. Bull Connor, the Birmingham police commissioner who sicked dogs on black demonstrators, defeated him that year for a seat on the Alabama Public Service Commission.

"Yeah, he hung a black man on me every stump," Folsom said. "That was his backbone, hang one on every stump. But all of them's like that, has been since the black folks first came in here, them folks that brought them in here. That was his campaign. That's right, Bull Connor won that."

In 1944, when Folsom won a race for delegate to the Democratic National Convention in Chicago, he traveled there with the Alabama delegation by train. One of the Pullman porters on board was E. D. Nixon, the Montgomery civil rights leader who later chose Dr. Martin Luther King, Jr. to lead that city's historic bus boycott of 1955 and 1956.

Nixon, years later, told Professor Carl Grafton about a conversation he and Folsom had on the train. Nixon quoted Folsom: "Let me tell you. The day is going to come when we will recognize the Negro."

At the Chicago convention, Folsom split with his delegation and voted to retain Iowa Progressive Henry Wallace as FDR's vice president. The majority of the Alabama delegation went for Harry Truman. Four years later, when Henry Wallace ran for president on the Progressive Party ticket, his campaign brought him to Alabama.

"The resentment against Henry Wallace in north Alabama was unbelievable," said Rex Thomas of the Associated Press, dean of the Capitol press corps in Montgomery. "When he got to Gadsden, a heavily industrialized city where unions had pretty much a liberal stance, he couldn't even get out of his car. He pulled up in front of the courthouse, and the car was surrounded, and people started throwing rocks at it, rocking the car. He just drove on."

One of Folsom's close political associates in his 1954 campaign for governor, John Drinkard of Hartselle, compared Big Jim's civil rights record with that of one of nation's most liberal governors at that time, G. Mennen Williams of Michigan.

"Jim Folsom was as liberal as Soapy Williams ever was," Drinkard told us. "I'd say he was twenty years ahead of his time for Alabama or the South."

The AP's Thomas said, "I think the guy was way ahead of his time, frankly, just about a generation ahead of his time because of the things he advocated. Some of the things almost got him impeached."

As governor, Folsom unhooded the Ku Klux Klan, commuted death sentences, sought to repeal the poll tax and register black voters. He condemned attacks on Freedom Riders, vetoed racial segregation and state right-to-work bills and raised old-age pensions. And in 1948, he opposed the Dixiecrat movement.

Shortly after the ruling in *Brown v. Board of Education of Topeka, Kansas*, the Alabama Senate passed a resolution demanding that Congress investigate and reveal "what part, if any, the Communist Party had in writing the U.S. Supreme Court school decision." Folsom opposed the resolution.

He ridiculed another resolution by the Alabama Legislature that declared the United Supreme Court rulings on civil rights cases "null, void and of no effect in Alabama."

"All this claptrap about the resolution is just like a hound dog baying at the moon and claiming it's got the moon treed," Folsom said.

Big Jim told us that in his first term as governor he rejected George Wallace's request to be speaker of the House of Representatives.

"I wouldn't take someone from a slave-holding county," Folsom told us, referring to south Alabama counties in the agriculture-rich black belt where slavery once flourished.

"I had to have somebody that I liked," Folsom said. "He wanted every little committee he could get, but the main thing he wanted was to be on the Board of Trustees at Tuskegee. The governor appoints one from the Senate and one from the House. I appointed him. Black folks couldn't vote on these boards. He wanted to politick these black leaders over the state, and later on he did. He'd cuss them on top of the table and play peters with them under the table."

Nearing the end of his third year as governor in 1949, Folsom went on radio with a Christmas message that was stunning for the time and place it was delivered:

"And so we founded in this country, great and far-reaching welfare programs. These programs were not created, nor are they operated, as a great leveler, but as an obligation of a democracy to its people, in order that the unfortunate may feast on more than crumbs and clothe themselves with more than rags.

"What has gone before us in the way of welfare work exemplifies rich rewards of human endeavor. But we are actually just coming of age, just beginning to scratch the surface in fulfilling the needs which are so widespread. So long as we have a hungry person, ill-clothed or without medical aid, we can take no pride in what has been done.

"It is good at Christmas for us to turn our thoughts to the neglected, because Christmas is a time to think of others and not ourselves. It is a time for us to ask questions of our inner self.

"It is indeed a proud thing to know that the people of this state are concerned enough about these questions to vote a giant hospital building program which will extend into every county in Alabama. This program is one of the greatest things that ever happened in Alabama, and its effect will be such as to make for a far healthier and happier people.

"Our Negroes who constitute thirty-five percent of our population in Alabama—are they getting thirty-five percent of the fair share of living? Are they getting adequate medical care to rid them of hookworms, rickets, and social diseases? Are they provided with sufficient professional training which will produce their own doctors, professors, lawyers, clergymen, scientists—men and women who can pave the way for better health, greater earning powers, and a higher standard of living for all of their people? Are the Negroes being given their share of democracy, the same opportunity of having a voice in the government under which they live?

"As long as the Negroes are held down by deprivation and lack of opportunity, the other poor people will be held down alongside them. . . . Let's start talking fellowship and brotherly love and doing unto others—and let's do more than talking about it, let's start living it.

"In the past few years, there has been too much negative living, too much stirring up of old hatreds, and prejudices, and false alarms. The best way in the world to break this down is to lend our ears to the teachings of Christianity and the ways of democracy . . .

"Before lasting peace will ever prevail in this world, nations have got to respect the laws of human decency which Christ preached in His teachings. Nations have got to become as families. They have got to gather around the cross of Christianity if good is ever to triumph over evil. And before nations can do that, the leaders of nations must be fired with the challenge to see that equal justice, equal opportunity, and equal freedom become a reality for every man, woman and child. . . ."

During the Montgomery bus boycott that started the civil rights movement in the United States, Folsom invited Dr. King to the governor's office for a talk. Later, Folsom said he encouraged the young black minister to adopt passive resistance. Big Jim also invited Congressman Adam Clayton Powell to the governor's mansion when he came to Montgomery to support the bus boycott. Professor Grafton quoted E.D. Nixon as saying Folsom gave Powell permission to make their meeting public.

"I had a drink with the governor," the New York congressman told the press. "I doubt I could have done that with the governor of my own state."

In the summer of 1975, the Alabama Civil Liberties Union awarded Folsom a lifetime membership. Alabamian Charles Morgan Jr., director of the ACLU national office in Washington, went home to make the presentation to Big Jim.

"The things we believe in," Morgan said, "he believed before us. The things we say, he said before us. The things we fight for, he fought for before us."

To later generations, Big Jim's meetings with Dr. King and Congressman Powell might seem routine examples of a governor's hospitality, but they were suicidal acts for a Southern politician of that day. He never won another election. The rising star in Alabama was George Wallace and his politics of race.

12

Disaster in the Last Thirty Minutes

DESPITE THE WHISKEY, liberal politics and a loose hand that made his friends rich out of the state till, Big Jim Folsom almost won a third term as governor in 1962.

"We had it won till the last thirty minutes," said Roland Johnson, who once again helped draw Big Jim's crowds as the lead singer and guitar picker with the Strawberry Pickers band.

There was no exaggerating this one into a joke.

If Big Jim had stuck with stump politics in the branchheads and county seats, he would have been all right. But on election eve, he bought saturation television coverage from border to border, from the Gulf to the Sand Mountains, and went before the cameras for half an hour with his wife and seven of his children seated beside him on a couch.

In Cullman, entrepreneur and town character Winfield (Bully) Moon watched the television performance with long-time Folsom aide John Drinkard. Big Jim's image came on the screen, and before he said anything, Moon exclaimed to Drinkard: "Goddamn, he's drunk!"

That was the prevailing opinion on election day. Big Jim missed getting into the runoff by about two thousand votes, and his opponent, George Corley Wallace, was launched on a career that would change the course of American politics.

One of Big Jim's problems on the TV program was that he couldn't remember the names of his children. But sober, Big Jim would have been in trouble that night. A strike by television personnel had forced the Folsom campaign to move the show from Birmingham to Montgomery, and when they got to the studio, a campaign film that was supposed to have taken up twenty-nine-and-a-half minutes of the thirty-minute show was missing. When technicians tried to show a brief segment of footage taken at a big Folsom rally in Mobile they ran it upside down.

But Big Jim was the biggest problem that night. Big as Folsom was, the cameraman had trouble keeping the lens focused on him because he kept standing up and staggering around the bare set, swinging the microphone and gesturing. He slurred his words and wound up his 1962 campaign howling incoherently about his opponents' "me too" politics and cooing into the microphone.

"Me too, me too, cuckoo, cuckoo, cuckoo," he signed off.

Grover Hall, editor of *The Montgomery Advertiser*, wrote an editorial calling it The Cuckoo Speech.

Until his death, Big Jim contended that one of his aides drugged him. In Alabama, you can still find people who think he was drunk, people who think he was drugged, and people who think he was drunk and drugged.

"Somebody may have given him tranquilizers to try to get him calmed down, and that could have had a bad reaction," said Rex Thomas of the Associated Press. "But he was drunk. The TV show was on Monday night. And Sunday morning, oh, the middle of the morning, he called me at home, and he was so drunk he couldn't talk."

Thomas said he talked with Big Jim's campaign manager, Herman Nelson, about Folsom's election eve TV performance.

"Herman said there wasn't any question the guy was just

falling down drunk, and they tried to get him to stay off of TV and put on a film, and Jim wouldn't agree to it," Thomas said.

Big Jim had been turning more and more to the bottle.

"He could drink more than any man I'd ever seen," said John Drinkard. "In the 1954 campaign, the one we won without a runoff, I drove him from Mobile, Alabama, to Cullman. He drank a fifth and a pint of whiskey without a bit of chaser. I took him to the front of his house. He got out and walked in, and he never staggered a damn lick. Three years later, two drinks made him drunk. His body chemistry just changed."

Drinkard was Folsom's driver in the 1962 campaign. But he had a more important job than driving. He was in charge of giving Big Jim his ration of whiskey, an ounce-and-a-half miniature bottle every three hours. Drinkard had two deputy sheriffs to assist him in keeping Big Jim from getting more than his ration of whiskey on the campaign trail.

"Early Death, that's what he called it," Drinkard told us. "He drank Early Times. He called it Early Death."

But the night Folsom went on TV, Drinkard was recovering from an appendectomy and wasn't there to ration his whiskey.

"I was in the hospital," Drinkard said. "I was afraid this would happen when I found him Sunday. He was definitely drinking on Sunday, and the boy who picked him up Monday morning and went from Cullman to Double Springs, Alabama, was an alcoholic."

Drinkard saw the telecast.

"I couldn't believe what I was seeing," Drinkard said. "I nearly pulled the damn stitches out of my stomach. Bully Moon was with me. When Jim came on TV, before he said a word, Bully said, 'Goddamn, he's drunk,' just like that. I didn't believe it. But he was. There was something definitely wrong with him."

Tom Cork, a former Alabama newspaperman and aide to State Attorney General Bill Baxley, was among those who believed Big Jim was drunk on TV. But he said, "The people here in Alabama do not deal in the calm, sane, Midwestern type politicians anyway. Jim, or any of them, might be capable of anything if they got enough liquor in them."

Finis Ewing St. John, Jr., a Cullman lawyer, had known Folsom since the 1930s, when Folsom moved to Cullman. St. John also had defended some of the Folsom crowd on criminal charges. "In my opinion," St. John told us, "he had some friends who could do anything."

Big Jim told us he had some campaign workers who wanted to see Wallace elected and that he learned after the election that some of his closest aides had bet heavily on the outcome with Las Vegas gamblers.

"They were playing for keeps," he said, "because they had a lot of money on it."

Folsom told of the night of the television program: "Hell, they got me there to introduce that damn program, and I thought it was going to be just a half a minute. They told me the film was gone. I said, 'Hell, I'd better get me something.' I had a Coca-Cola and I went on live. I drank the Coca-Cola, and a fellow, a doctor friend of mine, supposed to have been, give me a pill. It was supposed to calm me down."

Jack Folsom was about twelve years old when he went on TV with his family.

"Pa appeared to be drunk, and drunk he wasn't," he said. "He wasn't drunk before he went on there. He started out in good shape, and about ten minutes into the show he started acting real funny and strange and goofy."

Others agree. Ted Bryant, veteran political reporter with the *Birmingham Post-Herald*, told us he talked with someone who was in the studio that night.

"This guy said that when Folsom came in, he was not acting that way," Bryant said, "that he sat down and they turned on those lights. The more he sat there the drunker he became."

We asked Big Jim if he was drunk.

"Hell, it didn't make no difference," Folsom replied. "I'd been shot, hell, on the stump plenty of times."

Wayne Greenhaw, a former Montgomery newspaperman, wrote the book *Watch Out for George Wallace*. He said Folsom "was the only man sane who could have beaten George Wallace."

Claude Duncan, former political reporter in Montgomery and a staff member of the Alabama Senate, told us, "If there's anything that ever changed the course of Alabama history, and maybe national history, it was probably that broadcast."

13

The Drinkard Boys Strike It Rich

THE FOLSOM CROWD DID more than play high-stakes poker at the mansion and drink whiskey with Big Jim. Some of them got rich.

"There's a few people who got rich under Jim Folsom, but he was definitely not one of them," said John Drinkard, one of three brothers from Cullman who were insiders in the Folsom administration.

Drinkard told us Big Jim once dropped a $50,000 state commission into his lap totally unexpectedly and said he turned down a Folsom offer that would have brought him more than $100,000 a year selling Seagram's Seven to state-operated liquor stores. This was at a time when the governor's salary was $12,000 a year.

When we interviewed Drinkard in April 1979 in Hartselle, Alabama, he worked as a car salesman at Abercrombie Chevrolet. Drinkard drove Big Jim around the state in two of his campaigns. He said he saw thousands of dollars change hands at the governor's mansion in poker games that Big Jim called "special sessions."

"I made more money out of the poker games than I did out of the administration," Drinkard said.

He told us he agreed reluctantly to drive Big Jim and help him control his drinking habit in the 1962 campaign. At the time, he said, he owned forty percent of a family Chevrolet dealership in Cullman and had made arrangements to borrow money from a bank to buy his brother Roy's sixty percent. Big Jim told him that if he would help him get elected governor again he wouldn't have to worry about paying off the bank note.

"That was the only time he ever admitted he had a drinking problem," Drinkard told us. "He said, 'I've got a problem, and you can keep people off me. You know how to handle it. I want you.'"

Drinkard said he refused but that Folsom summoned him back: "Jim said, 'John, I'm going to make a flat proposition to you. If you make that campaign with me, I'll sign that damn note, and if elected, I'll see that you get enough business from the state of Alabama to pay that damn thing off.'

"I reached over and shook hands with him. People may tell you they can't be bought, but that was the equalizer there."

Drinkard had been a salesman all his life and was selling tractors and other machinery on the side while he worked as Folsom's driver. He said that one day, Folsom asked him to be at the governor's office at six o'clock in the morning.

He showed up on time, delaying his departure on a long-planned fishing trip up a remote river near the Gulf Coast, a hundred and forty miles from the Capitol.

"I kept on waiting, and kept on, and kept on," Drinkard said. "Hell, it got to be ten o'clock. It got to be eleven o'clock, and I wasn't in to see the governor."

Drinkard told the governor's executive secretary, O.H. Finney, he was leaving. Finney asked him to wait and have lunch with Folsom at the mansion at noon, but Drinkard refused.

"I said, 'I'm going fishing,'" Drinkard said. "So I went fishing. To get to this fishing hole, you had to travel twelve miles up the river. We went out and caught a few fish and were cleaning and dressing them when I heard the damndest noise I'd ever heard in my life coming up the river. It was twelve damn boats.

He had every game warden, every conservation officer, every state trooper in that damn area, and they had them damn boats, and here he come up the river.

"It was real muddy up there, and he started to get out of the boat and fell on his ass, got mud on him. And he had the sheriff of Baldwin County with him. Right between his legs was a five-gallon crock of wildcat whiskey that the sheriff had confiscated off of somebody. Well, from then on, the rest of the night, we cooked the rest of the fish and fed everybody. We had the five gallons of whiskey. I think maybe there were ten gallons of it. I remember the five he had between his legs. That was his.

"He spent the night. We had a small poker game. He didn't say a damn word. He wouldn't go fishing with us the next morning. So I left to fish. He waited until about noon when I got back and said, 'I'll tell you what. You haven't got talking on your mind, but when you get through fishing, I want you to come by the office, by God. I want to see you.' I said, 'Okay.'"

When he returned to Montgomery, Drinkard said, he went to the governor's office in his fishing clothes, and Big Jim took him into the state finance director's office:

"He told the finance director, 'I want you to give those tractors to John's company. How much is involved? About how much commission do you think John will make out of it?' The finance director said, 'He would get about fifty thousand dollars.' Jim said to me, 'Okay, the fifty thousand dollars is yours. And the next time I tell you to come by the governor's office, you come.'"

John Drinkard's brothers may have won the 1946 governor's election for Folsom with a hearse.

Roy Drinkard was part owner of a chain of fourteen funeral homes at that time. Bill Drinkard, an embalmer, was directing Folsom's campaign. Later, Bill Drinkard held several top jobs in the Folsom administration, including finance director and head of the Board of Pardon and Parole. Roy Drinkard told us about the hearse one afternoon at his office in Cullman.

Unmarried at the time, Big Jim had a love affair with a Birmingham hotel office worker, Roy Drinkard told us, and she got pregnant. When Folsom failed to marry her, the young woman threatened to go to the press. Rumors of the affair leaked out just before the Democratic primary, and reporters were trying to find the woman. The Folsom campaign was frantic. A barrage of news stories at that crucial time would have defeated Big Jim, who had not yet perfected the art of confession.

Roy Drinkard told us that his brother Bill and a lumberman financing Folsom's campaign, Bryce Davis, tricked the woman into riding around for two days in a Drinkard Brothers hearse.

"They told her they were going to meet Big Jim and it had to be in secret," Roy Drinkard said. "And I think they did meet him at one time. But they mostly rode her around over the state until the primary was over. It was pretty high stakes, you know, for the Drinkard boys."

Bill Drinkard, later killed in a car wreck, ended up with powerful and high-paying jobs in both Folsom administrations, and Bryce Davis became liquor czar of Alabama as alcoholic beverage control chairman.

In his 1977 book, *A New Life to Live*, William Bradford Huie wrote about the young woman and the son she bore. He said the woman, Christine Johnston, a bookkeeper and cashier at the Tutwiler Hotel in Birmingham, got out-of-court settlements totaling $35,000. Huie said the boy was Jimmy Putman, who grew up to be six-feet-five in his bare feet.

"I helped him get his first job when he got out of high school, and he's a Folsom," Roy Drinkard told us.

When Bryce Davis was liquor czar, he and Roy Drinkard roomed together year-round at the Jeff Davis Hotel in Montgomery. Drinkard said Davis arranged for him to get a dollar for every case of Jim Beam bourbon sold in Alabama. Drinkard said the first check he received from Jim Beam was for $40,000, but when his wife found out it was liquor money she wouldn't let him keep it.

"I said, 'What do you want me to do with it?'" Drinkard told us. "She said, 'Send it back.' So I sent it back and got it made out to her brother-in-law, God love him. And he, fool-like, told his wife. So I sent it back to the Beam Company the second time, and I got it made out to Ross Clark, Jim Folsom's brother-in-law and Thelma's husband. He couldn't tell his wife.

"He said, 'Better not try to cash that in Montgomery. I'll

see you next week.' The next week he didn't get to come, nor the next week, nor the next. About the fourth or fifth week, I went to his funeral. Ross committed suicide before I got the money. I saw that check three times. I saw it in my name, I saw it in my brother-in-law's bureau drawer, and I delivered it to Ross. I don't know why he committed suicide. I didn't send flowers."

Roy Drinkard told us he lost out on another deal with the Folsom administration. He was chairman of the Cullman Industrial Development Board and said he had arranged through Big Jim to use state road equipment to grade the site for a new King Edward cigar plant. But State Auditor Ralph Eagerton reported they were violating the law, and Big Jim didn't fulfill his promise, Drinkard said.

"I was in the middle," Drinkard said. "The King Edward people were not demanding, but firmly asking, that the work be done. And the governor, having promised it, failed to deliver. So finally, after a year, I confronted him in the mansion. I carried the state senator, the state representative and my brother Bill Drinkard with me. I told the governor to keep his word. He said he couldn't. I said, 'You got to.' He said, 'I can't.' I said, 'You're just a liar, governor.' He said, 'No, I'm not a liar.' I said, 'You are. You won't do what you said you'd do.' So he said, 'You just get out of my house and stay out.' I said, 'This is not your house. It belongs to the taxpayers. I'll stay here if I like.'

"So he stood up, six-foot-eight, you know, and I went for the kitchen. They were frying two quail in the kitchen. I said, 'I'd like two.' So a trusty from the prison served me two quail at the table, and I ate them. I stood up and about that time, the governor came in and asked for his quail. I didn't know there were only two in the house. He said, 'Where are my quail?' The trusty said, 'Mister Roy et 'em.' The governor said to me, 'You son of a bitch, you get out of this house and don't you ever come back to Montgomery as long as I'm governor.' I said, 'I got no way to go.' He said, 'Ride the bus.' I said, 'I don't have any way to get to the bus station.' He said, 'Winston will carry you.' That was his chauffeur.

"So they put me in the big Cadillac, the number one, and started to the Greyhound Bus Station. I was sitting in the front seat, and I said, 'Winston, what is this?' He said, 'Mister Roy, that's a telephone.' I said, 'A telephone in a car?' You've got to realize this was in '48. He said, 'Yes, sir, just try it. Who do you want to call?' I said, 'Do you know the governor's number?' He said, 'Yeah,' so he rang him up, and the governor answered the phone, and I took the phone and said, 'Governor?' And he said, 'Yeah.' I said, 'This is Roy. I still say you're a lying son of a bitch.'"

Drinkard never did get to the Greyhound station. He said he persuaded Winston to return him to the mansion, and he spent the night in a small guest house in the back yard.

The trappings of power of the governor's office never awed Roy Drinkard. He said he and the mayor of Cullman, Bill Nesmith, went to Folsom's office in the Capitol to ask a favor and found George Wallace, then a state legislator, waiting to see Folsom to seek appointment as circuit judge. Drinkard said they waited in the anteroom for two days, but the governor never showed up.

"Bill Lyerly, the governor's personal secretary, let us in the governor's private office," Drinkard said. "He had a bunch of marbles on his desk and a sign up there that said, 'I got the marbles. Talk to me.' We sent down to the supply room and got a big piece of chalk, and we drew a big circle on the Persian rug in front of the governor's desk. We got the marbles down off that desk. Bill Nesmith, George Wallace and I played marbles for the next two days. Wallace sure could shoot those marbles, stick with his taw, you know."

After Folsom's first term ended in 1951, the Gordon Persons administration indicted several members of Big Jim's crowd. It indicted Roy Drinkard for perjury after he denied to investigators under oath that he received $1,500 to arrange a state inmate's parole. Drinkard was acquitted when the prosecution's key witness failed to appear to testify.

Roy told us he was a close friend of J. Hoyt Shepherd, the crime boss of the $50-million-a-year liquor, gambling and prostitution racket in Phenix City. The little Alabama border town is across the Chattahoochee River from Columbus, Georgia, and Fort Benning, a huge Army base that supplied Phenix City with an active and gullible clientele on paydays. The town was known as the nation's Sin City. Then Albert Patterson, Alabama's attorney general nominee, was assassinated on Phenix City's main street in 1954. After that, the Alabama National Guard moved in to clean up the town.

Some of Phenix City's leading citizens were convicted of murder and other crimes.

Roy remembered spending the night at Shepherd's Phenix City home before the cleanup. He recalled that Shepherd stationed armed guards in pillboxes outside his house and stashed automatic weapons under his baby's crib.

Another of Roy's acquaintances in Phenix City was Jimmy Matthews, Shepherd's partner in the crime syndicate.

"The last time I saw them, " Roy said, "they came to see me."

That was when some of the cases growing out of the Phenix City cleanup were on appeal before the Alabama Supreme Court, Roy said.

"They came over here to see me with a very simple request," Drinkard told us. "That was to bribe the Supreme Court."

He said he turned them down.

"They said, 'Who are we going to get to do it if we don't get you to do it for us?'" Roy recalled. "I told them, 'Man, no sir. You ain't talking to me.'"

Drinkard was a good Baptist. He was nominated for deacon of the First Baptist Church of Cullman just before a countywide liquor referendum. His pastor was circulating a dry petition to counter the wets and asked Drinkard to sign. When he refused, the pastor asked Drinkard to withdraw as a candidate for deacon. Again, Drinkard refused.

"He stood up and said, 'Mister Drinkard, how do you expect to vote wet and run for deacon of the First Baptist Church?'

"I said, 'Pastor, I guess I'll have to run on the wet ticket.'

"I was not elected."

When Drinkard was in the funeral business, his chief competitor in Cullman was Raymond Higdon, who worked for Moss Funeral Home, Drinkard said. He tried to hire Higdon with a huge bonus, but Higdon turned him down.

"Boy, he is the type of guy who lives to serve others," Drinkard said. "There was no way to compete with him. At night—and he still does it—if there's a storm and the power goes off and people are up the pole and it's hailing, why he goes out there and shimmies up the pole to carry them a thermos of hot coffee. He'd borrow money to loan it to somebody that needs it. I decided if we couldn't get him to go to work for us we would just have to get him elected to public office. We talked him into running for sheriff. He was sure to be elected."

Drinkard said they got up $300 to pay Higdon's qualifying fee, and they decided to have a little fun with him:

"We went and told him, 'Now, Raymond, you know how the sheriff's office is run?' He said, 'Yeah, you get some deputies and you enforce the law.' We said, 'Yeah, but you've got to turn your head once in a while. There's a certain man who has had all the bootlegging rights for years because he elected the sheriff. Now, are you going to lock him up and break that up?' He said, 'Yes, sir. Yes, sir. I'm going to dry this county up.' We said, 'Oh, don't say dry it up. This is going to be a natural for us. We'll buy liquor in Birmingham and haul it in in a hearse. We'll be the wholesalers. We won't ever be known. And you've got to turn your head.'

"He said, 'I got to do that to be sheriff?' We said, 'Yes you have.' And he said, 'Boys, what y'all say ain't going to work. When I'm sheriff, I'm going to look at y'all like anybody else. I hope you don't give me any trouble. But I tell you this, you'd just as well chalk your feet and toe the line because if you haul liquor in here I'm going to lock you up.'

"We had to get Raymond out of the sheriff's race. We got him qualified for tax collector. We gave him that $300, and he swept the field. He's been tax collector ever since."

We asked him if that got Higdon out of the undertaking business.

"No, sir," Drinkard said, "he stayed right up there. He handled more funerals than he ever did. He became more of an influence. We got out of the business."

Drinkard told us to make sure we looked up Ruby Folsom, Big Jim's baby sister and former mother-in-law of George Wallace. Ruby was a six-footer, and Cornelia was taller than George. When Cornelia told her mother she planned to marry Wallace, big Ruby was quoted as exclaiming, "Why, honey, he ain't titty high."

"She said she was misquoted about George Wallace," Drinkard told us. "She said, 'I never said George was titty high. I said he was *about* titty high.'"

14

Alabama's Jewel: Big Ruby

WHEN WE ARRIVED IN Montgomery, old newspapermen who had known Ruby Folsom through the years told us about her. After her short career as Alabama's First Lady, Big Ruby had remained in Montgomery where she became a folk figure. Ruby's daughter, Cornelia, also was Alabama First Lady when she was married to George Wallace.

"Big Ruby stories are a dime a dozen," said Tom Cork, a political consultant and former Montgomery newspaperman. "I love this one best because I happened to be sitting there. After Cornelia and George got married in '71, there were all kinds of hangers-on who would walk in and out of Ruby's house day and night. She just kind of ran an open house.

"For all her faults, the woman did have a heart, and still does have a heart of gold. Strangers would come to the door, and she wouldn't refuse anybody: *Come on in, there's something on the stove cooking.*

"If they had any whiskey, that was good. If they didn't: *There's Archie. Give them a drink.*

"You would meet all kinds of strange people. I went over there one night, mainly because I wanted to take my girl friend—she's my wife, now—to see Audrey Williams, Hank's widow. She was over there. My wife had heard stories about her and wanted to meet Audrey Williams. So we went over there. We didn't get to talk to Audrey very much. She was zonked out of her mind.

"But there were ten people sitting around the living room, all of us, including me, very drunk. I happened to be sitting on one side of Ruby, and there was another fellow who was relatively sober sitting on the other side. I never did get his name. I don't know anything about him except this was the first time he had ever met Ruby. He was from out of the state. He was obviously some type of hustler, trying to get in on something with the governor's mother-in-law or some type of thing.

"He was just being so polite, and it was impossible, it was totally different from anybody else's behavior around there. Everything Ruby was saying, he would just agree with: 'Oh, Miss Folsom, you're so right. You're so smart.' She would say the most outrageous things in the world. So as the evening wore on, Ruby got drunker and drunker and drunker. She's got this habit where the chin will come to rest on that magnificent bosom. And she will stay there like that, and she will catch everything you say every now and then. And maybe a few seconds later, she will raise her head and respond to it.

"So this fellow, he was really just talking down the country to her. She nodded off. In a minute, he said, 'And Miss Folsom, I want you to know that I met your daughter, Cornelia, and not only is she a lovely lady, and not only is she very beautiful, she has an exquisite figure.'

"Ruby didn't respond. This fellow said something else. I was kind of watching Ruby for her response. Then she lifted her head, and looked at him kind of bleary-eyed, and said, 'All us Folsoms got big titties.'"

Ray Jenkins, then editor of *The Alabama Journal*, told us, "Most of Ruby's stories have no particular point to them. They are just funny. I'll give you a perfect example. I was sitting in

Tom Johnson's house one Saturday morning. He is editor of the *Montgomery Independent*, a little weekly newspaper here, and lives next door to Ruby. She came walking across the yard. She is an enormous woman, about six feet tall, very vulgar. Johnson looked out across the lawn and saw her coming toward his house, and he said, 'She's not drinking. This is going to be trouble.'

"She came in and was in a very surly mood. She was that way when she didn't drink. They had just had her at the kill-or-cure place, which she defined as kill you or cure you. So she was off the booze. She never stays off of it more than a few weeks. But she was off of it this particular morning, and in a very sour mood, and cussing, 'Goddammit, George Wallace won't even send a state trooper over here to pick up his mama-in-law.'

"She wanted to go over to the governor's mansion. That's when George and Cornelia were still married. I said, 'I'd be glad to take you, Ruby, but all I've got is this little old car.' I had a Triumph Spitfire, which is practically a motor scooter. I said, 'I don't think you could get in there.'

"She had some scruffy old poodle dog with her. She said, 'Oh, yes, I can get in it if you will take me over there.' It wasn't but a few blocks from where we were. She managed somehow to get in that car. Of course, I'm pretty large myself, and she's about as large as I am and weighs more than I do. And that dog got in there. I was afraid that damn little car was going to collapse.

"Anyway, we got over to the governor's mansion. I stopped out front. I didn't want to drive up into the driveway and make a spectacle of myself. She said, 'Go on and drive up in the driveway.' So I took her on in, drove her right smack up. The guard there saw who we were and waved us on in, and I pulled right up to the very doorsteps of the governor's mansion.

"Ruby started to get out. She strained, but she couldn't get out. It got more and more embarrassing. I said, 'I'll help you, Ruby.' And I got out, and I pulled on her, and she still couldn't make it. The guard saw us and he came up and here both of us were pulling Ruby, and the dog barking, and what have you. I was scared to death George Wallace was going to wheel out there and start laughing at me and pointing at me: 'Ah, Jenkins, I see you picked up somebody.'

"But he didn't come out. At one point, she said, 'I reckon we're just going to have to call a crane.' We finally got her out of there, and I got away from there as fast as I could."

Jenkins said Ruby had been invited to a Christmas party in his neighborhood and couldn't find the address.

"She got the wrong house," he said. "And she has always got a boyfriend. They are usually strange characters who don't have much to say, just errand boys who go to the liquor store for her. So she and her boyfriend showed up at our neighbor's house, looking for this Christmas party she was supposed to go to. The neighbor told her, 'No, you have the wrong one.' Ruby said, 'Well, you're having a party. We'll just come in and go to this one.' So she barged right on in and made a shambles of the party."

Jenkins said, "She's kind of a tragic person. She's capable of breaking down and crying frequently. She's an older woman, but she looks pretty good. She had a face lift, and I complimented her on it. She said, 'Yeah, I really like it. I like it so much I'm thinking about having my body tightened up, too.'"

Claude Duncan, a former political reporter and a member of the state Senate staff, was a confidante of Ruby and Cornelia. Duncan told us Wallace and Cornelia became alarmed during his 1972 presidential campaign because Ruby was telling family secrets they wanted kept out of the papers.

"During the campaign, Cornelia and George made Ruby swear off talking to the press," Duncan told us.

He said that Eleanor Randolph, then with the Washington bureau of the *Chicago Tribune*, was trying to get an interview, but Ruby wouldn't talk to her. Randolph was about as tall as Ruby but a great deal younger and better looking. She was not above using Southern belle wiles to get a story.

"I told her, 'Just go out there and knock on the door, and if Ruby's there she'll talk to you.' So Eleanor went out to her house. Ruby was very cautious. Eleanor wanted to buy her dinner, buy her a meal, buy her drinks. Ruby told her, 'Well, this is Wednesday night, honey. I reserve Wednesday night to go out to the Diplomat, drinking with my friends.'

"Eleanor used her charm and told her how much she had heard about Miss Ruby all her life, read about her, wanted to talk to her, buy her drinks. Ruby finally said, 'Well, come on, honey. Let's go out to the Diplomat. Maybe I can get you laid, too.'"

Later, Eleanor confirmed the story for us and added to it: "While I was at her house, Big Ruby brought out bourbon in tea glasses for us to drink. I never had seen people drink tea glasses full of bourbon before. I told myself that I could die if I was not careful. Finally, she said let's go over to the club at the Holiday Inn, and we did. I was taking lots of notes, and the *Chicago Tribune* was buying and Big Ruby was drinking. After a while my notes got to be scriggly lines. The next day, when I could get up out of bed, I had to call my office and tell them I had a lot more research to do on the story. I had to stay in the hotel three days to get over being out one night with Big Ruby. But it was a wonderful, wonderful story. You can't miss when you are talking to her."

After Eleanor's story was published in the *Chicago Tribune* and other newspapers across the country, Duncan said, "Cornelia told me, 'Hell, I was trying to keep all that from even getting in my book. Eleanor went out there, bought her two drinks, and she told her everything she ever knew.'"

Eleanor told us, "I was down there again and saw Big Ruby and she said, 'I am not supposed to talk to you.' But she told me, 'I just love the PTL club and every morning I promise the Lord I'm going to stop drinking, but by about mid-day I start backsliding.'"

We found Ruby sitting at a table in Crockmirers bar in south Montgomery. She told us she had just spent $3,000 to dry out at an alcoholism treatment center in Statesboro, Georgia. She was drunk.

"I drink Jack Daniel's and water," she informed us. "This is cocktail hour. You get two for the price of one, you lucky buzzards."

Ruby, who was sixty-six years old, was at the table with a much younger, effeminate man who said he was writing a biography of country singer and song-writer Hank Williams. When he went to the bar to get another round of drinks, Ruby mocked his flouncy manner and confided to us in the noisy bar, "What I need is a man's man."

While we sat trying to interview Ruby, having to shout our questions in her ear, Cornelia and another woman came in. Cornelia showed her mother a ring she had received from a man as a gift. But obviously disgusted that her mother was drunk again, Cornelia and her friend chose another table and soon left the bar.

Ruby stayed on, flirting with men at several other tables and insisting on telling us intimate details of her life. She told us that Cornelia owed her beautiful singing voice to the fact she was conceived the night her mother saw Nelson Eddy sing "Indian Love Call" in a movie in Evergreen, Alabama.

"Damn it, I wanted a baseball team, and I only had two," Ruby said. "Charlie didn't want to have any children. He loved me so much, but he didn't want any children. So I tricked him into two."

"How did you do that?"

"You know, the night I got pregnant with Cornelia, he was singing," she said, pausing to do a weird imitation of Nelson Eddy. "Isn't it 'Indian Love Call'?" she said. "I went home that night, and my husband was asleep. I was so passionate I took advantage of him."

She said she later met Nelson Eddy when he performed in Birmingham and told him how she got pregnant with Cornelia.

"I gave him credit for it," she said.

But Eddy seemed offended by the story, she recalled.

"That's when I realized he was a queer," she said.

Ruby's father died of poison whiskey when she was six. A strict, teetotaling Baptist anyway, her mother asked each of her seven children to sign a pledge in the family Bible that they would never touch a drop of whiskey. Only Big Jim and Ruby signed. Although Thelma never signed the pledge, she took up her mother's mantle against whiskey and became head of the Elba Temperance Committee.

Big Ruby said she had reached her full height by the time she was thirteen years old. She told us about her awkward childhood, growing up in Coffee County. She said she developed a complex over her height.

"I knew I had to have the best personality," she told us. "I had to do everything the best, and I did. I always wanted to be in show business."

She said her husband, Charles Ellis, left her when she took Cornelia and her son, Charles, and went to live with Big Jim in Cullman after his first wife died and left him with two small girls.

We kept trying to get Ruby out of the tumultuous bar so we could interview her in the quiet of her apartment, but she kept ordering rounds of drinks and getting drunker and drunker. When we finally succeeded in getting her up and on her way out, she lurched toward a table of men and launched into a conversation, the only word of which we picked up was "poontang." She was having the time of her life.

We went to the Carriage Hills Apartments, where Ruby and Cornelia were staying temporarily after a fire at Ruby's house. Ruby settled into a big living room chair and told us, "The Folsoms drank. I have a hollow leg, and I drink, and I'm a Folsom. I'm not proud of it, and I don't fight it. As long as you love them, and you spend your whole life getting jobs for people and helping them. . . ."

Her voice trailed off.

"Everybody loves me," she said. "I know I'm loved. Whiskey is here to stay. I'm sorry about it. In a way, I'm not. But I think it's better to be legalized than to drink poisoned liquor, like people were drinking."

Then she turned remorseful and weepy, remembering her brother Carl, who was killed on Luzon in World War II.

"Honey," she said through her tears, "he must have had one like that. He drove the women crazy. It's a damn shame the Lord took him. He had one this long, and he knew how to use it."

Before we left, Ruby had not sobered up, but her tears had dried. She told us how she wanted to be buried.

"I don't want no lily in my hand," she said. "Put a glass with some Coffee County branch water and bourbon in it. Dress me up, put a bottle of Jack Daniel's on my left hip, put my left hand on the bottle, and I'll be ready for Heaven."

IV

IV

George Wallace and Other Barbour County Bourbons

EARLY IN HIS CAREER, George Wallace calculated that Jim Folsom was right about the race question in Alabama. Wallace knew that after World War II, blacks were going to demand and get the right to vote in the South. He thought it was proper to allow blacks that right as long as they voted for him.

So he hitched a ride on the Folsom bandwagon, hoping to cash in on the votes of poor whites, blacks and union members. Wallace's timing was bad. In the 1950s and 1960s, Alabama turned out to be an unfortunate precinct for a liberal candidate for public office. Wallace decided Folsom was wrong.

Loss of a governor's race was enough to switch Wallace to a proved Alabama political philosophy—hardcore racism. He got elected.

As governor in the 1960s, Wallace read the frustrations and anger of the American people. He tried to ride that discontent to the presidency. But Wallace's practice of blatant racism back home in Alabama was too much of a handicap for him in the politics of the nation. Instead, Republicans mined the seam of voter dissatisfaction and moved into the White House.

Late in life, paralyzed by a would-be assassin's bullet, Wallace realized Big Jim had been right after all. Running from a wheelchair, Wallace won two more terms as governor, his third and fourth. That was a record in Alabama. His winning margin in his last election came from black voters.

The South's greatest switch-hitter was man enough to say he was wrong.

But the gadfly of Alabama politics and Wallace's tormentor, Shorty Price, accused the governor of being afraid to fight him. Even if Price was "shorter and littler" than Wallace when he was in his prime.

Shorty never made it into high office. But he may be the only man in Alabama who ever made money running against George Wallace.

15

The Little School Children

In 1975, when George Corley Wallace, Jr. was governor of Alabama, the state's general fund was about out of money, but the separate education fund was bulging with a $150 million surplus. Wallace wanted to divert $48 million for highways and mental hospitals.

"Of course, the educators were bad against it," political consultant Tom Cork told us. "They raised hell. They lobbied. They got the Alabama Education Association to come up to the Capitol. They had every teacher in the state, you know, to call their representatives and the press. All these educators were talking about was, 'The poor little school children are going to suffer.' The little school children this. The little school children that. 'They're not going to have any milk if Governor Wallace has his way. Not going to have any books.'

"So the bill got hung up in the Legislature, and Wallace called about seven of the legislators into his office. He started off very calmly, 'Now, gentlemen, I think I have offered here what is a good sound program to help us out of this emergency, and it will not hurt education in the long run. I just want to hear your views on it. I think what I proposed is good. If you will examine it very carefully, I think you will agree with me. I don't know why you oppose me so. I want to hear every one of your views on it.'

"And every one of them just sounded like a parrot. They said the same thing. They said, 'Oh, governor, these teachers have been calling us about the little school children. We just can't go against the little school children.'

"The governor said, 'Yes, I understand that.' He asked the next legislator, and he said the same thing: 'Oh, I'm telling you, they brought a whole bunch of little school children to see me, you know, and they said all these little school children are going to suffer if you do this, and we're going to beat you the next time you run.'

"The governor says, 'I understand.' He goes on to the next one. He listens to them all. All of them were alike."

Cork interrupted the story to tell us: "I need to give you this little tip note of information. About a month before this issue had come up, they had a local referendum in Montgomery about raising taxes for the schools. They wanted to put a half mill on, something like that. They had a local vote on it, raising taxes for the same purpose, little school children, see. It was beat about ten to one. Just beat the hell out of it."

He went on with his story:

"The governor very calmly listened to all the legislators he had called into his office. When they got through, he said, 'I'm going to tell you something. Y'all keep talking about the little school children, how they're going to suffer, how the people are going to get mad at us. I want to tell you a little story. Right here in Montgomery, about a month ago, they had a vote on this issue over raising taxes for schools. All these educators went on TV, and they told everybody, 'If you don't vote for this tax increase, the schools are going to shut down, and the little school children will suffer. They ain't going to get no education. You'd better vote for this tax increase or these little school children are going to suffer.'

"That amendment was beat ten to one, and I'll tell you why. It was because the average Alabamian has spent eight hours working out in the hot sun, comes in at five o'clock in the afternoon, he sits down in front of the TV set, mad as hell, all hot and sweaty, and he's got a beer in one hand and a baloney sandwich in the other. And he turns on the TV, and some educator in some three-piece suit comes on the air and says, *If you don't vote this tax increase, the little school children are going to suffer.*

"Now I'm going to tell you what that fellow watching that TV thinks. He says, *Fuck the little school children.*"

Wallace still hadn't convinced enough legislators to pass the bill, so he went on statewide television with three fruit jars sitting in front of him. Two were empty, and the third was spilling over with nickels. The political device he used to make his point was stolen right off the stump from Big Jim Folsom. Scooping up some coins from the spillage, Wallace dropped a few into each of the empty fruit jars to illustrate that the fat, greedy educators could spare a few nickels to get the poor farmers out of Alabama's mud and to help the mentally sick.

As Wallace anticipated, angry mail poured in to legislators opposing his bill, but enough of them were still afraid of the little school children lobby that he still didn't have enough votes to pass the bill. Following his three-jar speech, Wallace threatened to start tearing up blacktop roads in counties represented by rebellious legislators. The next day, one of the legislators got a call from back home, and a constituent told him, "George has got the tractors next to the road."

His bill passed.

Former Montgomery newspaper editor Ray Jenkins told us Wallace's sales pitch on another of his pet programs.

"It was '77, may have been '78, but Wallace was trying to put through some bills to really grind down the Alabama Power Company. And the power company was very much concerned about it. I think the power company also knew it had the Legislature pretty much in its hip pocket. It is common knowledge that the power company retains legislators and pays them fat fees, and they look after the power company's interest in the Legislature. But in any case, Wallace was really pushing for this package of bills dealing with the rate base and things like that.

"And so he was calling all the legislators down one by one, really putting the heat on them, as he did in his crucial fights. He called down these two black legislators from Birmingham, U.W. Clemon and J. Richmond Pearson. And by this time, Wallace had pretty much shed his racist image, you know, and he could sit down and talk comfortably with a black legislator. He had these two black senators down from Birmingham.

"Generally speaking, you will find the black legislators from Birmingham are pretty much part of that establishment up there, and this was no exception. They would vote with the Birmingham Chamber of Commerce's legislative package more than against it. And Wallace was well aware of this. But he was putting the heat on them to pass this utility package.

"And he was relating this story to me, and Wallace is at his very best when he is very scornful and sarcastic. He said to me, 'I was talking to these legislators and told them, *Now, senators, this is the kind of bill that will really help your people more than anybody else. It is designed to help the poor people.*'

"At this point, Wallace said they told him, 'Governor, we understand what you are fighting for. But we are concerned about your no-growth policy.' That was what the power company said, in effect, that Wallace was instituting a no-growth policy. And he paused, and said to me: 'No growth! I can hear it now, out there in that poolroom in Bessemer, some black poolroom in Bessemer, where one guy says, *Eight ball in the side pocket, motherfucker. You know, I'm concerned about Governor Wallace's no-growth policy.*'"

George Wallace was born in the south Alabama hamlet of Clio on August 25, 1919, and got his political start sixteen miles away in Clayton, one of Barbour County's two county seats. Clayton was a drab town of a couple of thousand people, squeezed in around a gray stone Confederate soldier towering over a small square in front of the courthouse.

Barbour County had two courthouses and two sets of county officials, one in Clayton and one in the prospering Chattahoochee River town of Eufaula on the Georgia line, twenty-two miles east. Barbour had only one set of county commissioners, but it had two sheriffs, two probate judges, two tax assessors, two tax collectors and two circuit court clerks.

Six other Alabama counties had two county seats to make it easier for citizens to transact affairs with their local governments, but it always seemed that Barbour County's politics demanded a courthouse at each end of the county to accommodate and absorb its sound and fury and violence. George Wallace's father, who served a term as county commission chairman, was remembered for chasing a man through the courthouse at Clayton brandishing a knife. He died at age forty while George, Jr. was attending the University of Alabama, where he got his law degree in 1942.

Wallace's grandfather was a country doctor and, for one term, probate judge, the most powerful political job in his end of the county. The grandfather was the strongest childhood influence on young George but could not convince him to become a preacher. Instead, the political arena beckoned.

It turned out to be the natural outlet for Wallace's aggressiveness. He boxed as a schoolboy, winning two state Golden Gloves championships, and was captain of the boxing team at the University of Alabama.

Wallace's younger brother Jack, a circuit judge, said that as a boy George would walk up to people on their porches, shake their hands and tell them that one day he was going to be governor of Alabama.

It was a reasonable ambition for a middle-class boy from Clio. Among Alabama's sixty-seven counties, Barbour was known as the Home of Governors. When Wallace was growing up he was aware that the county had furnished three governors. And when he returned from Army Air Corps duty in World War II and got himself elected to the Legislature in 1946, Alabama had its fourth Barbour County governor, Chauncey Sparks from Eufaula.

From January 1963 to January 1987, two more Barbour Countians were governor for eighteen of those twenty-four years. They were George Wallace and his late wife, Lurleen. Wallace was elected to a record four terms. And in 1966, when he couldn't succeed himself, he persuaded Alabama's voters to elect his wife.

Lurleen served two years of a four-year term before she died of cancer. By law, she was governor; in reality, her husband was governor.

Soon after he was elected governor, Wallace set out to change the country and get himself elected president. In 1964, he made the first of his four races for the White House.

Never a more rambunctious soul than George Wallace ever hurtled himself onto the political stage, bobbing and weaving, strutting and scowling, gnawing and scratching. None had a greater love for politics and power and for running for office than the dark-eyed, cigar-chewing, demonic little man, barely five-feet-six.

Even after Arthur Bremer shot him down at a Maryland shopping center in 1972 and made him a paraplegic, Wallace campaigned in a wheelchair. He ran for president a fourth time and was elected governor twice more.

Wallace and liberal Senator Wayne Morse of Oregon once got into a name-calling contest. Morse called Wallace a punk. Wallace replied, "I'd rather be a punk than a pink," and suggested that Morse should have his head examined.

In a speech on the Senate floor, Morse read from a Veterans Administration medical report that qualified Wallace for a ten percent pension from the Air Corps for a service-related mental disability: "He was tense, restless, and ill at ease, frequently drummed the desk with his fingers, changed position frequently, sighed occasionally and showed a tendency to stammer, resulting in the diagnosis of anxiety reaction."

Wallace retorted, "Well, at least I have a paper that certifies I have ninety percent of my faculties, which is more than Wayne Morse can claim."

There was no denying Wallace influenced the politics and

policies of the nation after the glory days of the Great Society in the 1960s.

"Yeah," he bragged with some justification late in his career, "now they all saying everything I used to say, ain't they? Talking about bureaucrats, inflation, taxes, saving the middle class."

The first indication that the nation was moving toward Wallace's politics came early in 1972 when he stunned the Democratic Party by winning its presidential primary in Florida over George McGovern of South Dakota, Hubert Humphrey of Minnesota, Ed Muskie of Maine, John Lindsay of New York and Henry Jackson of Washington.

"When we went to Florida, my opponents were talking about the perfectibility of man," Wallace said. "When we came out we were all talking about busing."

From the start of his career, Wallace had a knack for pinpointing people's frustrations and convincing them he could do something about it, or if he couldn't, that he was on their side. In 1952, after six years in the Legislature, he ran for judge of Alabama's Third Judicial Circuit, cashing in on the frustrations of World War II GIs.

Wallace ran against Preston Clayton, for whose family the town of Clayton was named. Clayton was a genteel, honorable man, from most accounts, who liked to ride Arabian horses. But he had one monumental political vulnerability. During World War II, he had been a lieutenant colonel in the Army. Wallace had been a sergeant.

Wallace campaigned the width and breadth of Barbour County telling voters: "Now, all you officers vote for Clayton, and all you privates vote for me." He won easily.

Wallace made his first race for governor in 1958 with the endorsement of the NAACP and the AFL-CIO. At that time, his politics was similar to Big Jim Folsom's, and he had been Folsom's south Alabama campaign manager in 1954, when Folsom won his second term as governor by a landslide.

But times had changed between 1954 and 1958. The Supreme Court had ordered that the South's public schools be racially integrated with all deliberate speed. Rosa Parks had refused to move to the back of the bus in Montgomery, and Dr. Martin Luther King, Jr. had become an international figure by leading a successful boycott against the capital city's bus system. President Eisenhower had ordered the 101st Airborne Division to enforce a federal court order to admit black students to Central High School in Little Rock. And civil rights officials from the U.S. Justice Department were moving into the South to require registration of black voters.

Frustrations among Southern white voters were growing, but Wallace had not read them quickly enough.

In the 1958 governor's race, the Ku Klux Klan endorsed Wallace's opponent, John Patterson, and worked in his campaign. After he lost to Patterson, a distraught Wallace disappeared for several days. He reappeared, gaunt but determined. He was widely quoted as saying to his cronies, "Boys, John Patterson out-niggered me, but I won't be out-niggered again."

Wallace denied the quote, but he was true to the words.

After his 1958 election defeat, Wallace had only a few months left in his term as circuit judge, but he made the most of it. He emerged as the fightin' little judge for Alabama's segregationists.

That put him on a collision course with a tough, young federal judge from the Middle District of Alabama, Frank Minis Johnson, Jr., his classmate and close friend at the University of Alabama Law School.

George Wallace and Frank Johnson were from opposite corners of the state and different heritages. Wallace was from the old slave-holding, cotton-growing black belt whose plantation owners led Alabama's rush to secession. Johnson grew up in the Free State of Winston, a fiercely independent, coal mining, moonshine-making county in the north Alabama hill country.

At the time of the Civil War, Winston Countians had no slaves, no plantations and no dog in that fight. When Alabama withdrew from the Union, Winston County tried to secede from Alabama. Winston was the only Alabama county to send more soldiers to the Union army than to the Confederacy.

One of Frank Johnson's great-uncles fought for the North against his own brother. After the Civil War, Winston County became a Republican island in solidly Democratic Alabama.

When Wallace and Johnson were law school classmates in Tuscaloosa, Johnson was married, and bachelor Wallace often visited him and his wife, usually at suppertime.

Montgomery author Wayne Greenhaw told us about a time when Johnson and Wallace teamed up to rescue the president of the law school student body from a stretch in the drunk tank at the Birmingham jail. Glenn Curlee of Elmore County was their friend in trouble.

Greenhaw said Curlee got drunk at the Alabama-Tennessee football game in Birmingham. And when Alabama scored the winning touchdown as time was running out, he smacked a policeman over the head with a rolled-up newspaper.

"The cops toted him away and put him in a paddy wagon, a big old black thing they called a Black Maria, to take him off to the clink," Greenhaw said. "Glenn hollered out to George and Frank, 'They're taking me away. I'm going to need a good lawyer now, and I'm going to need a good witness. Y'all come on down.'

"So they followed him down to City Court at the jail. At the time, they had night court. It was about ten o'clock at night. There was some judge on the bench who was from Haleyville, which is where Frank Johnson was from. Frank and George flipped a coin to see which one was going to represent Glenn. Frank won. He was going to be the lawyer, and George was going to be the witness.

"George took the witness stand and said, 'I know this man doesn't use alcoholic beverages. He is a clean cut, fine fellow. We're in law school together. I've been knowing him for years and years. He has never done such a thing, your honor.' At the end of the hearing the judge said, 'Well, I find this boy not guilty.'"

Afterward, Greenhaw said, the judge invited the three boys to his home for drinks.

"The judge turned to Curlee and said, 'We have some Coca-

Cola out there for you,'" Greenhaw said. "All night, Frank and George sat out there drinking whiskey and beer with the judge, and old Curlee was sipping Coca-Cola."

In 1952, Johnson was Alabama campaign manager for Dwight Eisenhower. The Republican president rewarded him with a federal judgeship in 1955.

Johnson collided with Wallace in 1958. Wallace had just lost the governor's race and had only a few weeks to go as circuit judge. The U.S. Civil Rights Commission sought the voter registration records in Wallace's home area of Bullock and Barbour counties. Wallace saw this as an opportunity to launch his new political strategy of race. He seized the records and refused to turn them over to federal agents.

Johnson ordered Wallace to surrender the records or show cause why he shouldn't be held in contempt of court. Although he was making political hay out of it, Wallace got worried that he might have to go to jail. It was Glenn Curlee's turn to repay a favor. He called Johnson at his home in Montgomery and asked if he would be willing to meet privately with Wallace. The judge agreed to do it.

In his book *Watch Out for George Wallace*, Greenhaw described the meeting of the old law school classmates:

"After eleven o'clock Wallace rang the doorbell of the judge's brick ranch-style house in a fashionable area of the town. When Wallace walked inside, he said, 'You've got my ass in a crack, Johnson.'

"The two went into Johnson's paneled den, had coffee, and Wallace said, 'If you'll give me a light sentence, you can find me in contempt. I know I wouldn't be able to spend more than a week in jail.'

"Without blinking, Johnson said, 'If you don't hand over those records, I'll throw the book at you, George.'"

Wallace struck a deal on Johnson's terms. In a face-saving sleight of hand, Wallace agreed to turn the voting records over to the county grand juries, which would give them to the federal agents.

From then on, Wallace referred to his old friend Johnson as

"an integrating, carpet bagging, scalawagging, race mixing, bald faced liar."

Later, as a candidate, Wallace said Johnson and other federal judges "couldn't try a chicken thief in my home county" and that "thugs and federal judges have just about taken charge of this country." He prescribed a remedy for them: "a barbed-wire enema."

It played well with the segs in 1962 when Wallace ran for governor again, this time against his one-time mentor, Big Jim Folsom.

Rex Thomas, the Associated Press' man in Montgomery for this entire era, was a remarkable reporter. He was a fishing partner of Frank Johnson and a drinking buddy of Big Jim Folsom but retained the friendship and confidence of George Wallace.

"Wallace was smart enough to ride that racial question into office," Thomas told us. "You know, this is a strange thing about George. I never believed, and I don't believe today, that George was a racist. He was an opportunist, which in some ways, I think, is even worse. Suppose George had run as a moderate. In the first place, he probably wouldn't have gotten elected. In the second place, who in the hell would have ever heard of him outside of Alabama? But when it became politically expedient to turn the other way, and black people started voting, you had to go after their votes. So he did it. He went over and spoke in Martin Luther King's church one night. So I think he's more of an opportunist than anything else."

One of Wallace's first campaign pledges in 1962 was: "I won't be drunk in the governor's office." Having fixed attention on Folsom's best-known habit, Wallace went on to campaign against his former friend, Judge Johnson.

An expert on mores in the Alabama Legislature, former Representative John Guthrie of Cullman, said Wallace gave up drinking while he was in the Legislature because he couldn't hold his liquor.

"He couldn't drink," Guthrie told us. "He'd go crazy as hell with just a drink or two, you know. And this is facts. So he more or less had to leave it, and he had to run on the sober idea."

In the 1962 campaign, Folsom and his strategists met to explore Wallace's weaknesses that they might exploit, and one strategist said, "Hell, he doesn't even drink." Participants in the meeting later told reporters that Folsom piped up, "George don't drink, but he's bad to fuck."

Insiders knew Wallace as a ladies' man, but it was a well-kept secret from voters. Rex Thomas said, "Actually, women would follow him like camp followers."

In a nasty divorce that ended Wallace's marriage to Cornelia in January 1978, she accused him of running around on her in his wheelchair. In September 1981, at age sixty-two, Wallace married Lisa Taylor, a platinum-blonde country music singer who had performed at his rallies. She was thirty years younger than Wallace. They divorced in January 1987.

The major issue of the 1962 campaign became Folsom's drink with the black New York congressman Adam Clayton Powell at the governor's mansion during the 1955 Montgomery bus boycott. It neatly tied up both of the things Big Jim was weak on, his drinking and segregation. Wallace rode that issue into the governor's mansion, with a lot of help from Folsom when he appeared on statewide TV in a stupor on election eve.

Wallace's inaugural speech in January 1963 was vastly different from Folsom's Christmas message of 1949. Folsom's message preached brotherly love; Wallace's rang with defiance.

"This nation was never meant to be a unit of one, but a unit of many," Wallace told a throng assembled in front of the Capitol as the Confederate Stars and Bars flew from a flagstaff atop the dome. "And so it was meant in our racial lives. Each race, within its own framework, has the freedom to teach, to instruct, to develop, to ask for and receive deserved help from others of separate racial station.

"But if we amalgamate into the one unit as advocated by the Communist philosopher, then the enrichment of our lives, our freedom for development, is gone forever. We become, therefore, a mongrel unit of one under a single all-powerful government. And we stand for everything, and for nothing.

"It is very appropriate then that from this Cradle of the

Confederacy, this very heart of the great Anglo-Saxon Southland, that today we sound the drum for freedom. Let us rise to the call of the freedom-loving blood that is in us. In the name of the greatest people that have ever trod the earth, I draw the line in the dust and toss the gauntlet before the seat of tyranny. And I say, Segregation now! Segregation tomorrow! Segregation forever!"

There has been a lot of speculation and controversy about who wrote Wallace's inaugural speech. He told us in an interview, "I wrote it."

Wallace was sworn in as governor with his foot on a bronze star that marks the spot at the top of the Capitol steps where Jefferson Davis took the oath as president of the Confederate States. From that spot, Wallace looked down upon the Dexter Avenue Baptist Church, where Dr. Martin Luther King, Jr. preached.

"Forever" lasted a hundred and forty-eight days in Alabama. Wallace was inaugurated January 14. On June 11, two black students, Vivian Malone and James Hood, enrolled at the University of Alabama in Tuscaloosa under protection of Alabama National Guard troops nationalized by President John F. Kennedy.

When the president's brother, Attorney General Robert Kennedy, visited Wallace at the Capitol in 1963 to negotiate integration of the University of Alabama, Wallace got the United Daughters of the Confederacy to lay a wreath over the star marking the spot where Davis had stood. Wallace said he "didn't like the idea of Bobby stepping on it."

16

Wallace for President

GEORGE WALLACE HAD A domestic policy when he became governor in 1963. What he needed was a foreign policy so he could run for president in 1964, and he needed it fast. Not long after he was inaugurated, he was invited to Washington, D.C., to appear on national television for the first time on *Meet the Press*.

"I've got to have a foreign policy," Wallace said to Grover Hall, a Montgomery newspaper friend, as soon as they were airborne for Washington. "Those boys are going to question me about my beliefs tomorrow. They're going to want to know what I think about things in this nation. And they're going to want to know about my foreign policy."

Wallace fidgeted the entire flight, fretting about a foreign policy. Hall, editor of *The Montgomery Advertiser*, rode with Wallace from the airport to their hotel. Wallace continued to fuss about a foreign policy.

The governor was still worried when he woke Hall early the next morning. He had to have a foreign policy.

In the car, as they rode to the television studio, the governor was getting frantic about a foreign policy. Hall ripped an article from an old issue of *The Wall Street Journal* and told Wallace that would be a perfect foreign policy.

Wallace read all the way to the studio and put the clipping in his pocket as he got out of the car and went inside.

When the live broadcast ended, a smug Wallace walked off the set and found Hall waiting for him in the lobby. Wallace struck a match, lit a long, black cigar and took a satisfied drag on it.

Taking the *Wall Street Journal* clipping from his shirt pocket, Wallace glanced at it momentarily, crumpled it up and dropped it in a trash can. Turning to Hall he said, "I don't need a foreign policy. All they wanted to know about was niggers, and I'm an expert."

Hall, who has since died, told Wayne Greenhaw about George Wallace's foreign policy, and Greenhaw told us. He wrote about it in his book *Watch Out for George Wallace*.

By 1964, Wallace was running for president and doing well in northern Democratic primaries of Indiana and Wisconsin. He almost won Maryland, after which he concocted a story he used thoughout his 1968 and most of his 1972 presidential campaigns.

He would tell his audiences night after night that when Maryland first reported its 1964 Democratic primary vote returns, "I was leading. Walter Cronkite came on the television and said, 'Wallace is leading!' A little later, the governor of Maryland came on the television and announced they were going to recapitulate the votes. A newsman from Baltimore said to me, 'Do you know what recapitulate means?' I said, 'No, I'm from Alabama. I don't know all those big words.' And the newsman said, 'You about to find out.' And a short time later, the governor of Maryland came back on the television and said they had recapitulated the votes, and Wallace was now running second."

Then with an indignant flourish and a curl of his lip, Wallace would impart to his audiences a warning: "Now, if somebody tells you they're going to recapitulate for you, you had better watch out, 'cause they are going to do something bad to you, or on you."

Wallace withdrew before the 1964 Democratic National Convention. But he was back in 1968, running for president as an independent against "pointy-headed liberals who can't park a bicycle straight" and "Washington bureaucrats toting briefcases with nothing in them but a peanut butter sandwich." His campaign cry was "send them a message," which foreshadowed the anti-government rhetoric yet to come from Jimmy Carter and Ronald Reagan.

Wallace's message carried a strong undercurrent of racism. His popularity in the national polls peaked at twenty percent, but he only got ten percent of the vote on election day. He carried Alabama, Georgia, Mississippi, Louisiana and Arkansas. Some politicians thought the effect of Wallace's 1968 campaign was to elect Richard Nixon because he deprived Hubert Humphrey of five normally Democratic states in the South.

But Wallace's biggest victories were still ahead. The ones he liked most were in Michigan in 1972 and Boston in 1976. The backlash and defiance that drove Wallace's campaign seemed to be a furious rising tide in 1972. Soon it was evident he was no longer only a regional favorite in presidential campaigns. He was winning Democratic primaries, beginning in Florida.

Wallace borrowed another idea from Jim Folsom. He put together a country and western band with high-paid Nashville talent instead of Folsom's home-grown Strawberry Pickers led by outfielder Roland Johnson. Instead of using Big Jim's suds bucket, Wallace passed Kentucky Fried Chicken buckets through his crowds to collect money.

"We're nickeling and diming our way across America," emcee George Mangum would yell, stepping high around the microphone in his white, pointy-toed cowboy boots. But a lot more than nickels and dimes were going into the chicken buckets. And the crowds got bigger by the day.

Lead singer Billy Grammer would come back on stage, picking his guitar, crooning mournfully of Dee-troit City . . . . "By day I make the cars, by night I make the bars. . . ."

He would interrupt the song to explain: "This is a song about an old boy who came up to Dee-troit City and he wants to go back home. But he can't go. Taxes so high he can't save enough for a ticket back. . . ."

The crowd would be so worked up it would be bedlam, nearly a riot, by the time Wallace got to the microphone to tell them about their grievances.

Detroit Mayor Coleman Young and other black leaders threatened to boycott the Michigan Democratic Party's annual Jefferson-Jackson Day fund-raising dinner if Wallace was invited in 1972. Wallace was not invited, but he held a competing rally in Detroit. The Democrats drew about two thousand to their dinner in Cobo Hall on the downtown riverfront. Wallace held a double-header at the State Fairgrounds auditorium seven miles up Woodward Avenue from Cobo. He spoke to ten thousand people, ushered them out of the auditorium and spoke to another ten thousand, while police were turning away thousands more.

And the next week, Wallace held another double-header in the General Motors company town of Flint.

But a shadow crossed these glory days for Wallace. As he campaigned across Michigan, a disturbed young man with a chilling grin was stalking him at rallies in Dearborn, Cadillac and Kalamazoo. Arthur Bremer, of Milwaukee, watched Wallace and waited for his chance.

On May 15, 1972, at a Laurel, Maryland, shopping center where Wallace had gone for a rally, Bremer shot the Alabama governor five times. The next night at Holy Cross Hospital in Silver Spring, Maryland, his wife Cornelia took the early edition of the Baltimore *Sun* to the hospital bed where Wallace lay. The headline said: "Wallace wins in Maryland, Michigan; hospital takes him off the critical list." Cornelia said she knew if anything could pull him through it would be winning two elections north of the Mason-Dixon Line on the same day.

Wallace had won fifty-one percent of the Democratic primary vote in Michigan. Ever afterward, he was fond of saying, "If I ever get run out of Alabama, I'd move to Michigan."

Before Wallace left the hospital in a wheelchair, his aides were already talking about him running for president in 1976 as "another Franklin Roosevelt."

His time had passed on the national scene, however, but not before victory in Boston. In the 1976 Massachusetts Democratic presidential primary, he ran second statewide but ran first in the city of Boston. The city's anti-busing sentiment was still steaming enough to give him a plurality of votes in the citadel of the Civil War abolitionists and the hometown of the Kennedys.

"Can you believe I carried the city of Boston!" Wallace marveled at nearly every campaign rally after that.

In our interview with him, Wallace was still reveling in that memory.

"They were just hysterical at *The Boston Globe* that I was going to win Boston itself, which I did anyhow. Even carried Beacon Hill!"

But 1976 was another Southerner's year. Jimmy Carter of Georgia won the Florida primary by telling Southerners they ought to send a president to Washington, instead of just a message.

Still bearing down when all was lost, Wallace made a pitiful sight in the final throes of the 1976 campaign, and never more so than at a night rally in Fayetteville, North Carolina. He was perched on an auditorium stage behind a bullet-proof shield on which his aides had hung a Wallace campaign sign saying, "Trust the people." Wallace waved a wet, chewed cigar, his face darkened and his lip snarling as he spoke, as if addressing unseen demons. "We need to bring back the good old electric chair," he roared to the packed auditorium. As a second thought—he had been trying to improve his image on the racial issue—Wallace added, "We ought to execute some of them of all races."

In the midst of one of the strangest performances of Wallace's career, a North Carolina good old boy who had stopped at the beer store on his way in, jumped up in the middle of the audience and yelled out, "Give 'em hell, George. I've got to go to the bathroom," and left.

Eventually, Wallace's 1976 campaign was reduced to press conferences in big cities where Democrats were holding primaries. One of his last appearances of the campaign was in California. The only newsman traveling with him was Drummond Ayres of *The New York Times*. Ayres had covered the Wallace campaign from the start. Wallace was seated in his wheelchair behind a table responding to questions of local reporters when Ayres broke in and asked, "Governor, I know you aren't running in California, but they have a ballot question out here on nuclear power. As president, that's an issue you would have to address. What's your position on nuclear power?"

Wallace looked up and rolled his eyes and said to the assembled reporters, "Do you think it would do me any good in California to answer a question from *The New York Times*?"

There was an awkward silence as Ayres tried to think of a rejoinder. He was saved by a local reporter who said, "Can't do no harm."

Wallace broke up with laughter and put his forehead down on the table in resignation.

Claude Duncan, then a Montgomery newspaper reporter, told of watching the demise of Wallace's final presidential campaign.

"We were on the plane with Wallace on the last day of the campaign in '76 in North Carolina," Duncan said. "He knew he had lost. He had lost Florida. He knew it was all gone, and we brought up that Raleigh *News & Observer* story where Carter had played his born-again card and played it big. We asked Wallace if he had seen it. He said, 'No.' He was quiet for a minute, then he said, 'Oh, you mean that one about spending all that time on his knees?'

"Governor Carter had said he spent more time on his knees than anything else, praying in his office. I said, 'Yeah, that's the one.' Wallace said, 'I didn't know he was a damn queer.'"

Duncan said he accompanied Wallace the next morning to speak at a Baptist church in Charlotte.

"I asked him what he was going to say," Duncan told us.

"He said, 'I'm going to tell them that Carter's so sinful that when they bury him they need to bury him face down, so when he starts to scratch he'll be headed home.'"

After Carter defeated him in the South, Wallace held his nose and supported him. Carter went on to win the Democratic nomination and a close presidential race against Gerald Ford.

Duncan said, "Wallace may have saved the Democratic Party in 1976 by going with Carter. Wallace could have cost Carter several states. I'm convinced that was one of Wallace's finest moments, staying in the party after getting beat. He had never done that in his lifetime that I know of."

Wallace's supporters in Georgia, including former segregationist Governor Marvin Griffin, helped elect Jimmy Carter governor in 1970 because he had led them to believe he was a conservative like they were. Wallace always thought he had a handshake pledge from Carter to help him in the 1972 presidential campaign. But angling for a presidential bid himself, Carter had turned his back on Wallace-style politics by that time. Wallace never forgave him.

After Carter was elected president in 1976 as a liberal Democrat, Montgomery reporters asked Wallace what he thought about the politics of the new Southern president.

"It's like watching your daughter coming in at four o'clock in the morning with a Gideon Bible under her arm," Wallace said.

In the long stream of history, Wallace may command no more than a few paragraphs, maybe a long footnote amplifying background to the U. S. civil rights movement. Certainly, he will not be in the running with Martin Luther King, Jr., who started out as a young pastor at the Dexter Avenue Baptist Church, the modest brick building that Wallace could see all those years from his Capitol office.

But alert historians will note that Wallace was unique as a notorious Southern politician. The South has had its switch hitters—politicians who began their careers with the noble hope of putting together winning political coalitions of blacks and whites and then, beaten down by white racism, switched to the politics of the "black peril." Best known among them were populist Thomas Watson of Georgia, after the Civil War, and Orval Faubus of Arkansas, governor when federal troops integrated Little Rock's Central High School in 1957.

Not until Wallace, however, had the South had a double switch hitter of note. Wallace started out with the NAACP endorsement and lost, switched to a strategy of making race his basic politics and got elected, but finally wound up with blacks praising him and providing him a winning margin in his last election.

Enough Alabamians to fill a great many of the state's football stadiums think Wallace never cared a nickel for anything but political opportunity.

But the evidence is that he began his epic political journey with an appeal to the common people.

Because of the state's failure to provide its citizens with equal protection of the law during Wallace's terms as governor, Judge Johnson's court orders probably had more influence on the state of affairs in Alabama than anything else. Johnson issued orders governing voting rights, school desegregation, property tax assessment, reapportionment, prisons and mental institutions.

But Wallace also saw the rising power of the black vote. Supporting Carter helped him turn back from the politics of race. It wasn't too long before Wallace was crowning and kissing a black beauty queen at halftime of the homecoming football game at the University of Alabama.

Wallace usually excused his past behavior by saying segregation had been "the way of life back then" and that "we didn't mean to hurt anybody." Alabama's black leaders, who had started the U. S. civil rights movement with the Montgomery bus boycott, judged by Wallace's actions that he repented.

He was elected governor for another four years in 1982 and ironically—even outrageously, for all that he had stood for—nudged forward Dr. King's dream that the sons of slaves and the sons of slaveholders would one day sit down together at the table of brotherhood.

When Wallace announced in 1986 that he would not seek a fifth term as governor, E. D. Nixon, one-time Pullman porter and the patriarch of the civil rights movement in Montgomery, expressed his regret.

"George Wallace has done more for black people than any other governor," Nixon said.

At a small restaurant on the square in Clayton, when George Wallace was riding high, you could eat lunch in the very shadow of the grey stone Confederate soldier standing up there with his rifle at parade rest. But the square has faded, and the restaurant is gone. And an old boy at the filling station on a corner in George Wallace's hometown will tell you that if you want something besides a hamburger at the dime store, or barbecue come the weekend, the only place in town is Caesar's Palace out on East College Avenue.

Clayton didn't have much of a high rent district, and if it did, Caesar's Palace wouldn't be in it. Out behind the low cement block building housing the Palace, rows of collards and turnips grew beside a clothes line. Inside, a black family served you ribs and chicken and fish and greens and candied yams and squashes and sweet ice tea, with hot peppers in jars of vinegar on the tables, and nobody cared what color you were.

17

Fightin' Shorty Price

ONE OF GEORGE Wallace's roommates at the University of Alabama was another famous politician from Barbour County, Home of Governors.

Shorty Price roomed with Wallace for one semester at the University of Alabama before World War II and helped Wallace in campus and Barbour county political campaigns. But when Wallace made his first race for governor in 1958 as "the fightin' little judge," he and Shorty had parted ways. Shorty, who described himself as "four-feet-twelve," ran against Wallace and followed him around the state harassing him at his rallies.

"Stand up, George, and let 'em see I'm littler than you, and tell 'em I can fight better'n you," Shorty yelled at Wallace.

Nobody called Shorty by his real name, Ralph. Starting in 1950, after he dropped out of the University of Alabama Law School in his last year, Shorty ran for governor, lieutenant governor, Congress, the state House of Representatives, delegate and alternate delegate to the Democratic National Convention and presidential elector. He never won an election.

In 1970, Shorty ran for governor on a platform to reduce the term of governor from four years to two.

"If you can't steal enough to last you the rest of your life in two years," Shorty said, "you ain't got enough sense to have the office in the first place."

In the 1970 campaign against Wallace, Shorty branded him "Little Jesus." Shorty kicked off his campaign by having his five-year-old daughter lead a Barbour County crowd in a cheer: "Shorty, Shorty, he's our man. George Wallace belongs in the garbage can."

For years, Shorty had been stumping the entire state of Alabama to try to get elected to statewide office. But in 1970, he kicked off his campaign for governor with a rally in his Barbour County home town of Louisville on Saturday, three days before the election. He said his campaign would be comprised of the kickoff on Saturday, church on Sunday, nailing up posters on Monday, voting on Tuesday and moving into the governor's mansion on Wednesday.

Shorty explained that he didn't want to peak too soon.

Harold Martin described Shorty as "a small, frog-shaped man" in a May 7, 1966, article in the *Saturday Evening Post* entitled "The Race of a Thousand Clowns." Martin said Shorty's wife, Delores, was "a doe-eyed blonde with a voice that strikes the eardrums like an ice pick."

"I know I'm low-down, but I didn't know I was shaped like a frog," Shorty croaked. ". . . How could anyone say such a nasty thing about my petite little blue-eyed blonde wife whose voice touched your eardrums like a feather or a whisper in the night?"

AP's Rex Thomas covered Shorty's political campaigns and antics for years.

"Shorty got arrested for pissing on the sidewalk in Montgomery," Thomas told us, "and they fined him ten dollars for disorderly conduct. And his complaint to the cops was, 'You treat horses and dogs better than you treat people.'"

In another encounter with Montgomery police, Shorty explained why he was pushing his car down crowded Dexter Avenue on inauguration day for a new governor. He told the officers he was too drunk to drive.

Shorty attended University of Alabama football games for years in a white dinner jacket and high silk hat. He also got drunk and led the crowd in cheers until police came and hauled him away. Birmingham police arrested Shorty for public drunkenness thirty times out of thirty-four years. When police arrested him in 1980, Shorty offered the defense that being drunk at a University of Alabama football game was a natural state.

Shorty prided himself in his frugality. He said he built the first house he and his wife lived in for $165, using scrap lumber, and claimed to have started his first race for governor in 1958 with $11.35 in his pocket. In 1956, he hitchhiked to Chicago with ten dollars spending money to attend the Democratic National Convention. Shorty said he hoped to borrow twenty-five dollars from George Wallace and sleep in Wallace's bed while he was out tending to convention business during the day.

In a book he paid to have published in 1973, Shorty said he arrived in Chicago at dawn, went into the lobby of the LaSalle Hotel and rang up George on the house phone. Shorty noticed that Wallace was irritable and gruff when he answered the phone and asked, "Why did you wake me up so early?"

"I told him I wanted a place to lie down," Shorty wrote, "and since he would be getting up soon, I'd like to take his place! He immediately informed me that his wife Lurleen was arriving that day so I could not rest in his room. He did not even invite me up for a drink, and I know he drinks. I said to myself, 'What a friend!' I politely walked over to a couch in the lobby, lay down, and took a nap."

Wallace turned Shorty down for the twenty-five dollar loan.

The next day, Shorty wrote, "George Wallace strode down the aisle to the Alabama delegation. There were about ten delegates present when he bleated out, 'Shorty, how are you doing financially?' . . . I replied, 'I'm doing okay. I'm still getting by.' At that moment, as everyone present was watching him, he reached into his pocket and he came out with his fist balled up.

He stuck his hand out to me and said in a high-pitched voice, so that everyone present could hear, 'Here, Shorty, take this $100 bill and enjoy yourself at the convention.'

"I was so startled that I automatically stuck my hand out to receive it. For some unknown reason, I turned around and opened up my hand. There I saw a wadded-up one dollar bill! I was so mad I could have bitten a nail in two. I started to spit in his face, but I didn't. I only stood there, quivering with anger and humiliation. It shocked me so I didn't even let "Bull" Conner and the other delegates know it was a one dollar bill instead of a $100 bill. I just walked away in order to cool off and come back to earth."

By 1964, Shorty again was supporting Wallace in political races. Shorty blanketed the Auburn campus with cards he had printed to tout Wallace's presidential campaign. The cards stated: "I'm for George Wallace all the way—Let's put a white man in the White House."

But that fall, Wallace backed Ed Blair for presidential elector against Shorty.

"I backed Wallace and Wallace backed my opponent, Ed Blair," Shorty wrote. "Blair won and I lost. The moral of this story is: Don't depend on George Wallace for a damn thing."

Shorty also was a free loader and bum. He bummed food and gasoline while campaigning for office and attending political conventions and sold copies of his book in advance to pay the printing costs. He sent lists of all his contributions to the Alabama secretary of state, including donations as small as a nickel given to him in the 1954 campaign for lieutenant governor by N.D. Killebrew of Eufaula. "Hog Eye" Chance of Union Springs gave him a dollar. Chick (Big Orange) Reaves of Eufaula contributed a dollar and a half in gasoline for Shorty's car.

On Shorty's list of contributors was one donation of "Good Luck" from "Some friends in Birmingham, Ala."

Shorty would go to public offices and pester people for campaign contributions of a dollar or two. Don Wasson, former Montgomery newspaperman who was at the University of Alabama with Shorty, told us, "Shorty ran just to raise money, get contributions and not spend anything on campaigns and live off that for several months.

"He was in Luverne one day, and he camped in Alton Turner's outer office all day, wanted to see him. Alton was floor leader under Wallace and chairman of the Finance and Taxation Committee. Alton's secretary had told Shorty that Alton was busy. And finally she got up and went in and told Alton, 'Either talk to Shorty Price or find yourself a new secretary. I've had all I can stand of this son of a bitch.'

"Alton got up and went out in the waiting room and said, 'Shorty, I know what you're here for, and I'm going to give you two dollars for your campaign. But you've got to make me one promise. Don't list me as one of your contributors.' And just like that, Shorty said, 'That'll cost you three dollars.'"

Rex Thomas told us that Shorty asked Republican Congressman Bill Dickinson of Opelika to send him ten dollars and told him he would send him a copy of his book.

"Dickinson sent him five dollars, so Shorty sent him half the book," Thomas said.

After Shorty had lost seven straight races, he beat out Coleman Brown for sixth place in a seven-man race for governor in 1970. Statewide, Shorty got 3,768 votes to Brown's 2,658. Newspaper editor Joe Adams of Ozark, Alabama, wrote a feature story on Shorty's victory, headlining it, "BEATS BROWN IN GOV. RACE."

The first of Shorty's losses came in 1950 when he ran for the Legislature from Barbour County. He ended up with a credibility gap. He was taking one of his campaign workers, Douglas Benton, from Louisville to Clio in a car that had a loudspeaker on the top for ballyhooing his candidacy. Benton's mother had taught Shorty in the first, second and third grades. Shorty said it was a Sunday, and he didn't use the loudspeaker because he didn't want to offend church-going voters, who frowned on any kind of work on Sunday.

"We went from Louisville down Highway 51 to Clio, and on the way down we passed the Pea River Church," Shorty wrote in his book. "They were having a dedication service to celebrate their new brick church, which we had just completed. As we passed by, I saw a cousin of mine, Jack Weston, and he threw up his hand and waved at me. I naturally waved back."

Shorty said one of his opponents put out the rumor that he had driven by the church with his loudspeaker blaring and had broken up the dedication services.

"Even Douglas' mother believed the rumor when she heard it, and I'm sure she voted for Sim Thomas against me," Shorty wrote.

After the election, Shorty said, he talked with Mrs. Benton, his former teacher, about the rumor, and said Mrs. Benton told him she believed it.

"I asked her why she hadn't asked her son, Douglas, if we had the loudspeaker on. She said, 'I did ask Douglas and he said you didn't.' I said to her, 'Don't you believe your own son?' She said, 'Yes, I do, but the rumor came so straight.'"

Delores Price, Shorty's wife, was the first woman to run for governor of Alabama. She was twenty-three years old at the time and would have been seven years too young to take office if she had won. That was in 1966, when Shorty turned his campaign into some real money. George Wallace couldn't succeed himself and was planning to run Lurleen as a stand-in for him.

Wallace's opponents remembered how Shorty had agitated Wallace in the 1958 race, and they figured he would be no less abrasive in 1966. They put up five hundred dollars to pay Delores' qualifying fee and bought the Prices some new clothes to campaign in. They also had campaign literature printed bearing a photograph of Shorty and Delores with their heads together under campaign slogans, "Two hearts that beat as one," and "The Prices are right."

Shorty and Delores were paid $130 a week to pursue Wallace throughout the state and heckle him at his rallies. Delores didn't finish the race. Two hours before the deadline for withdrawing, Shorty asked for her $500 qualifying fee back. Taking a dig at Lurleen Wallace's candidacy, he said, "I do not believe that any woman can be elected governor of Alabama."

With the money, Shorty paid off $581.12 he owed in back income tax.

"Shorty was a real pest, and he was persistent as hell," Rex Thomas told us. "He showed up at Auburn University on Governor's Day after Wallace was elected, and the president of the university was Ralph Draughton. Ralph was the kind of guy who looked like everybody's father. He was the last man in the world you would ever expect to say anything off-color.

"Now, this I know, because I was standing there. I was as close to Ralph as I am to you. Shorty had showed up in Ralph's office and was trying to get a free ticket to the luncheon. Ralph didn't know how to handle Shorty, and he just ordered him out of his office, out of the building and off the campus.

"Well, you don't get rid of Shorty that easy. Shorty bummed a ride out to the airport and caught Wallace coming in and put the arm on Wallace. And of course Wallace knew how to get rid of him. He said to Shorty, 'Yeah, yeah, you can be my guest at the luncheon.' And that was it. He was through with Shorty.

"Shorty's back on campus, and when George and Lurleen arrived on the campus, the ROTC was firing a salute to the governor, and everything was very, very, very stiff and very formal, and everybody was standing at attention. Draughton was standing at attention. Draughton's wife was standing on one side of him, and I was standing on the other. He looked back over there, and there was Shorty Price. And Ralph said very audibly, 'Aw, shit.'"

V

V

Happy and Orval: Marching to Different Drummers

WHEN THE UNITED States Supreme Court ruled in 1954 that the public schools must be integrated with all deliberate speed, the white South went into shock.

Some white Southerners called for massive, violent resistance. Others who could read history took a calmer approach. They had learned what happened after 1861 when General Beauregard fired on Fort Sumter.

Two Southern governors chose different ways of dealing with the crisis. They were Happy Chandler of Kentucky and Orval Faubus of Arkansas.

Chandler and Faubus had similar backgrounds. Both grew up as poor country boys. They went to college and came to political success early in their states.

At crucial points after federal courts ordered schools integrated in their states, they acted with different instincts.

When black children were threatened with violence, Chandler sent a National Guard force big enough to overwhelm a town. The black children entered school without a scratch or a ruckus.

The opposite happened in Arkansas. Faubus ordered Arkansas National Guardsmen to prevent black children from entering Central High School in Little Rock. President Eisenhower sent federal troops to escort the black children into the school, but Little Rock became a symbol of Southern resistance for those who had not learned the lesson of Fort Sumter.

After his political star rose and then plummeted, Faubus returned to the Arkansas mountains whence he came. There he scrambled to earn a living. His place in history, perhaps unjustly, will be remembered only for his days of defiance.

Chandler went on to become a member of the United States Senate and commissioner of baseball. He made it possible for Jackie Robinson to integrate big league ball.

But Chandler came to an ironic end because of the race issue. Somehow, mysteriously, he never figured out how to talk about black people without offending them and others.

18

Happy Chandler, Kentucky Squire

THE COLOR BARRIER IN major league baseball fell in a log cabin in Happy Chandler's back yard in Versailles, Kentucky. Chandler proudly showed us the spot.

The cabin, made of walnut logs, with walnut paneling, four upstairs bedrooms and three baths, is quite different from Abe Lincoln's, over in Hodgenville, but log it is. And it was there, in January 1947, that Chandler and Branch Rickey made the decision that allowed Jackie Robinson to play second base for the Brooklyn Dodgers.

It was a bold stroke that opened the door for Roy Campanella, Willie Mays, Hank Aaron, Bob Gibson, Roberto Clemente, Reggie Jackson and other black stars to share in the gold and glory of the national pastime.

Chandler, a former Kentucky governor and United States senator, had been commissioner of baseball for two years when he and Rickey met in the cabin. Rickey was owner of the Dodgers.

The sixteen major league club owners, meeting in New

York, had just voted, 15–1, to keep baseball all-white, the lone dissent coming from Rickey. He rushed to Versailles from the meeting.

"Branch Rickey had a boy that he felt was capable of playing in the major leagues, and indeed he was," Chandler told us. "The rest of them didn't have a fellow they thought could play. So they had a meeting in New York that was supposed to be advice to me. I didn't need it. I didn't ask for it."

Chandler was seventy-nine years old when we visited him, in the spring of 1978, and he had never doubted the wisdom of the Jackie Robinson decision.

"I said to myself, I'm going to have to meet my maker some day, and he's going to ask me, 'Why didn't you let this fellow play?' And I'm going to say, 'He was black.' And he's going to say, 'I don't think that's enough.'"

The old Kentucky squire was a church-going Episcopalian who believed in heaven and hell.

"I was afraid the Lord wouldn't let me in if I didn't let Robinson play," he said. "I wasn't present when the Lord gave out the colors, and by God, I wasn't going to rely on that color business. . . . I felt like I had to do it."

Chandler added, without bitterness, "I've never gotten any credit for it. But there's no way they could do it without me."

Actually he did get credit where it counts, from Jackie Robinson. A letter Robinson wrote to Chandler in 1956 is among Chandler's papers at the University of Kentucky.

"I will never forget your part in the so called Rickey experiment . . . ," Robinson wrote.

Black baseball had been loaded with talented players for years, as black fans knew but white fans refused to believe. Superb black players before Robinson had sought a chance in the major leagues, but Chandler's predecessor as baseball commissioner, Judge Kennesaw Mountain Landis, had blocked them, Chandler told us. He said he had seen the records in the commissioner's office that prove it.

"For twenty-four years, Landis wouldn't let blacks play. They always wanted to play. The owners were afraid, for example, that they'd have a riot and burn down the Polo Grounds because the Polo Grounds was in Harlem. They were fixed in their ways. They just didn't want the black boys to play. It's as simple as that."

The color barrier kept Leroy (Satchel) Paige, one of the all-time great pitchers, out of major league baseball during his best years. Paige admitted to being forty-two years old, and some people thought he was much older, when he finally got to play with the Cleveland Indians in 1948.

"Satchel told me that he would have won thirty games a year for thirty years if I'd come along earlier in his career," Chandler said. "And he probably would have. Satchel told me he had two pitches, the bat-dodger and the hesitation. I told him to stick with the bat-dodger. That sounded good enough to me."

Because he had been a successful Southern politician, Chandler said his decision to let Robinson play came as a surprise to the baseball world.

"They thought I would go the other way, because my grandfather was second sergeant in Morgan's cavalry, and I'm a Democrat and a Southerner, and he was a Southerner and a Confederate. My wife's a Confederate. They thought I wouldn't make that decision, but I did."

Corydon, the little town in northwest Kentucky where Chandler grew up, was half black and half white, Chandler said.

"We never had any trouble," he said. "We never had what you call nigger trouble. It never occurred to me. They loved me and I loved them."

He said he told Rickey at their historic meeting "to bring Robinson in and we'd keep a close watch on him."

"And we did," said Chandler. "He said, 'How are they going to treat him?' I said, 'Just as another ballplayer, no better, no worse.'"

As he promised Rickey, Chandler stood by Robinson after he joined the Dodgers in 1947. Chandler said some players and managers rebelled.

"They threatened Robinson," Chandler told us, "and when they did, I threatened them. Ben Chapman said one time, 'Wait till he comes to Philadelphia, and I'll make trouble for him.' Ben Chapman was from Birmingham, Alabama. I wired him. I said, 'If you make trouble for him, I'll make trouble for you.'"

Chandler said the Dodgers' Dixie Walker, another Southerner, threatened to boycott if Robinson played.

"The greatest amount of help Robinson got from any ballplayer he got from Peewee Reese from Kentucky," Chandler said. "Young Peewee Reese helped him more than anybody else. Reese is from Louisville."

With Reese at shortstop and Robinson at second, the Dodgers had one of the best double-play combinations in baseball.

Robinson was a good choice to break the color line because he was a college graduate, very intelligent and a ballplayer who couldn't miss, Chandler said.

"But he was pretty difficult," Chandler recalled. "Not only didn't a lot of the white boys like him, a lot of the black boys didn't like him once they got in. He had a chip on his shoulder, and I don't blame him. Everybody was on him, you know. But he had an obligation, too, not to show the umpires up. He had some showboat in him."

Another of the early black players with the Dodgers was pitcher Don Newcombe.

"He and Don Newcombe didn't like each other," Chandler told us. "And Newcombe lost a World Series game one time when Tommy Heinrich hit a home run in the last inning. Cal Hubbard was umpiring. Cal Hubbard was a Confederate and from Missouri and an All-American tackle who played at Green Bay. Robinson had been down at second base all day making choke signs, directed toward Cal Hubbard. Cal hated his guts."

After Heinrich crossed the plate with the winning run for the New York Yankees, Chandler asked Newcombe if Hubbard's umpiring had cost the Dodgers the game. He said Newcombe told him no, that Hubbard missed maybe one call all game.

So Chandler telephoned Dodger manager Burt Shotton.

"I said, 'Burt, do you need Robinson to play second base for you tomorrow?' He said, 'Oh, yes, commissioner, why?' I said, 'I thought if you didn't need him to play, I don't need him to umpire. I've got enough umpires. I thought I could give him the day off.' He said, 'Oh, please, commissioner, don't do that to me.' I had no intention of doing it, but I was going to shake him up. I said, 'You take care of that, Burt. Tell him this for me, if he does the same thing tomorrow, I'm going to stop the game and take him out. That's all I'm going to say about it.'"

In another instance, Chandler said, Robinson complained to him about Leo Durocher when Leo the Lip was the Dodgers' manager.

"Robinson said, 'Durocher called me a son of a bitch,'" Chandler recalled. "I said, 'What did you do about it?' He said, 'I called him a son of a bitch.' I said, 'Then maybe you're both sons of bitches, and that makes you even. Just go on from there.'"

Chandler said Durocher was a good baseball manager "who didn't have much common sense or practical sense."

In a 1948 game, Chandler remembered, "Durocher and Jocko Conlon were standing at home plate kicking each other's shins. Jocko, a great National League umpire, had his shin guards on. He was kicking Durocher on the bare shins, you know. He was barking Durocher's shins real good. Finally Durocher figured out he was in a losing match. He retreated."

Chandler had suspended Durocher for the 1947 season.

"I said Durocher's conduct was detrimental to baseball," Chandler recalled. "He had a wife—oh, he had five or six wives—but he had this one who was lovely. Her name was Grace. She was a dressmaker in St. Louis. And the year I suspended him, I was sitting in Yankee Stadium at the opening of the season. That was '47. This pretty girl came and stood in front of me, and she wanted to remonstrate with me for suspending Durocher.

"I listened to her, and she conducted herself ladylike. I said to her, 'Grace, what I did was not intended to be offensive to you, and I'm awfully strong for women who support their husbands. But it's done, and he's going to have to stand aside.'

"Well, a year later, Durocher had courted and married Laraine Day. And I'm in the same place in Yankee Stadium the first week of the season, and this pretty girl comes and stands in front of me again. She stuck out her hand and said, 'Commissioner, you knew he was a son of a bitch all the time, didn't you?'

"And I said, 'Grace, I didn't say that, you did. But what a difference a year makes.'"

Actor George Raft also approached Chandler on behalf of his old friend Leo. Chandler said, "I asked him if he owned a baseball team. He said, 'No.' I said, 'I won't talk to you then.'"

Whoever gave Happy Chandler his nickname knew what he was doing. He was a short, muscular man, about five-feet-eight, who grinned constantly. But the real reason people called him Happy was the way he laughed. It was the kind of gurgling sound that comic strip artists pencil in as "yuk-yuk-yuk."

Chandler seemed to be a contradiction. His grin gave him an oafish appearance at times, but he had canny insights into institutions and people and a sure, nervy instinct for decisive action.

He thought of himself as a conservative politically. In 1942, as a United States senator, he voted to continue the poll tax that had inhibited black voting in Southern states, even though Kentucky did not have a poll tax. In 1968, he wanted to be George Wallace's running mate on the American Independent Party ticket, but Wallace chose retired Air Force General Curtis LeMay instead. Chandler also was given awards by the American Daughters of the Confederacy and took pride in his grandfather who fought for the Confederacy in the Civil War.

His grandfather had a scar on his heel that he said came from a Yankee bullet at Shiloh. Chandler said he asked his grandfather if that didn't mean he was wounded while running. He said the old man replied, "Son, at Shiloh, everybody was running."

Chandler said his grandfather also told him, "Boy, we could have whipped those Yankees with cornstalks. Only thing was, the Yankees weren't using cornstalks."

But the grandson of the old Confederate didn't run from one of the great issues of his day, no matter what his motivation.

Chandler put his mark on two landmark civil rights accomplishments, the toppling of baseball's racial barriers and the peaceful integration of Kentucky schools in 1956, when the rest of the South was engaged in massive resistance to the court-ordered change.

Chandler sent National Guard troops into Sturgis and Clay, two towns in his home area of western Kentucky, to integrate the public schools.

"The mayor of Clay, Herman Clark, was my good friend and I'd known him all my life," Chandler said. "He called me and said, 'Albert, no niggers are going to school here.' I found this out, and you'll find out, too, if you're going to have trouble, it will be where they know you best and where they've known you the longest.

"Herman owned Clay. He owned the town. He was the richest fellow in it. He told me, 'Albert, I just called you to tell you wasn't no nigger going to school here,' and I said, 'Herman, I know you own that town, and I know if you make up your mind, why you'll make trouble for us. But this is the law. It's not my job to put blacks in the school, but if they show up, it's my job to see they are protected. And I'm not going to let you keep them from it. I'm not going to let anybody stop them.'

"I sent three thousand National Guardsmen down there, and a tank, and the attorney general."

The 1950 census put Clay's population at 1,291.

"I had more soldiers than they had people," Chandler told us.

Chandler said he used the same military tactics as Nathan Bedford Forrest, a Confederate general from Pulaski, Tennessee, sometimes credited with founding the Ku Klux Klan.

"They asked Forrest how he won his battles," Chandler told us, "and he said, 'I got there fustest with the mostest.' Hell, I got there fustest with the mostest. Early in the morning, I had three-thousand National Guardsmen, the adjutant general and everybody."

Speaking of the now deceased Herman Clark, Chandler told us, "Before he died, he called me and said, 'Albert, I was foolish, and you were right. I'm sorry.'"

"What would have happened if every Southern governor had done what you did?"

"Pretty soon it would have all been over," Chandler replied.

Yet Chandler seemed oblivious to racial sensitivities. He used the terms "boy" and "nigger" repeatedly.

Nor had he learned his lesson ten years later, when he again used the word "nigger" in a newspaper reporter's presence at a meeting of the University of Kentucky Board of Trustees in the spring of 1988. In the outcry for his resignation as a board member, only the support of Governor Wallace Wilkinson saved him.

"I am not going to condemn a lifetime of achievement—achievement in the fight for civil rights—for a moment's indiscretion," Wilkinson said.

Happy Chandler started that life as a country boy, son of the town handyman in Corydon. His mother abandoned the family when Chandler was five years old. Happy thought she was dead until he went looking for her grave in Florida when he was thirty-five years old and found her living with another husband. He emerged from the poverty of his boyhood with a combative nature, driving ambition and righteous self-confidence that made him a governor, a senator, a baseball commissioner and an extremely wealthy man.

Rather than become a minister, as his father wished, Chandler went into politics.

From his youth, Chandler had believed any American boy could grow up to be president of the United States, and he expected to do just that. He worked his way through Transylvania College in Lexington, Kentucky, and attended the Harvard University Law School for a year before completing work on his law degree at the University of Kentucky.

He said he played football, basketball and baseball at Transylvania and played professional baseball and coached high school and small-college football for several years as a young man. A high school coaching job brought him to Versailles in 1922, and he never left. He married a teacher at the high school, Mildred Watkins, in 1925, a year after he graduated from law school. From 1932, Chandler held directorships and other offices with insurance companies in Kentucky and Georgia.

Chandler was elected to his first office, in the Kentucky Senate, at age thirty-one, singing *When Irish Eyes are Smiling* and other Irish ballads on the stump. After he was elected, he entertained his fellow senators in the state Capitol with his tenor rendition of the old Al Jolson tune *Sonny Boy*.

Two years later, Governor Ruby Laffoon put Chandler on his ticket, and Chandler was elected lieutenant governor at age thirty-three.

But the governor soon found out that Chandler never let friendship get in the way of his ambition, something other politicians would discover later. When Laffoon took trips out of Kentucky, Chandler assumed the powers of governor and began appointing his own people to state jobs. On one of Laffoon's trips out of the state in 1935, Chandler called a special session of the Legislature and enacted the state primary law under which he was elected governor that year. When Laffoon returned and found out what Chandler had done, he tried to have the law rescinded, but it was too late.

When Chandler took office as governor, he was thirty-six years old. He resigned as governor in 1939 and had himself appointed to fill a vacancy in the United States Senate, where he remained until 1945. He resigned from the Senate to accept appointment as commissioner of baseball.

Chandler said he changed jobs so he could "pay my debts and pay my taxes and send my children to school." His income jumped from $10,000 a year in the Senate to $75,000 a year in salary and benefits as baseball commissioner.

The club owners fired Chandler in 1951 and named Ford Frick to succeed him.

"They wanted a vacancy in the commissioner's office, and they soon had one," Chandler wisecracked.

In 1955, twenty years after he first was elected governor,

Chandler won another four-year term. In a political career spanning three decades, Chandler lost only a 1938 race for the United States Senate against Alben Barkley, later vice president under Harry Truman.

Despite his accomplishments in politics and sports, Chandler gave us the impression he felt he had somehow fallen short. But we concluded that Happy Chandler was no fool.

"My rise was not unanticipated," Chandler told Gail Green of the *Lexington Herald-Leader* in a 1978 interview. "It was my destiny. I even thought I was going to be president for awhile . . . and would have been except for the opposition of the Louisville *Courier-Journal*."

He told us, "They tried their best to make a clown out of me. They didn't hurt me in Kentucky. I had more circulation in Kentucky than they did."

The nickname Happy turned out to be a handicap for him when he sought the Democratic presidential nomination in 1956.

"I got the nickname in college: Happy Chandler," he said. "A nickname is something your friends give you, and there's not much you can do about it. If they had called me Stinky I'd be stuck with it."

More than two decades later, Chandler still thought he would have made a stronger candidate than Illinois liberal Adlai Stevenson, who won the nomination for a second time but lost the election to Dwight D. Eisenhower.

"I don't want to be too harsh with him," Chandler said of Stevenson, "but I don't think he could have beaten Tom Thumb with a broadaxe."

Chandler gave us a tour of his house at 191 Elm Street in Versailles, which Kentuckians pronounce "Vur-sales." From the shady street, it looked like an ordinary ranch-style home, but it turned out to be huge, nearly square in shape, with four rooms panelled in butternut wood specially milled for Chandler from trees cut in the Kentucky mountains. The entire house, including a full, furnished basement, was expensively appointed. Chandler hired a cabinetmaker to do the interior when he built

Courtesy of *The Tennessean.*

Jim Cummings living it up at the state convention

Courtesy of *The Tennessean.*

Cummings regales Governor Lamar Alexander with another outrageous tale.

Courtesy of *The Tennessean.*

Two-thirds of the Unholy Trinity press their point. L-R: Education Commissioner J. M. Smith, Representative McAllen Foutch, Jim Cummings and I. D. Beasley

Courtesy of *The Tennessean.*

Mister Jim in his element, the Tennessee General Assembly

Courtesy of *The Tennessean.*

Pete Haynes entertains President Kennedy and the First Lady.

Courtesy of *The Tennessean.*

No crowd was too small for Tennessee's Prentice Cooper.

Courtesy of Herman E. Talmadge collection, Richard B. Russell Memorial Library.

Gene Talmadge bids Godspeed to a constituent bound for the Chicago World's Fair.

Courtesy of Herman E. Talmadge Collection, Richard B. Russell Memorial Library.

Old Gene proves they love a man in the country.

Courtesy of *The Atlanta Journal and Constitution.*

M. E. Thompson drives home a point about the high cost of maintaining three governors simultaneously.

Courtesy of *The Atlanta Journal and Constitution.*

Marvin Griffin always saw the humor in any situation.

Photo by Ken Elkins.

In his last days, Big Jim Folsom couldn't always persuade voters to heed his invitation: "Y'all Come."

Photo by Ken Elkins.

The gang at the Bessemer pool hall would have loved Big Jim's game.

Photo by Ken Elkins.

The crowds still turned out to see Big Jim when he could no longer see them.

Photo by Tony Triolo.

Big Ruby Folsom has a heart as big as a basketball and hands big enough to palm one.

Photo by Ken Elkins.

George Wallace with a big cigar and large helping of skepticism

Photo by Ken Elkins.

Shorty Price rolls with the Crimson Tide.

Photo by Remer Tyson.

Happy Chandler among his books and his memories

Photo by Billy Bowles.

Orval Faubus takes a break between bank customers to talk about his days in high cotton as Arkansas governor.

Photo by Joe Clark, HBSS.

Junebug Clark on the phone at Dal Gulley's General Store

Courtesy of Ruth Henderson Ellis.

Bad Bill Henderson in a quiet moment

Photo by Tony Spina.

Ruth Henderson Ellis hasn't forgotten the lessons Bad Bill taught her.

Photo by Tony Spina.

Detroit gunmen met their match in Cumberland Gap's Ruth and Ottis Ellis.

Courtesy of South Caroliniana Library.

Cole Blease, South Carolina's pardoning governor

Courtesy of South Caroliniana Library.

Cotton Ed Smith, without the traditional cotton boll in his lapel

Courtesy of *The State*, Columbia, S.C.

Barnwell ringleaders Edgar Brown (L) and Sol Blatt

Courtesy of *The Atlanta Journal and Constitution.*

Johnny Popham still loves the rogues.

the house on a rock foundation in 1960, using thick beams salvaged from old buildings in Cincinnati.

"It's a right comfortable place," Chandler said with a satisfied grin, "come the revolution."

Upstairs and downstairs, the house was filled with framed photographs documenting Chandler's life in sports and politics. Early photos showed him as a young baseball pitcher.

"I pitched for Transylvania College against the University of Tennessee in 1920," he said, directing our attention to an old photo with an inscription on the bottom. "Look at the score in that game."

"Ten to four. You beat the University of Tennessee?"

"I beat 'em," he said. "Wore 'em out."

He pointed to another framed picture: "There's my team at Lexington. I played in the Bluegrass League."

"Which one is you?"

"Right there," Chandler said, pointing to a grinning face on the photo. "He was *happy*, wasn't he?"

The house was a museum of Happy Chandler mementoes from famous people, and Chandler told us we missed three million pieces he had already given to the University of Kentucky. But everywhere we looked—on walls, desks, mantles, bedside tables—we saw framed photos, letters, autographed baseballs and other personal gifts from people Chandler had met around the world. Ben-Gurion, Moshe Dayan and Mahatma Ghandi. Ty Cobb, Honus Wagner, Joe Dimaggio and Ted Williams. Douglas MacArthur, George C. Marshall, George Patton and Richard Byrd. Babe Ruth, Jack Dempsey and Connie Mack. Bob Hope, Bing Crosby and Irving Berlin. Albert Schweitzer, Eleanor Roosevelt and Pope Pius XII.

And Cactus Jack from Uvalde, Texas.

Chandler informed us that John Nance (Cactus Jack) Garner owned downtown Uvalde, bought and paid for with poker winnings he amassed in Washington, D.C., while moonlighting as a congressman, speaker of the House of Representatives and vice president of the United States. He was vice president under Franklin D. Roosevelt from 1933 to 1941. Years after he resigned as speaker and got himself elected vice president, Garner lamented that he had given up the second most powerful job in the republic to take one "that didn't amount to a bucket of warm piss."

"He was something special," Chandler said. "He told me he made $100,000 playing poker while he was in Washington, and he went down and bought downtown Uvalde with the money. Yeah, bought the whole damn town. He and I were just as close as a dead heat."

John L. Lewis, president of the Congress of Industrial Organizations, described Garner as "a poker-playing, whiskey-drinking, labor-baiting, evil old man," Chandler said.

"Garner just chuckled," Chandler recalled. "It tickled the hell out of him."

Happy Chandler and Cactus Jack Garner were unlikely companions. Chandler was a non-smoking, non-gambling teetotaler who told us he had never taken a drink of whiskey, beer or wine in his life. Chandler said one of his grandfathers "wasted a good estate with riotous living." Chandler's father made him promise not to drink, and he told us he kept that promise. He also had been a member of the Episcopal Church in Versailles longer than any other member except Mildred Chandler, his wife.

Mildred Chandler seemed a likelier companion for old Cactus Jack. She liked to drink, play poker and bet on the horses. She often visited Caesar's Palace in Las Vegas, where the Chandlers' son Dan was second in command of the casino.

Mrs. Chandler told us that the late Harry Byrd, Sr., the courtly United States senator from her home state of Virginia, had the Chandlers pegged. He'd said: "Happy gets all the votes down in Kentucky. He gets all the church people, and Mildred gets all the gamblers and drinkers. They work both sides of the street."

Because of her husband's career, Mrs. Chandler had the opportunity to drink with some pros. Her husband said Cactus Jack Garner "liked to strike a small blow for liberty every day to keep his industries running. His small blow for liberty was a water glass three-fourths full of red liquor with no chaser, just drink it down."

Another pro was golfer Walter Hagen, Happy Chandler's partner at a tournament in Louisville. Mrs. Chandler said she saw Hagen pour a water glass nearly full of whiskey and toss it down just before walking out on the course.

She laughed. "About the first two holes, he was blind."

"But on the third," her husband said, "he got an eagle."

"After that, he just burned up the course," Mrs. Chandler said.

"I shot a seventy-two on my seventy-ninth birthday," Chandler boasted.

"Have you felt his muscles?" Mrs. Chandler asked us. "They're hard."

Mildred Chandler invited us inside to strike a small blow for liberty. She opened a liquor cabinet containing a lot of bottles, most of them nearly empty.

"That gal does all the drinking for my family," Chandler said.

"Y'all see the colored man that was helping me this morning?" Mrs. Chandler asked us. "Every time I have a bottle set out here, I'll look at it, and it's down a little bit."

She said the suspect was Porter, an ex-convict who first came to work for the Chandlers in the governor's mansion. There, he met his wife, Ellavee, also serving a prison sentence when the Chandlers selected her to work for them at the mansion.

"She killed one, and he killed two," Chandler told us.

It is a tradition among Southern governors to have state prisoners as household help.

"It's nearly always murderers," Mrs. Chandler informed us. "The police say that the reason for that habit is that murder is a crime of passion, and they screen the murderers that they send to the mansion. We had about fifteen."

"We wouldn't want a thief," Chandler said.

"You can't afford to have a thief," his wife said. "You can't afford to have people who are in for almost any other crime that you can think of."

The tradition is based on the belief that murderers who kill in anger seldom kill again, and that they make the safest servants for governors and their families.

Neither of the Chandlers could tell us Porter's and Ellavee's last name, although they had known the couple for more than twenty years. Chandler pardoned Porter and Ellavee after they had served out their sentences in the governor's mansion. He said the pardons restored their citizenship and permitted them to vote. After the Chandlers left the governor's mansion in 1959, Porter and Ellavee came to Versailles and worked for them. When we talked with the Chandlers, Ellavee no longer worked for them, and Porter worked only occasionally, as a handyman for Mrs. Chandler.

"Happy's always been quite liberal," Mrs. Chandler told us.

"Not too liberal," Chandler said. "I'm liberal with other people's money."

"I know," she said, "but you see what you did with Jackie Robinson."

"Well, I felt I had to do that," Chandler said. "I was afraid the Lord wouldn't let me in if I didn't do that."

It was getting on toward supper time.

"Mama, is there anything for these boys to eat?" Chandler asked his wife."

"No."

"No?"

He said to us, "I'm sorry. If we had the niggers. We just can't get the niggers."

Before we left, Chandler told us about his valedictory speech when he left the Kentucky governor's office for the last time in 1959.

"I said, 'I don't want y'all to blame anybody else for anything that I've done. I don't know what the verdict of mankind will be with respect to my conduct here.' But I said, 'I was sober, and I meant to do every damn thing I did.'"

19

Orval Faubus' Dogwood Winter

A MOUNTAINEER wearing a straw hat with two long feathers in the band walked up to the teller's window of the War Eagle Branch of the First National Bank of Huntsville, Arkansas, and peered at us sitting behind the counter beside the teller.

"Who you got back there, Orval, bank examiners?" he asked the teller.

Sitting on a tall stool behind the teller's window, Orval Faubus assured his customer that we were not federal agents examining his books. The customer was one of Faubus' Huntsville neighbors. Faubus cashed his check and put it in a Roi Tan cigar box beside rolls of quarters, dimes and nickels.

When the customer left the one-teller branch bank, Faubus turned back toward us and resumed talking about his rise from nearby Greasy Creek in the Ozark hills to the governor's mansion in Little Rock, where the deep carpets reminded him of walking barefooted on new-plowed ground.

We interviewed Faubus in 1978 on a chilly April morning when the mountains were white with dogwood.

"We always have a cold spell while the dogwoods are in bloom," Faubus told us. "They call it dogwood winter."

Twenty years earlier, a Gallup poll had listed Orval Eugene Faubus among the ten world figures that Americans admired most, along with Dwight D. Eisenhower, Winston Churchill, Albert Schweitzer, Billy Graham, Harry Truman, Douglas MacArthur, Richard Nixon, Jonas Salk and Bernard Baruch. At that time, Faubus was in his second of a record six terms as Arkansas governor. The previous record had been three terms, held by a politician lucky enough to be named Jeff Davis in the years after the Civil War.

We found Faubus down on his luck. He had left a job running an Ozarks tourist attraction called Dogpatch U.S.A. and was teller, manager and the only employee in the War Eagle branch bank the morning we interviewed him. Formerly the owner of the *Madison County Record* in Huntsville, Faubus had lost his newspaper to his ex-wife, Alta Faubus, in a divorce settlement.

Just before we arrived, he had made headline news in Alta's paper by knocking a camera from the hands of *Record* editor Carol Hargis Whittemore and kicking it down the courthouse stairs. Whittemore, Alta's niece, was at the courthouse covering the trial of Faubus's second wife, Elizabeth, on charges of speeding, improper passing and fleeing from a state trooper.

That was big news in Huntsville, a town of only 1,287 people but a metropolis compared with Greasy Creek. The two communities are only thirty miles apart, but the only route when Faubus was growing up was over rutted, all but impassable mountain roads. Faubus told us he got to Huntsville, the county seat, only twice in his youth, the first time to testify as a witness before a grand jury, the second to stand examination to become a teacher when he was eighteen years old.

That was 1928, which also was the year he finished grammar school. He was twenty-four when he completed high school, and had already taught for six years in one-room, eight-grade schools in remote communities with such names as Pinnacle, Yellowhammer, Accident and Bald Creek.

Those were hard times. For food, the Faubus family trapped rabbits, which they called "Hoover hogs," salted their own hams and picked wild huckleberries for pies.

While he was still in grammar school, Faubus chopped wood to make cross ties for ten cents apiece.

"That's why I became a liberal," he said with a grin.

Later on, in the toughest times of the Depression, Faubus hopped a freight and joined his father as a lumberjack in Washington state for about a year.

Both Orval and Alta, a Baptist preacher's daughter he courted and married when she was nineteen and he was twenty-one, traveled the country in the summer as migrant workers, although that term hadn't been coined yet.

The greatest influence on the young Faubus was his father, Sam, who went only to the fourth grade but read *The Tulsa Tribune* and the writings of Robert Ingersoll and admired Eugene V. Debs, the American Socialist labor leader who organized railroad workers.

Sam Faubus headed a Socialist union—really a political club, with ten cents a month dues—in Greasy Creek and espoused such radical views as women's suffrage, the eight-hour day and Social Security. His opposition to World War I got him indicted under federal sedition laws.

But old Sam was a determined man. When he was dying of Hodgkin's Disease, he continued to hoe his garden on his knees, crawling from row end to row end, his son told us.

It took World War II to improve Orval Faubus' lot. He enlisted in the Army and got his second-lieutenant's bars in Officer Candidate School at Fort Benning, Georgia, finishing first in a class of 208.

"That's when I lost my concern about competing," Faubus said.

The former governor was sixty-eight years old when we interviewed him, with gray showing in his hair and his open-neck shirt hanging a little off his narrow, slouched shoulders, giving him the appearance of having lost weight.

He told us he'd had a new pacemaker implanted in his chest

and that he wanted to move for his health to a better climate in the Southwest as soon as he could find an oil sheikh to pay the $1.1 million he was asking for his house, which he built on seventy acres on a bluff overlooking Huntsville.

It was a magnificent 6,400-square-foot house with a cedar-shake roof, built of redwood, glass and native stone in the Frank Lloyd Wright style. The house had caused a big controversy when Faubus built it as he left the governor's office in 1967. He said it cost less than $100,000, but his political opponents said it cost $280,000 to build and $60,000 more to furnish. Faubus' salary as governor had been $10,000 a year, and Republicans wanted to know how he could afford a $280,000 house.

"I saved my money," Faubus told reporters.

His recent adversity had taken away none of Faubus' independent Scot spirit. He was open, smiling, working to make a living, carrying on in the manner that his late father once described to an interviewer: "Orval never liked to be looked down on. Never asked nobody to hoe his row, sharp his ax or light his fire."

Faubus became a world figure when he called out Arkansas National Guard troops to stop nine black students from being admitted to Central High School in Little Rock in 1957. President Eisenhower federalized the National Guard, taking it away from Faubus, and sent in 101st Airborne troops to enroll and protect the black students.

Faubus' action at Central High School went against everything he had stood for in the past. Sam Faubus had valued education above all else. Orval Faubus adopted those values himself. He was elected governor by poor Arkansas chicken farmers who felt they were being discriminated against by the wealthy aristocrats of Little Rock. One of his first acts as governor and head of his party was to enlarge the Democratic State Central Committee by six members and fill the vacancies with blacks.

Just before the Central High crisis, White Citizens Council leaders assailed Faubus as an integrating liberal.

By 1957, five of Arkansas' six state-supported colleges, including the University of Arkansas, had been desegregated.

Faubus' son, Farrell Eugene Faubus, attended an integrated college, Arkansas Tech in Russellville. Arkansas had desegregated more school districts than all other states in the South combined.

Why Faubus took the action he did at Central High has been a mystery through the years. His critics said he did it because he knew it would assure him of a third term as governor and put him in the Arkansas history books with Jeff Davis.

And it did prove popular with the public, not only in Arkansas but nationwide, as the Gallup Poll showed. Faubus carried every Arkansas county in the 1958 election and went on to win the governor's office three more times.

But his action brought scorn upon him and Arkansas. The photograph of a lone black schoolgirl in sunglasses, walking with dignity past a jeering crowd of enraged white adults, flashed around the world on wire service photofaxes. It had much the same impact as later photos of snarling dogs attacking black demonstrators in Birmingham, and helmeted sheriff's deputies on horseback clubbing black marchers at the Edmund Pettus Bridge in Selma. It galvanized whites all over the country in support of the black children and speeded up racial integration.

Faubus insisted to us that in 1957 he wasn't worried about winning a third term. In the months before the Little Rock crisis flared, he had never been more popular, he said.

"My main concern," he said, "was that nobody be hurt or killed and that we not have any violence such as that which occurred in some other places, like Clinton, Tennessee, and places in southern Illinois, and Texarkana, and Mansfield, Texas. I didn't want any rioting through the streets, with broken windows and looting and violence, and I thought I had to do something to prevent it.

"And I'm still convinced I did. Subsequent events, when violence broke out in more than two hundred major cities from coast to coast, long after Little Rock, are proof that the potential was there. I think any fair-minded person would have to recognize that."

He said he had two goals and achieved both: to avert killings, serious injuries and property damage, and to force the federal government to back up its own court orders, which he was still insisting, as late as 1988, were illegal.

"I've always said I regretted that it occurred—*after* it occurred," he told us. "I don't regret any decision I made, because there hasn't been a window broken yet in Arkansas, no riots, no looting.

"Look at Washington, D.C. The smoke from burning buildings drifted over the White House and the Capitol for three days, and they showed them on television carrying out all those television sets and goods. It happened in Detroit. It happened in Chicago. It happened in Watts. Nothing like that happened in Arkansas."

Nothing in Faubus' past had suggested he might do what he did at Central High. In his first race for governor in 1954, he had to fight charges that he was a Communist. Faubus entered that race a nobody but deprived incumbent Governor Francis A. Cherry of a majority of the vote in the Democratic primary and forced a runoff. Faubus promised Arkansas' broiler growers, the backbone of the state's economy, he would drop the two percent sales tax on chicken feed and told poor people he would make it easier for them to qualify for welfare payments.

Cherry panicked. A few days before the runoff election, his campaign revealed that Faubus as a youth had attended radical Commonwealth College in Mena, Arkansas, whose student body was about one-third Communist, one-third Socialist and one-third independent. During the McCarthy era of the 1950s, the U.S. Department of Justice had labeled the college a "Communist line" school.

Cherry's campaign smear backfired. The *Arkansas Gazette*, which had supported Cherry, ran a page-one editorial criticizing him. As a combat-decorated infantry officer in Europe in World War II, Faubus had led troops in the Rhine and Marne crossings. To counter Cherry, he went on the attack. He gave the press a copy of a telegram challenging Cherry to "say that I'm subversive, and we'll stand or fall on this issue."

Faubus told us that his telegram said: "If you say I'm subversive I'll sue in the courts of my native state."

Using a speech written by Harry Ashmore, executive editor of the *Gazette*, Faubus went on statewide radio.

"I'm just as American as the cornbread and blackeyed peas on which I was reared," he told the voters. "I'm just as free of subversion as the spring that flows from the mountain to form the White River."

Faubus delivered the radio speech from a microphone set up at home plate in a windy ballpark outside Pine Bluff with only a few people in the stands to watch, most of them poor, middle-aged women.

"I could see the older women in the audience crying, wiping tears out of their eyes," Faubus told us. "So I knew I was selling. The telegram and that speech turned the tide. Harry Ashmore had helped to write the speech. He later became my bitter critic."

Ashmore later wrote about Faubus: "He has about as much tact as a mother skunk."

In *Arkansas*, a history of the state that Ashmore wrote during the nation's bicentennial, he said Sam Faubus never granted interviews to reporters after the Central High crisis, but that he criticized his son in sharply worded letters-to-the-editor he sent the *Gazette* under the pen name Jimmy Higgins.

Before he quit talking to reporters, Sam Faubus spoke out strongly for racial equality from the 160-acre Greasy Creek farm he homesteaded.

"I think the Negro ought to have his chance," Sam Faubus said after his son was elected governor in the 1950s. "He's guaranteed it, just like us. Here's the whole point: If you keep the Negro down you'll have to stay down with him."

In his Arkansas history, Ashmore wrote that Sam Faubus had a theory about his son's motivation in calling out the troops to block school integration and that it wasn't racial prejudice. Old Sam believed the leading citizens of Little Rock looked down on his son as an interloper in the governor's office and that

Orval resented it. It reinforced a suspicion Orval harbored that these community leaders deliberately designed a school integration plan that would send poor white children to school with blacks downtown and leave rich, suburban white kids in segregated schools.

After we interviewed Faubus at the bank, he moved to Texas for his health and underwent heart surgery again. Doctors implanted another pacemaker in his chest.

Later, he and his wife separated and he moved back to Arkansas. His wife was raped and murdered in Texas by a man who confessed to the crime.

Faubus ran for governor for what he said was the final time in 1986, losing to the incumbent governor, Bill Clinton. In November 1986, Faubus, at age seventy-six, married a forty-four year old first-grade teacher and moved to Conway, Arkansas. He still had not found a buyer for his magnificent house on the bluff in Huntsville and had turned it over to his brother, who was charging admission for tours of the house.

And in 1987, the Arkansas Nine—the black students who integrated Central High School—held their thirtieth reunion. Most of them had gone on from Central High to become successful. One was assistant dean of the School of Social Work at UCLA. Another was an investment banker who had served as assistant secretary of labor in the Carter administration. Others had become teachers and writers and government workers and housewives.

Whatever the explanation for Orval Faubus' actions in the Central High crisis, he had no illusions about fame and power. In his two-volume biography, *Down from the Hills*, Faubus quoted an unknown poet in his dedication:

The rust will find the sword of fame,
The dust will hide the crown.
Ay, none shall nail so high his name
Time will not tear it down.

VI

Cumberland Gap: Copper Coil and Gunpowder

IT WAS THROUGH THE treacherous and beautiful hills and hollows of Cumberland Gap that Daniel Boone, in the hire of Eastern Seaboard land speculators, led a procession of risk-taking adventurers to the west.

Three states, Virginia, Tennessee and Kentucky, converge at the Gap. They drew their lines there and left its inhabitants to their own devices. Their devices included a lot of copper coil and gunpowder.

Labored volumes have been written trying to wring out a definition of the Southerner and what sets him apart. In a few short paragraphs, Tennessee novelist Jesse Hill Ford succeeded. Certainly he had these mountain folk pegged when he wrote this:

"The longer I live the more convinced I am that the white Southerner is a Scottish problem. . . . The white Southerner has taken to himself many features of the Scottish character, including a streak of independence which many outsiders feel contains elements of incipient criminality. A number of insiders tend to agree.

"Scotland gave the South its border struggles, its tradition of feuds and grudges, its foredoomed and frustrated longing for independence, not merely from the Crown but from any sort of government whatsoever, be it county, city, parish, commonwealth, state, or a federation of states. Where else but in Scotland is the poaching of fish and game so well thought of as it is in the South?

" . . . How he loves secrecy, sacrifices, and demon rites. What won't he do when pushed? Ask any American professional where the best soldiers come from. . . . Ask the same question in the United Kingdom . . . .

"The Southerner's class consciousness is also, it seems to me, Scottish and not English. A man's a man for a' that.

"When Scots were driven off the land to make way for sheep, and then set upon the trail of exile which took them first to Ireland and afterward to the New World, their spirit and culture took hold in the American South. It flourished here and it continues to sing and riot and to hold forth in story and legend."

Ford was writing about the South at-large. But his words seem particularly applicable to the men and women who ventured into the mountains with a flintlock rifle, an ax and nothing else but the grit in their craw.

Their descendants continue in the old ways, hunting and trapping in the hills, farming the hollows, and making the best moonshine whiskey on the face of the earth. They are an accommodating people. Accommodating but dangerous.

20

Chalk Gambrell's Mule

NOTHING HAD PREPARED us for what we found at Cumberland Gap. Our first stop there was on the Tennessee side of the Gap at the home of Junebug Clark in Powell Valley.

Besides having an interesting name, Junebug was a storehouse of mountain lore. We went to see him at the suggestion of his brother, Joe Clark, who grew up around the Gap and made his fortune by photographing whiskey stills instead of operating them.

Joe left the Gap as a young man and took a job as janitor at J.L. Hudson's Department Store in Detroit. Photographs of moonshine stills and mountain weddings that he took with a twelve-dollar Kodak on trips home proved to be his ticket to a new career.

When we interviewed Joe at his home in a northern Detroit suburb, he was seventy-two years old and enjoying his reputation as the Hillbilly Snapshooter. He had spent twenty-two years shuttling back and forth between Detroit and Lynchburg, Tennessee, taking pictures of distillery workers and town characters for Jack Daniel's whiskey ads in *The New Yorker* and other national publications.

Joe Clark said his brother, Junebug, could tell us about people like old Bill Colson, who died in a church gunfight. Joe said Colson and his boys, in a feud with a neighboring clan, holed up inside the church and found themselves surrounded.

"Old man Colson got mad," Joe told us, "and said, 'By God, I'm going out and get 'em.' Out the church window he went with guns blazing."

For the old man's funeral a couple of days later, his son Bill laid him out in a fine chestnut coffin, Joe told us.

"Young Bill said, 'I want him to go through hell a'crackin' and a'poppin'.'"

Joe also suggested that we ask Junebug about a coal miner who swapped his wife for a mule, and a moonshiner who killed seventeen men.

So when we got to Cumberland Gap, we headed straight for Junebug's house.

He was a talkative, forthright man of sixty with a sardonic turn of mind. We talked with him far into the night in his living room overlooking the gorgeous Powell River Valley. To help entertain us, he invited over his lifelong sidekick, Glenn Sharp. We also were joined by Junebug's son, Doug, home on a visit from Venezuela, where he was teaching farmers how to grow tobacco.

Junebug descended from a line of horse traders. He and his buddy Glenn started a trading business of their own during the Depression of the thirties.

From the Great Lakes to the Gulf, they practiced the ancient art of trading on the road. They drove their truck up and down the middle of the country, bargaining, buying, swapping and selling. They dealt in mule-drawn farm machinery, washpots, pigs, wheat, corn, land and anything else they could buy low and sell high.

"Anything you got," Junebug told us. "If it's in good shape, there's somebody, somewhere, wanting it. I don't care what it is. If it's a knitting needle, if it's a good knitting needle, there's somebody, somewhere, looking for it."

Doug Clark brought up the wife-swapping story before we got a chance to ask about it.

"That was Chalk Gambrell who done that," Junebug said. "Traded his wife for a mule."

Junebug and Glenn said they had known Gambrell for forty-five years, since they worked at a coal mine on Straight Creek outside Pineville, Kentucky, in 1932. They lived in the company boarding house that Gambrell operated.

By coincidence, Junebug had talked a few days earlier with a coal vendor who claimed he and a bunch of other old boys had witnessed the trade that assured Gambrell a place in Cumberland Gap history.

As Junebug remembers the story, Chalk Gambrell's wife had left him for another man, and one night a bunch of Chalk's friends started razzing him about it.

Until then, Chalk had accepted her decision. She already had been at the man's house two or three days. But someone in the crowd said, "Chalk, why don't you do something about that?"

They knew Chalk had an old pistol.

"Just go over there and kill him," one of Chalk's buddies said.

"Yeah, that's the thing to do," suggested another.

So Chalk set out for the man's house with his pistol, and his friends followed. When they got there, Chalk went inside, and his friends waited for the gunfire.

It never came. After fifteen or twenty minutes, they saw Chalk and his rival come out the door and head for a little shed behind the house.

They went into the shed, and in a few minutes, out they came, leading a mare mule. They put a harness on the mule and hooked her up to a sled. Then they came back to the house and loaded a stove onto the sled.

When Chalk with his mule, sled and stove, joined his

friends in the shadows, one of them asked him, "What happened, Chalk? You didn't shoot him."

"No," Chalk said. "I got this mule, sled and stove for my wife."

There's an addendum to the story. After Chalk had sold the mule, his wife came back to him.

Junebug said the coal vendor told him, "He knew his wife was coming back. He'd just beat that man out of the mule, just robbed him. Got that mule for nothing."

"He was quite a character," Junebug said of his old friend Chalk.

"Would Chalk tell us about that trade?"

"I just don't know," Junebug said. "I don't know whether he would or not. I'm satisfied he'd tell me about it if I'd get to talking about it and ask. But you just go in there as a stranger, never seen him before, I don't know whether he would or not."

We spent four and a half hours the next day looking for Chalk Gambrell. At a store along Straight Creek, we finally got directions to his house from Corbet Saylor and his son Wendell. They told us the same story we had heard the night before from Junebug Clark and added details. They said that Gambrell's first name was George and that Chalk was a nickname he probably picked up in the mines. They informed us Gambrell traded his wife, Mossie, to another coal miner, Ernest Eldridge, for a mule.

"What kind of mule was it?"

"Just a mare mule," Corbet Saylor said.

He told us Gambrell and Eldridge, who had died a few years earlier, had lived near the Saylor store for years.

Wendell Saylor said he had talked to Gambrell about the swap "and he would laugh. He thinks it's all a big joke."

Corbet Saylor said, "George is funny. Maybe he wouldn't come around with all of this, but it was put in the paper."

The Saylors' version of the story differed in one detail from the earlier version. They said that Mossie and Eldridge raised a family. She had returned to live with Gambrell earlier that year but died within the month, the Saylors said.

Before we left, Wendell Saylor related a story about Frank (Granny) Reed, a local politician who ran for office at every opportunity but never won an election:

"He was out in the country here trying to electioneer a bit and come to this old house, and this old woman was out in the yard chopping wood. So he stopped and got out and said, 'Ma'am, let me help you cut that wood.' So he cut the wood for the lady, carried it to the house, opened the door, and there sat his opponent churning milk."

We thanked the Saylors and headed out to find the man who traded his wife for a mule.

Following the Saylors' directions, we found Gambrell, a little man with tobacco stains around his mouth. He was seventy-three and coughing from black lung disease incurred in his years in Kentucky coal mines.

He confirmed that he had met Glenn and Junebug when he ran a boarding house the coal mining company in the thirties. He also confirmed that Mossie had died of cancer a month earlier.

"Mr. Gambrell, somebody over at Straight Creek told us you traded your wife for a mule one day."

Gambrell guffawed.

"Naw, buddy," he said, "That's just—Granny Reed started that stuff. Why it was in the *Herald*, in the *Herald* up in New York City."

"The *New York Herald*?"

"It shore was, buddy."

"Did he do it as a joke?"

"Yeah, more than anything else. There wasn't nothing to it."

He laughed again.

"A fellow asked me about that in Chicago when I was up there, got acquainted with him, he said he heard it, or read it in the *Herald*, the *Chicago Herald*. It must have been in every paper. I don't know how it got up in there like that, but it did."

21

Little Respect for The Living and None for The Dead

BACK AT JUNEBUG Clark's, we saw his sardonic side when he started telling us about the killings, and about a Kentucky valley just west of Cumberland Gap so violent the people thought they lived in South America.

"There was a moonshiner over there killed seventeen men," Junebug told us.

"How did that happen?"

"He aimed the gun at them and pulled the trigger."

"In fights?"

"Yeah, uh huh."

"What was his name?"

"Bill Henderson," Junebug replied. "They called him Bad Bill Henderson."

"Is he still alive?"

"No, they shot him down right at his front porch."

Junebug's flippancy reflected the casual acceptance of the violence in this no-man's land whose rich green beauty masked the harshness of its slopes and toughness of its people. Here,

Tennesseans, Kentuckians and Virginians set aside state allegiances to go about the business of surviving. They refer to where they live as "this country."

Junebug was not dealing in hyperbole. Before we left, we discovered people who did, because of the violent nature of the land, believe they lived in South America.

We told Junebug and Glenn Sharp we were astonished that one man could remain out of the penitentiary long enough to kill seventeen people.

"Well, it keeps the population down," Junebug said. "Maybe this fellow didn't want the country to get overpopulated."

"If you're a law abiding citizen, what do you do to avoid getting shot in a place like this?"

"You stay home mostly," Junebug said.

"What's at work here that a man can kill a lot of people and never go to jail? Is there some unwritten code?"

Glenn said, "They claim they got so many in jail they got no place to keep them. So maybe they'll give them six months or a year and turn them out, you know."

Doug Clark, Junebug's son, broke in: "Some of this was a long time ago, Glenn."

"Yeah."

Junebug said, "Yeah, but there's some of them happening today, too."

"A year or two ago," Doug recalled, "Carey down here—they killed him and the man never did go to jail."

Almost before his son finished, Junebug jumped in. "Well, they shot this Sutton boy. They shot him in two in the middle, you see, and the fellow never did—. "

Interrupting, Doug said, "That man over in Middlesboro killed three and never did go to jail a day."

"This fellow over on Ridge River," Junebug chimed in, "killed this thirteen-year-old boy. I don't think he ever served a day."

In their impromptu litany of violence, they volleyed tales of death like tennis players at the net. Yet this conversation between father and son was so casual they might have been discussing new model trucks.

"But what's at work here? Surely the jails aren't too crowded to hold cold-blooded killers?"

Glenn Sharp tried to explain: "After they kill and bury them, why they forget them. Most people forget them. They don't have much respect for the living and none for the dead. That's about the size of it."

Junebug told us about the thirteen-year-old. "A fellow just across the river, about three miles from here, I guess, killed a thirteen-year-old, then just picked him up and throwed him out front. And his mother come along two or three hours later and found him. Happened about a year ago. He didn't serve no time. They give him two years, but he didn't serve none of it."

"Why didn't he serve the sentence?"

"He didn't want to, I don't reckon. I don't know."

"Boy, you get the paper here," Glenn said, "and there's a string of arrests *that* long in it, you know. And most of them are dismissed."

"If you're a man, and you kill a thirteen-year-old boy, what's the defense? What was the defense in that case?"

"The boy needed killing," Glenn replied. "I think that's what they said."

He asked Junebug and Doug, "Wasn't they a'peddling dope or something and he caught onto it? What was the story on that?"

"The boy was supposed to have been peddling dope for him and squealed on him," Junebug replied. "They caught the boy with the dope, and he told them that he got it from this fellow."

"Oh."

We had learned another lesson about the Gap. No one was more detested than a snitch.

"Around here, they are a whole lot like Silas Culp," Junebug said. He turned to Glenn. "How many Silas claim he killed?"

"Eleven."

"Eleven men," Junebug repeated. "Some tourist came through here. Silas had a little beer joint down here."

"Fisherman's Hole," Glenn said.

"Fisherman's Hole, they called it," Junebug echoed, turning again to Glenn. "There was four or five killed at Fisherman's Hole, wasn't there?"

"Oh, yeah."

"This fellow came through," Junebug said. "He was looking at the old hills here and said, 'Silas, what do these people do, what do they raise around here?' 'Aahh,' Silas says, 'they raise little bitty corn, few potatoes, and they raise a little hell sometimes, too.' That fellow got out of there and got gone in a hurry."

Glenn described Culp. "He was a great big fellow. He was big around. He wasn't very long. But he wore a big old black hat all the time."

"He was mean as a snake, too," Junebug said.

"Oh, Lord, killed eleven that they knowed about," Glenn said. "And he had a boy there. They had a big fight out there one night in front of the place, and this old boy, oh, he whipped the tar out of a bunch of them. He said he'd have killed one of them but he knew his pap would rare at him. That's all that kept him from killing him. He didn't want his pap to rare at him."

Doug Clark suggested to Glenn, "Tell them about your cousin Arnold Sharp."

"Oh, Arnold," Glenn said. "He lived down the valley here. Hauled milk to Harlan, and he was built just like, oh Lord—."

"Harlan, Kentucky?"

Doug answered us. "Yeah, bloody Harlan."

"He was the stoutest fellow in this country," Glenn said. "He could do just about anything. He was kindly short and stocky, and every part of him was a muscle. He was taking milk up there, and he said he kicked some man's dog, and this man didn't like it. I think maybe there was a little bit more to it than that. But anyway the man came out there and he shot Arnold five times with a .45 pistol, and he was still standing when the man got done shooting."

"And he lived over it, too," Junebug told us. "He stood up for five .45 automatic slugs and never did fall. He hit him every shot."

Glenn said Arnold, with the bullets in his belly and arm, walked to a pickup truck to drive himself to the hospital. The truck owner came out of his house and asked Arnold, "You want to go to the hospital?" Arnold replied, "I need to go."

"So he took Arnold up to the hospital, and he got over it," Glenn said. "He was out in a little while. All he had was a stiff arm."

"Bloody Harlan," Doug said. "That's just a joke. There's been more people killed in Pineville, a whole lot more, than in Harlan."

Celebrated in films and folk songs, Harlan got a national reputation for violence during bloody union strife in its coal mines in the thirties and forties.

"Yeah, that's a joke, bloody Harlan," Doug said.

"Harlan got plumb jealous of this place around here for a long time," Glenn said. "They got way behind."

Much of the violence was connected with the Gap's leading industry, making and hauling moonshine whiskey. This chief export from Cumberland Gap flowed along a trade route that ran south to Knoxville and north to Cincinnati, Cleveland and Monroe, Michigan.

Claiborne County, on the Tennessee side of Cumberland Gap, sent forth more than its share of the export. Junebug and Glenn knew the county well. They had lived there, in the Powell River valley, most of their lives.

"Down here at Speedwell, every other house had a still in it," Junebug said. "They were trying to get enough money to go to the store and get something to eat. They really made the whiskey."

To move the whiskey north out of Claiborne County along U.S. 25E, the moonshine cars had to run a gauntlet through a half-mile stretch of Virginia. If haulers got through into Kentucky, they found the law more cooperative.

Charlie Redmond was a feared revenue officer in the Virginia strip. His army of agents commanded a respect not accorded lightly in the Gap.

"They came down there in force," Glenn recalled. "Boy!

They were a boogerish-looking gang. They had big belts around them, straps across their shoulders, cartridge belts. If you had a pistol or something in your car you were subject not to get all the way through."

"If you were with Kelly Rogers you'd get all the way through," Junebug said, setting off a round of laughter.

Junebug explained about Kelly Rogers: "There were about five or six old boys had a wreck in a car about halfway down the steep hill here below my house. I guess they were going as fast as they could. That was back in Prohibition days. Glenn's cousin knocked on the door. He was breathing so hard he couldn't talk, and he was scared to death, too. I had to tell him to rest a minute before he could tell me what was wrong. He kinda got where he could breathe a little bit, talk a little bit. He said, 'Come quick! We've had a wreck down here, and Frank is hurt bad, and there's some more of 'em hurt.'"

"Frank's my brother," Glenn explained.

Junebug resumed, "I jumped in the car and tore out down there. There was a guy, Basil, laying up there on the bank. Frank was there, he was bloody as he could be, his face was. Kelly Rogers was there. He was noted to be a mean fellow. He got killed later on."

"He killed his daddy," Glenn said.

"He killed his daddy," Junebug said. "Thought his daddy killed his mother. He had a pretty bad name. They said, 'Get Frank to the hospital.' I said, 'Up there's one on the bank looks in worse shape than Frank is.' 'No, no, Frank's in the worst shape.' So we loaded Frank up, and Kelly got in with me. When we got in the car, the first thing Frank done was give me his pistol. I knew Kelly always carried a pistol, but I didn't know how many he had.

"So we were going out of Cumberland Gap, up the mountain there, and there's a road that turns and goes up through Virginia. If there was one revenue officer, there was twenty-five, right there in the forks of the road. They stepped out in that road all around. There were revenue officers everywhere. They had the road blocked."

"Charlie Redmond was out there?" Glenn asked Junebug.

"Yeah, they just swarmed around that car. Charlie Redmond and them Wootens. One-arm Wooten was in the bunch. And his brother. I don't know who all they were. Anyway, there was a bunch of them. And that daggone Kelly didn't have one pistol out, he had two. When they stopped that car, he jumped out with a pistol in each hand, and he said, 'We're going to the hospital, and we're going *damned quick.*' That's what he said, 'We're going damned quick.' He said it right that way.

"Well, I just knew right then they were going to mow us down, because they were all around. Up over us and everywhere. Kelly was armed with two pistols in his hands and I had Frank's pistol. They cleared out and let us by, and I never made no more trips with Kelly Rogers."

22

Bad Bill Henderson of South America

BAD BILL HENDERSON was known for his pretty daughters, smooth sour mash whiskey and the notches on the stock of his box magazine Winchester rifle. But in 1923, he met a Methodist evangelist who bailed him out of the Pineville, Kentucky, jail and changed his life.

Junebug Clark said the preacher was Hiram Milo Frakes from Branchville, Indiana.

"He'd go to the jail, and he'd meet these people and talk to them and try to get them to live better and do better," Junebug said. "He met Bill Henderson in jail. And Bill told him, 'Preacher Frakes, I'd like for my kids to live better than I do, than I have, and enjoy life and have more, be better educated.' So when Bill got out of jail, Hiram Frakes went home with him. Bill had a little log building about ten-foot square that he kept his cow in, and he turned his cow out, and Hiram Frakes started a little church and a school."

Junebug said his brother Joe heard about the school back during the Great Depression and on a trip home from Detroit decided to photograph it. There was hardly any road to the wilderness community just north of the Tennessee-Kentucky state line west of Cumberland Gap. But on a winter morning, they headed out for the school anyway. Leaving their home in Powell Valley, Tennessee, they drove in Joe's Chevrolet, which had lost its running boards.

"It was in what is now known as Frakes," Junebug said. "At that time, it was called South America. It got its name back many, many years ago when they were having so many revolutions and uprisings in different parts of South America. And they named that territory in there South America."

They had a blacktop road for the short distance to Fonde Mountain across the Kentucky border, within six to eight miles of Frakes.

"I was driving, and we got to the top of the mountain," Junebug recalled. "We turned off on this gravel road, and it just went right straight down. I stopped and said to Joe, 'You see down there? When we go down there, we're not coming back.' Joe said, 'What do you mean?' I said, 'There ain't no way. Do we go on or don't we?'"

Junebug said Joe wanted the pictures.

"He kind of scratched his head and said, 'Let's go.' We didn't get five miles before we were done hung up. We set there a little while, and somebody come along walking. Somebody came out of the house. We all pushed and we got going and we done that all the way into Henderson Settlement. They had changed the name of the place to Frakes by then. They named it after this preacher. They changed it from South America to Frakes."

Joe Clark got his pictures, but it was a week later before they could get out. A snowstorm prevented delivery of supplies to the community, even by mule and wagon.

"They had a government surplus truck somebody had given them," Junebug recalled. "It pulled with all four wheels. They told us that in another day or two they'd have to try to get out and get a bunch of groceries. So they got about fifteen men and loaded the car in that truck, and it took us out of there."

Junebug said Joe's photographs of a mountain wedding in

Frakes later appeared in *Life* magazine. One of the pretty teen-aged girls pictured in *Life* was Mabel Henderson, an attendant to the bride and daughter of Bad Bill.

The moonshiner's dream for his children was realized in Mabel. When we interviewed her in the spring of 1977, she was sixty years old and living near the Henderson Settlement School that Reverend Frakes opened in 1925 on land Bad Bill donated. Bill had bought the land for $2,400 he made from a memorable moonshine whiskey sale at Christmas.

Until the moonshiner and the preacher collaborated to establish a high school in Frakes, schooling in that mountain valley ended at the eighth grade.

Mabel was a member of the fourth high school graduating class of the Henderson Settlement School in 1935. She went on to earn a bachelor's degree from Berea College in Berea, Kentucky, and a master's degree from Union College in Barbourville, Kentucky. At the time we interviewed her, Mabel headed the art department and taught English at Bell County High School near Pineville.

She had sons—the grandsons of Bad Bill Henderson—studying for degrees at Dartmouth College and the University of Kentucky law school. The law student, Warren, survived a bullet wound in Vietnam.

Like her brothers and sisters, Mabel grew up working in her daddy's business. She said they pitched in to carry corn and water to his stills and bring mash back to fatten their hogs. They also learned to dodge the law.

"We couldn't make a path," she told us. "We weren't supposed to go the same way two times. We had to jump from one rock to another."

Her mother, Lou Alice Henderson, headed the sales force in the family business.

"She said she sold enough liquor from behind the door to drown us all," Mabel told us.

Bad Bill worked in the coal mines but didn't like it, his daughter said. He had to travel a long way to get to the mines, and besides, she said, "Making whiskey was faster money."

The bad road out of the hollow didn't hurt the sale of Bad Bill's whiskey.

"He didn't have to get it out of here," Mabel said. "People came in and got it and took it out themselves. We had people from Pineville. We had the law that came in here and bought it from my dad. Moonshining was the main industry. My dad made the best moonshine in the country, so that brought up this feud. He had his own secret recipe, and these other guys were jealous because they couldn't sell their liquor as well as he could. They would report him to the law. Now the law—the men in Pineville who were supposedly the law—would buy my dad's liquor because they liked it, and they would arrest him later."

"Why did people call your father Bad Bill?"

"In this feuding and all, he had notches on his gun of men he had killed. In self-defense. It wasn't murder. I don't think he just outright murdered anyone. But he did kill a number of men in self-defense."

"Do you know how many he killed?"

"I've heard reports that he had ten notches on his gun. He spent much time in the hospital because he was shot by men who tried to kill him. He was shot in the back several times."

The feuding was always over whiskey or moonshine territory, never politics, she told us.

"It's easy to buy votes," she said.

She remembers hearing the gunfire at her father's still when Gilbert Maiden, one of Bad Bill's business competitors, shot him through the chest.

"I was playing with some neighbor kids before I went on home," Mabel recalled, "and we were playing in an old empty house when we heard the shots. We didn't think anything about them, but we started on down toward my house, and we were met by my sister, and she said my daddy had been shot. Those were the shots we heard."

Mabel said that at times her father could go out on his porch only after dark.

"You see, back in those days," she said, "the old-time way of washing was in a wash pan out on the porch. And you had a pitcher of water there. He hardly dared go out there and wash his hands because he was a target. People would be lying around waiting for him to come out so they could shoot at him. You can understand now why they call this a wild place, probably. It's no longer that way. Now, we have even worse stuff going on. Back then, that was good honest stuff going on."

Mabel said she was in the fourth grade before she knew where she lived. That's when she started studying geography.

"I grew up thinking we lived in South America. Old-timers would argue you—even now, some will—that they lived in South America, not in North America. And the little community joining us—you saw the pictures here of a wedding—that's in Germany right down below us."

She explained: "The people were rather suspicious of strangers. Anyone who was strange was supposedly a revenuer come back to arrest somebody. One reason the community was rather wild was because there was no law back in here. It was survival of the fittest, mostly. But we got along. We had our own churches and our own little schools, country schools. Teachers were sent here from town, and they boarded with local people. Just up to the eighth grade. We had no high school."

In 1923, Hiram Frakes came over the mountain from Pineville on horseback and moved in with Bad Bill and his family. Frakes had only an eighth grade education when he left Branchville, Indiana, a small hill country town on the Kentucky border southwest of Louisville. He was preaching at a church in Pineville when he met Bad Bill Henderson.

Pineville is a coal mining town. The seat of Bell County, it gets its name from the Pine Mountain Range that looms over the town so ominously that outcropping boulders must be held in place by huge chains to prevent a rock slide from wiping out the town. Pineville sits in a deep bend of the Cumberland River. Just before we arrived, the river had overflowed its banks by sixteen feet and washed mud into the second floor of downtown buildings and the courthouse.

As part of Frakes' ministry, he visited prisoners in the Bell County jail, where he met Bill Henderson, then fifty-seven years old and growing lame from gunshot wounds. The evangelist was moved by the aging moonshiner, talking about his dreams of a better life for his children back home in the hollow.

Despite his reputation as a killer, William M. (Bad Bill) Henderson was the closest thing that Henderson Settlement had to a pillar of the community. His father, James Henderson, gave the land for the two-room Henderson Hall grammar school. For a brief time, Bad Bill was a deputy sheriff in Tennessee.

Bad Bill's daughters were proud of their father. They described him as a warm family man who taught them discipline but never laid a hand on them. He played games with them, they said, and sat in front of the fire late into the night spinning tales of his exploits. In his later years, after he got religion and patched up bad feelings with old and dangerous foes, Bad Bill enjoyed a convivial relationship with his neighbors.

Mabel told us her father didn't mind people addressing him as Bad Bill.

"He was a great hand at jokes," Mabel said. "We used to go see my aunt. It would take us a half day to get there because he would talk with everybody who passed, and stop and see them. He was a great talker and joked a lot."

Wiley Maiden's family feuded with Henderson for years and competed with him in the moonshine business. Wiley told us Bad Bill once peppered him with a ten-gauge shotgun. But even Wiley described Henderson as "an accommodating man."

Reverend Frakes talked with the county judge before accepting Bad Bill's invitation to establish a high school in Henderson Settlement.

"It was very wild place, it had a wild name," Mabel said. "The judge said, 'It's at your own risk. I wouldn't advise you to go back in there. There's a lot of moonshining and a lot of killings.'"

When Frakes came riding into Henderson Settlement in 1923, Mabel said, "There were only two ways to get anywhere: the L.E.W., leave early and walk, or the T.M.W., two mules and a wagon."

Henderson had a house full of children but took Frakes into his household.

"That was his headquarters," Mabel said. "He stayed at our house about all the time. He tells the story about sleeping with my dad, and my dad keeping a gun handy beside the bed. Mister Frakes told the story, here was a preacher sleeping with a moonshiner."

Mabel said Reverend Frakes got Bad Bill to promise he would quit making whiskey.

"But I think he made a little moonshine after that," she said.

There was never any doubt, however, about the esteem in which Bad Bill held Hiram Frakes. In 1928, Bill named his youngest son Hiram Rufus Henderson.

"He was named for Reverend Frakes and the jailer in Pineville," Mabel said.

Eventually, Frakes and his wife built a home in the Valley. Frakes died about two years before we interviewed Mabel Henderson. She said they took him back home to Indiana for burial in Branchville. But his memory lingered strong.

"Mister Frakes was a leader," Mabel said. "He was a good speaker, despite the fact he had very little education. He could hold people spellbound. His heart was in his work. He thought of this place all the time. He had his faults, but any improvement you see in this community, if you go back to the source of it, you will find Mister Frakes working at it."

Frakes' students not only learned they lived in North America, they got to see some of it. Frakes organized his students into quartets and took them around the country to sing and raise money for the school. Mabel said that on a trip to Washington as part of a quartet, she had her picture made with President Herbert Hoover at the White House.

Using ten cents an hour labor, Frakes built a school that included dormitories for orphans and children from broken homes and destitute families. On Sundays, he preached in the school.

Frakes' high school closed in 1976, a year after his death, but the grammar school remained open. The dormitory also stayed open for needy children, some coming from as far away as fifty miles, in Harlan. The high school students transferred to the new consolidated Bell County High School outside Pineville, where Mabel Henderson taught. Now, even on snowy winter days, a school bus can negotiate the black top road across Fonde Mountain.

Bad Bill was killed on the morning he locked away his gun. He had differences with a stepson, Marion Overton, over a property boundary line, and at the request of the boy's mother, Lou Alice, Bill locked away the Winchester rifle in his corn crib and was hauling manure to a potato patch on that spring morning in 1932.

When her father was shot, Mabel was fourteen years old. She told us about the dispute.

"It was over land," she said. "Marion got up drunk. This was weighing on his mind, evidently."

Overton killed Bad Bill out by the barn and shot and wounded Bill's son-in-law, Ottis Ellis. Seventeen-year-old Ruth Henderson Ellis, Bad Bill's daughter and Ottis' wife, saw the shootings from the house.

Mabel, who was away and did not witness the killing, said that after he was shot, her father "knew he was going to die. Marion shot him in the chest. He put his hat under his head, folded his arms and said a prayer."

A court sentenced Overton to life imprisonment, but Mabel said he served only about eight years and was released. The last she heard, he was in a mental institution in Danville, Kentucky.

Bill Henderson was sixty-six years old when he died. Hiram Frakes preached his funeral.

But before Bad Bill was killed, Frakes engineered a peace meeting between Henderson and his chief adversary in the moonshine wars, Johnson Maiden, another pillar of the community.

"This old man Johnson Maiden was his main feudist," Mabel told us. "He died just awhile back. He was over a hundred years old. He and my dad became friends before my dad died. Mister Frakes had them meet. I was there. I remember my dad was shelling corn, and Johnson came in. That was right during this hot feuding they were having, too. I don't know how Mister Frakes ever maneuvered it, but he got Johnson there and prayed with them. And Johnson sat down to help my dad shell corn. And they got to telling old-time tales, from way back. Oh, they were enjoying each other."

"Did Johnson Maiden and your dad ever exchange shots?"

"They may have exchanged shots, but they never hit each other. They carried guns for each other."

"Are any of Johnson Maiden's sons still living around here?"

"There's Wiley Maiden," Mabel replied. "He's still causing trouble. He's an older man. He shot a boy in the leg the other day. He's mean, always drinking. He may be in jail, I don't know. The law was looking for him."

"Any other Maiden brothers still here?"

"There was Luke, but he was killed a few years ago. He set down with a group of people who were gambling. They shot him."

Before we left to look for Wiley Maiden, we got the address of Mabel's sister Ruth Ellis, who lived in Detroit. Ruth's husband, Ottis Ellis, had become a Church of God preacher in the Motor City.

Mabel informed us that Ruth and Ottis were recuperating from bullet wounds suffered in the back yard of their home near downtown Detroit when three gunmen tried to rob them.

Bad Bill would have been proud of Ruth, his favorite daughter.

"My sister had a gun," Mabel said. "She shot one of them, after she was shot through the stomach."

At Mabel's suggestion, we went down to the old Frakes School and asked a uniformed security guard patrolling the grounds where we might find Wiley Maiden. He asked if we were "the law." We tried to convince him that we were newspaper reporters, and showed him our press cards, which unfortunately were signed by the Detroit chief of police. He spotted the chief's signature right away and was more convinced than ever that we were undercover agents.

As if warning us, he said that within the last three months Wiley, then seventy-three years old, had shot two people. He shot one young man in the foot at a party and another man through the jaw.

"I don't fool around with 'em," the security guard said. "If they don't fool around with me, I don't fool around with them. He's mean in his old days, I know that."

Finally, the security guard told us that Wiley's daughter Ruby was married to Mack Jones and gave us directions to their house.

But he advised us, "I wouldn't just go up there and knock on the door. If I was going up there, I would park across the road and blow my horn real loud."

We thanked him for the information and advice. As we were leaving, he told us, "Y'all must really want him bad."

We decided to *telephone* Ruby Jones.

Over the phone, Ruby Jones told us her father was in Monroe, Michigan, staying with her brother, Stirl Maiden. She gave us Stirl's telephone number and a Monroe address on Gruver.

"My father is old time," she said. "He believes the way to settle things is with a pistol."

That night, we set up camp in Pine Mountain State Park overlooking Pineville. Park ranger Stanley Reed told us he grew up in the area and had returned after retiring as an Army officer. He said his father was a union organizer at the coal mines and that his brother "drove the getaway car for him."

We told him we had driven over to Frakes that day. He was familiar with the road.

"That's a bad ass road," the ranger said. "A deputy won't hardly ride down there unless he's got a posse."

23

Wiley Maiden On the Lam

SEVENTY-THREE-YEAR-OLD Wiley Maiden was on the lam. When we found the dangerous old moonshiner at the home of his son Stirl in Monroe, Michigan, he had just cut a deal with a judge back home in Kentucky so he could stay out of the penitentiary. He was homesick, but there was a little problem back there. The law wanted to talk to him about two shootings and three weapons possession offenses, all in a three-month period.

Maiden was luke warm about Michigan: "The water's no good, too many goddamn 'skeeters and not enough hills, bud. I've got a good farm down there. Well, it's all right up here. If you've got a pretty good gun, I don't see no trouble with these people."

He talked to us on May 28, 1977, readily agreeing to let us tape record the conversation. Maiden took us outside in Stirl's big back yard at 3847 Gruver in Monroe, hometown of the late General George A. Custer. Wearing Liberty brand overalls and a bright yellow shirt, Maiden sat under a willow tree in the yard, chewing grass stems as we talked. His face was covered with a day's stubble of beard. One tooth was showing. He had thin white hair.

Wiley Maiden looked like what he was, a mountain man who worked forty-nine years in the coal mines and came out with black lung disease and no pension. He was drawing $308 a month in disability payments for the black lung, plus Social Security payments. As a young man he carried 135 pounds on a five-foot-nine frame. He now weighed 205. Maiden said he made moonshine for forty years.

We asked Maiden if he had ever been shot other than the time Bad Bill Henderson peppered him with a ten-gauge.

"No, that's all the time I was shot."

"Did you ever kill anybody?"

"Oh, I shot a couple of fellows this year, a while back."

"What was that all about?"

"Well, just got into it." Maiden gave himself a little congratulatory chuckle. "I shot a fellow for robbing me. Howard Overton."

He pronounced the name "Hard Orton."

"He took two hundred dollars off'n me while I was asleep," Maiden said.

"This take place back home in Kentucky?"

"Yeah, he lives in Middlesboro. Come over there and stayed all night with me and took a couple of hundred dollars off me, catching me asleep. The next morning, I got up, went down there to get us some beer, and I looked in my pocket book and I seed my money was gone. I knowed there hadn't been nobody else up there."

As Maiden told the story, his anger returned.

"I had give the son of a bitch a ton of coal and had helped him deliver his oil. I come back to where he was and said, 'Bud, I lost some money.' Said, 'You stole my money, buddy, right out of my pocket.' I said, 'You shore as hell ain't getting away with it. If you don't give me my money I'm going to shoot hell right out of you.' He said, 'You wouldn't do nothing, you goddamn son of a bitch, you wouldn't shoot nobody.' So I shot him right through the mouth with a thirty-eight special."

He pronounced the last word "spatial."

Maiden said he got his money back: "I made him give it back to me. I told him, 'If you don't give it back, goddamn if I ain't going to shoot you again right in the head. He pulled it out and handed it to me, and blood was pourin' from him."

"Did he recover?"

"I took him to the hospital. Yeah, he got all right."

"The shot knock his teeth out?"

"Didn't have no teeth. Cut his tongue in two. Don't think he can talk plain no more."

Maiden, lively for his seventy-three years, said the second shooting occurred while he was partying with young people in his house trailer near Frakes, Kentucky.

"There was about ten or fifteen young fellows come by, and four or five girls," Maiden said. "We was all having a good time, drankin' moonshine. One of them got up and kicked the couch over. I told him, 'Buddy, goddamn, don't be a'kickin' my stuff around. It costs money to buy stuff.'"

"This was in your house?"

"Yeah. He stuck his foot out, said, 'Old man, go ahead and shoot me.' When he said that, I poured it to him, right through the foot."

Maiden laughed heartily.

"The goddamn state police come up. The girls took him off down on the road, took him out and turned him over to the state police, and they took him over to Pineville."

"What was his name?"

"Murray. Henry Murray. He was, I guess, about twenty years old."

"What were all of you doing there at your house, frolicking or playing poker or what?"

Maiden replied, "We wasn't playing no poker."

"Just having a good time, drinking moonshine?"

"Yep," Maiden said. "They took him off to Pineville and put him in the hospital."

"Were there any hard feelings about the shooting?"

"No, I went down the next morning to see the boy. I told him, 'Here, bud, is a carton of cigarettes and ten dollars.'"

"Why did you give him ten dollars?"

"I thought he might need something while he was in the hospital. He told the state police the next morning, he said, 'I shot myself.' I hated I shot him, but he wanted to see how it felt."

Maiden laughed again.

"And I poured it to him."

Our interview with Maiden was conducted over a barrage of constant crowing by roosters penned up down the slope of Stirl's back yard. With his teeth gone, his mountain accent and the roosters competing mightily with him, it sometimes was hard to understand what Wiley was saying.

"Boy, you've got the chickens out here. Does Stirl raise them?"

"Fights 'em," Maiden said.

"Around here?"

"All over," Maiden replied. "I went to a fight the other night down in Ohio."

We asked Maiden if he came to visit Stirl because of the two shootings.

"No, I come up here because they took a damn pistol off of me down there."

He told us about a telephone call he had received from a judge in Kentucky offering a deal that would keep him out of the state penitentiary if he would return.

"The judge told me, called and told me, to come on back. Said he'd give me sixty days and six months good behavior and turn me loose. I'll go on back. I come up here to keep from serving it. I damn sure wasn't going to the penitentiary. I got it made up now."

Maiden said he was familiar with the Pineville jail.

"I been in jail, I guess, seventy-five times. Never paid my drunk fine in all my life."

"Seventy-five times?"

"Yeah, but I hit pretty bad luck down there for the last three months. I had three goddamn pistols took off me in two months' time."

"Why do you carry a gun?"

"Hell, if you had three brothers get killed for nothing, wouldn't you think you needed a gun? I sleep with one under my head at all times down there."

"You sleep with a gun at your head?"

"Maybe two of them. And every time I step out I take a gun with me."

"You keep your gun on a table by your bed?"

"Under my pillow. I ain't going to let somebody kill me for nothing. If they kill me, they're going to have to do over half the damn fighting. I ain't going to be fooled with."

We returned to the question that had puzzled us since the first time we stepped into Cumberland Gap.

"Mister Maiden, with all these killings in that valley, how is it that nobody goes to jail?"

"Yeah, they kill one another. I've got three brothers that got killed there."

"Why don't people get prosecuted?"

"They lawed 'em, but the damn crooked courts would turn 'em loose. I'll tell you about the state of Kentucky. If you got money, you got it made. If you ain't got no damn money, you're better off shooting 'em."

"But doesn't anyone go to prison for killing somebody?"

He looked at us as if it were an absurd question.

He said an acquaintance killed his brother Troy when he was only eighteen.

"What was that about?"

"I couldn't ever figure what. They always seemed to be good friends."

"Did he go to prison?"

"He beat the case."

"Who were the other brothers of yours who got killed?"

"Luke Maiden, he got killed down there. He was about forty-five, I think."

"Who killed Luke?"

"Ralph Thacker."

"What was that about?"

"Over a damn election, I think. Yeah, couldn't have been nothing else."

"What happened to Thacker?"

"He beat the case."

"All these are shooting cases?"

"Yeah."

"Who was the other brother of yours who got killed?"

"Tony. He got shot right in the mouth with a P-thirty eight. Sowders killed him, Clyde Sowders."

"How old was Tony when he got killed?"

"Sixty-two."

"He was older than you?"

"He was the oldest in the bunch."

"How many boys in your family?"

"There was eight of us."

"How many are alive now?"

"Two."

"How many girls in the family?"

"Three."

"How many of your sisters are alive?"

"All of 'em."

Maiden told us his father, Johnson Maiden, had died of kidney failure earlier that year at age 105.

"He had a Browning automatic shotgun at the head of his bed when he died," Maiden said. "He died down at Frakes, at his own home down there."

"Did your father and Bill Henderson ever shoot at each other?"

"No. I think one was afraid of the other'n. One watched the other'n all the time."

"Your father kept a shotgun at the head of his bed when he died? Would anybody want to shoot a man a hundred and five years old?"

"Yeah."

"They *would*?"

"Yeah, that Clyde Sowders wanted to kill him."

"What was that all about?"

"Me and the old man went over there one Sunday," Maiden

replied. "Me and Clyde was drankin'. He took the old man out, as we started to leave, took the old man out and showed him an old still cap out on the porch cut all to pieces. He said, 'Johnson, could a man fix that?' My dad said, 'No.' Sowders said, 'Yeah, you can fix it like it's new.' He said to the old man, 'You a goddamn fool.' When Sowders said that, the old man shot him before God could get the news."

Maiden laughed at the story.

"Your daddy was a hundred years old when he did that?"

"Yeah."

"Your daddy shot him before *what*?"

He snickered: "Before God could get the news."

Maiden said that when he realized his father was going to shoot Sowders he had tried to grab the old man's gun.

"I couldn't catch that old man," Maiden said. "He done had him shot. Somebody asked Sowders, 'Why didn't you kill that old man,' that lawyer did. Sowders said, 'Hell fire, I didn't have *time* to kill him. He was too quick fer me.'"

"Did Sowders have a gun?"

"Yeah, but he didn't have time to use it."

"Did your father pull his pistol from his pocket?"

"He pulled it out from under his overcoat. Shot him square through, an inch below the heart."

Sowders survived. When we talked to Maiden, he said Sowders was serving fifteen years in a Tennessee penitentiary for shooting a man in the back at Jellico.

"Was this the same Clyde Sowders who shot your brother Tony?"

"Shot him right in the mouth with a P-thirty-eight. Broke his neck in three pieces. Tony stuck his head in the car and said, 'Bud, you got a flat.' Sowders shot him right in the mouth. All the damn smoke and powder burns right in his mouth. Sowders got seven year out of it."

"You say the only time you were ever shot was by Bad Bill Henderson?"

"Uh huh," Maiden said. "That Bill Henderson was a pretty tough guy. I think he killed about eighteen men."

"Why was he so tough?"

"Raised that way, I guess."

"He made moonshine?"

"He made whiskey, sold whiskey," Maiden replied. "He was awfully tough, Bill Henderson was."

"How did he kill people?"

"He was a dirty man, dirty as hell. He'd waylay you and shoot you any way he could."

"What did he use, a rifle?"

"A rifle. Pistol, too," Maiden said.

"What kind of rifle?"

"It was a box magazine Winchester."

"What kind of pistol?"

"It was a thirty-eight special. He shot me and my brother Tony one time with a ten-gauge shotgun, at about two hundred yards."

Maiden said he had lent a shotgun to Buster Partin, thinking Partin was going hunting. Instead, Maiden said, Partin used it for a killing. The victim was Bill Partin, no relation to Buster but married to Bad Bill's sister-in-law, Maiden said. Henderson blamed Maiden for supplying the killer with the shotgun.

Maiden told us he was innocent.

"I dug the grave, me and another man," he said.

Maiden said that after the funeral, "Me and my brother was up on a hill, hunting around, and Bill Henderson fired on us with a ten-gauge shotgun. It was damn meanness. He hit me in the arm, up here, and it run out down here."

He showed us where the pellet had entered and exited.

The next day after that shooting, the Maidens scouted out Bad Bill's still and returned home and waited until the following Saturday, when they knew he would be boiling off a run. That morning, a well-armed party of Maidens set out for Bad Bill's still.

"When we come in sight, he went to shooting," Wiley told us. "And Gilbert Maiden shot him right square through with a thirty-eight Winchester. Cut Bill *down*."

"Who was Gilbert Maiden?"

"First cousin to us."

When Gilbert Maiden's rifle shot struck him, Bad Bill tumbled off a cliff and broke his pelvis, Wiley said.

"I seed his feet going over a cliff eighteen feet high, bud." Wiley laughed.

"You didn't get a chance to shoot at him, right?"

"I wasn't going to stick my head over that cliff," Maiden said.

Reverend Hiram Frakes acted as peace-maker between Bill Henderson and Johnson Maiden, patriarch of the liquor-making Maiden clan. The families lived within hollering distance of one another, and at one time Bad Bill and Johnson Maiden made moonshine together. Over the years, bad blood developed between them, and at the time of the shootings they competed fiercely for moonshine customers.

"My dad lived down there 105 years," Wiley said. "And you know they never did catch that man, and he made liquor all his life."

Unlike Bad Bill, old Johnson Maiden never killed anyone.

"He shot several, bud, but luck was he never killed nobody," Wiley told us.

"But Henderson respected your father?"

"Had to."

Wiley said, "That old man didn't take no foolin' off of nobody."

He told us about a dispute between his father and Bad Bill when they were making liquor together in Tennessee. He said Bad Bill threatened to "fox somebody" who had angered him at the still.

"What do you mean by 'fox somebody.'"

"*Fox* 'em," Wiley explained, "that meant kill 'em. That was his word."

Wiley said, "Henderson said that two or three times, and the old man knowed Bill was going to shoot somebody in a minute. He got up and said, 'Bill Henderson, you ain't going to fox no goddamn body,' and jobbed him right in the belly with a forty-five. 'I don't want to hear that word no more.' Henderson was beside John Evans. Said, 'John, get my mule, I'll go home.'"

The reconciliation between Bad Bill and Johnson Maiden occurred at Henderson's place.

"Old Frakes come up on us," Wiley recalled. "The old man was settin' there. Frakes said, 'I've come up, Mister Maiden, to get you to go down and make friends with Bill Henderson.' The old man said, 'Make friends with Bill Henderson? I ain't never had nothing against Bill Henderson.'"

Frakes and Johnson Maiden went to Bad Bill's place and found him shelling corn.

"My old man had his gun in his right hand," Wiley said. "Every time you seen that old man, you seen that rifle. The old man went over and got him an ear of corn and commenced shelling. He asked Henderson, 'Bill, why in the hell did you send this man up here? You said make friends. I ain't got nothing against you. Are you mad at me?' Henderson said, 'No.' He was getting over that shot Gilbert give him."

Wiley recounted, "Henderson said to the old man, 'The one thing I'd like to ask you, Johnson, keep Tony and Gilbert out of this country.' The old man said, 'I don't keep none of my boys no goddamn place. They can come home when they want to. This is their home just the same as it's your'n, Bill. I can't do that. As fur as being afraid of you, I ain't a goddamn bit afraid of you. I ain't got nothing ag'in you.' Henderson said, 'Yeah, I know that.'"

Like everybody else around Cumberland Gap, Wiley Maiden had a lot of Bill Henderson stories to tell.

"He killed two of them Mayhan boys and burnt 'em," Maiden said. "Off Fox Creek. They was over there snitching on him for moonshining. He got them down there, him and old man Alvis Partin, and killed them and burnt 'em up. They just piled a damn big log heap on 'em and set 'em afire and burnt 'em up."

Maiden said that Bad Bill escaped arrest by faking his death.

"He stayed dead about eight year, I think, Bill did. His family took the casket out there and buried it, preached his funeral. Bill was dead."

The recollection tickled Maiden.

"Everybody knew he was alive, though?"

"No, they didn't know that," Maiden said.

"You didn't know he was alive?"

"Yeah, I knowed it. I knowed where he lived."

"Well, why didn't you tell the law?"

"We didn't snitch on nobody," Maiden replied. "We don't allow snitching down there."

He laughed ominously.

"If you snitched you wouldn't last long."

If anyone had a reputation rivaling Bad Bill's in the Cumberland Gap area it was the Ball family.

"The toughest men we had in that country were the Balls, Alvie Ball and Floyd Ball," Maiden said. "Yeah, they were tough. But they didn't make 'em no tougher than old Bill Henderson."

More than once, the Ball family shot up the courthouse in Pineville during trials.

"If they was going to have a trial in court, they would get up and kill the man, the judge, too, if he fooled with them," Maiden said.

Junebug Clark and Glenn Sharp had told us about the Ball family. They said members of the Ball family once ran Middlesboro, Kentucky, the largest town around Cumberland Gap. Members of the family served as mayor, sheriff, and in other positions of power.

"If they got mad at you, they'd send a policeman to kill you," Junebug told us.

The Balls owned the Wabash hotel, a Middlesboro landmark famous for vice. The Quarterhouse at Fork Ridge, southwest of Middlesboro, was a competing honky-tonk.

The Ball forces and Bad Bill Henderson clashed one night at the Quarterhouse in a battle that people in Cumberland Gap still talked about three-quarters of a century later. Maiden said the Quarterhouse operator, Lee Turner, had hired Henderson and his brother-in-law, Johnny Frazier, as guards.

"They run a big whorehouse up at the Quarterhouse and were selling whiskey," Maiden said. "The Balls were selling it in

Middlesboro, see. They wanted the Quarterhouse tore up. Sent old Charles Sessions and about sixteen men up there and burnt 'em out. They killed women and all. Bill got back on a hill, him and Johnny, in a crag. They took rifles and shot the hell out of 'em. Run 'em off."

"How many people were burned up in the fire?"

"I don't know, five or six. Old Charles Sessions set that Quarterhouse afire. He was a peg-legged man. Bill Henderson shot him, went down and took that peg leg off and throwed him in the fire and burned him up. I've seen him pick his teeth many a time with that damn peg leg. He'd take his knife and plane him off a sliver . . ." Maiden laughed ". . . and pick his teeth with that man's leg."

"How many did Henderson and Frazier shoot?"

"About six or seven."

One of the men Bill Henderson killed on another occasion was an Italian coal miner he had arrested while working as a deputy sheriff at Pruden, Tennessee, on the Kentucky line not far from Middlesboro. Versions of the killing differ greatly. Wiley Maiden's version was that it was cold-blooded murder.

"He was a crippled fellow," Maiden said. "Henderson walked him up on the mountain there and turned on the next fork ridge to Big Springs. Old Bill told him, 'You better get a drank, bud.' Said, 'It's the last drank you'll ever get.' The man had a stick to walk with. He laid down at the spring and got a drank and got up and turned around, and Bill shot him right between the eyes with a thirty-eight special."

"Why did Henderson shoot him?"

"Damn meanness. He had a warrant for him, taking him to jail. He didn't want to go over there to Tazewell to take him to jail. Had to walk across there. He had him on the other side of the mountain and shot his brains out."

Maiden said Bill loaded the corpse on a black mule, "like a damn hog," and took the body back to an encampment of about fifty Italians at the coal mine.

"He told them, 'If one of you cheeps or says a goddamn

word, I'll fox you,'" Maiden said, laughing. "'I'll kill you.' There wasn't nary a one said a word."

Maiden's version of how Bad Bill Henderson died also differed from versions within the Henderson family.

"Bill's stepson killed him," Maiden said. "Marion Overton killed him."

He pronounced the name "Marn Orton."

Maiden said Overton got into a fistfight with several of Henderson's relatives, including new son-in-law Ottis Ellis, married to Ruth.

"They thought Marion didn't have nary gun, and he went by Bill's house the next morning," Maiden said. "Old man Bill said, 'What in the hell is all this hooray about, Marion?' He said, 'That's what I'd like to know, old man.' Marion went back and set his foot up on a sled where that old man was hauling out manure. And old man Bill's son-in-law, Ottis Ellis, come running down and jerked out a big knife and cut Marion's hat open. Marion come out with that thirty-eight special and shot Ottis Ellis square through."

At that point, Maiden said, "Bill started to run—he had a gun settin' there, started to go get it—and Marion jumped between him and that gun. Shot him three shoot-throughs with a thirty-eight special. Old man Bill told Marion, 'That's all. You're the man that killed me dead.' He laid down. He didn't fall."

Maiden said Bad Bill was the third man killed in that hollow.

"They nicknamed it Dead Man Hollow."

Bill Partin was also killed there, Maiden said.

So was Dick Roach.

"He swapped his woman for a big white hoss," Maiden told us. "Roach met up with a fellow and said, 'I'd like to trade this woman to get me a good hoss.' The man said, 'All right.' He got off that damn hoss, Roach rode off, and that woman cussed hell out of that fellow and knocked him in the head and followed her man on up, and he kept the hoss."

He laughed aloud.

"Her name was Martha Roach."

Wiley Maiden is not one to hold a grudge.

"Old man Bill Henderson was always good to me," Maiden said. "That one time, he tried to shoot me. But we got a pair out of that. We shot his ass off. He was an accommodating man. But he'd swear a lie on you as quick as he opened his mouth. You couldn't law him."

"Why not?"

"He would swear a lie to prove he was innocent," Wiley said. "Never was stuck a damn time in his life. He always had some way to get out of it. Sentenced one time to six months in the penitentiary for walking off from jail up at Pineville. The governor pardoned him before he left the jail."

Bad Bill Henderson "wasn't no damn badder than no damn body else in that country," Maiden said. "You go down there and you can find some of them fellows you'd think wouldn't fight a thing. They'll fight a circle saw and it a'running."

A hulking Army bugler discovered that many years ago, when Maiden was seventy pounds lighter, a lot faster and just as mean. Maiden was an Army recruit at Camp Meade, Maryland, relaxing in the barracks while he waited to be issued his uniform.

"I was setting there on the bed, and a big old guy, a bugler, come and knocked me over three of them. I went back over to my squad room. I said, 'Come over here and try it again, you big son of a bitch.' I heard him a'coming. I had an old Barlow knife about *that* long, yeah, *that* long. I eased that thing open. He come through the door. I hooked that blade under his belt and it come out right there."

Maiden pointed to his crotch.

"It split underwear and all. Boy, he went down them steps a'gettin' it. He went down and told the supply sergeant and the clerks, 'That goddamn son of a bitch tried to kill me.' The sergeant said, 'You're *going* to get killed.' Said, 'I told you about that fellow. You ain't going to run over them Kentucky fellows and knock them around without getting killed.'"

The company commander summoned Maiden.

"He said, 'Let me see your knife.' Said, 'Man, you could kill a bear with that thing.' Said, 'The way we fight here, we fight fistfights, bud. We don't fight with no guns or no knives. When you knock a man down, let him get up before you hit him again.' I said, 'I couldn't stagger that big son of a bitch.' You know that damn fellow never bothered me no more. We got along like two brothers."

As we were winding up our interview under the willow tree with the gamecocks crowing in the background, Wiley extended us an invitation.

"Come on down, boys, and I'll let you sample a gallon of good moonshine."

"We might take you up on that."

"I've got a gallon setting down there. I guess eight or ten gallons setting back there in them woods. Ought to be getting good now."

He laughed.

Wiley told us he had made moonshine for about forty years.

"Yeah, you take a good sack of meal and a sack of malt, and you get your corn and about fifty pounds of sugar. Let that work about eight days, and then put it under a good copper outfit and run it off slow. You can drank it like dranking water, won't burn you, won't even make you sick. But it'll make you so damn drunk you can't crawl."

Wiley said he hadn't made any moonshine in about five years. He said he quit because he got caught twice. Before that, Wiley said he had a friend inside the revenue office.

"Head revenue man," Wiley identified him. "Yeah, I saved his life one time. My brother, Tony, had a thirty high-power, had it on him, fixing to kill him. I grabbed that gun down and took it away from him."

After that, Wiley said he would get special treatment when the revenue agent found his still.

"He'd knock the bottom out of a barrel, didn't knock the still down. Take my worm out from about here to that house and stick it under a log and go on. Some of the fellows said to him, 'Hey, you ain't lawin' that goddamn Maiden.' Said, 'That goddamn revenuer's a friend to him,' and he was. Yeah, I sold him many a gallon of whiskey."

Wiley turned philosopher: "Yeah, it pays to have friends, boys. If you ain't got no damn friends you ain't got nothing."

24

"She Don't Mean Any Harm By That Gun"

SHE HAD TO PROP THE shotgun on a fence rail to shoot it, and the kick knocked her down, but she got her man. Ruth Henderson was only ten years old when she fired that shot, knocking Wiley Maiden out of Bad Bill's chicken roost.

"They always depended on me for thangs like that," she told us.

We interviewed the seventy-three-year-old daughter of Bad Bill Henderson in November 1987. She and her seventy-seven-year-old husband, Ottis Ellis, were living in a big, comfortable home on the west edge of fashionable Indian Village near downtown Detroit.

Ruth was only a little girl in Kentucky when a master taught her to shoot. Some people put the count a little higher and some a little lower, but by Ruth's count, her father killed seventeen men.

"Lord have mercy, he could shoot," she said. "You could flip a dime in the air, and he could shoot it out of existence. My daddy was a perfect shot. They wouldn't let him enter a shooting match, a turkey shoot. They knew he would win every time."

Every Christmas, Bad Bill laid in a supply of ammunition in their home up a Kentucky mountain hollow just west of Cumberland Gap.

"He used to practice us every Christmas how to shoot. He started us to practicing shooting—I must not have been over ten years old. He practiced us all my life to shoot. I can shoot a gun. People say, 'Aren't you afraid?' I ain't a bit afraid."

These words sounded strange coming from this jolly little woman not five feet tall, with a nearly toothless smile and a friendly manner. The years had changed her from the pretty teen-aged mountain girl who watched from the house as her step-brother shot her father down in the barnyard in the spring of 1932. When we interviewed her in 1987, Ruth was a woman narrow at the shoulders and flared in the middle, giving her the appearance, when seated, of one of those inflatable toy trolls that bob upright again after being punched. She was a little hard of hearing and wore plastic-rim glasses that gave her an owlish look. She had on a purple, flowered dress, a hairnet and multicolored crocheted house shoes.

"She's a nice little lady," said Ottis, Ruth's husband of fifty-six years, "She don't mean any harm by that gun."

Ottis referred to a five-shot Smith & Wesson thirty-eight caliber revolver his wife keeps handy and loaded with blunt-nosed cartridges that she described for us: "Them would cut your head off. These bullets, they explode. You can't miss with them hardly."

Like Ruth, Ottis had changed over the years. He was no longer the quick-tempered mountain boy shot down that spring morning in 1932 as he went to the aid of Bad Bill Henderson, just before he was killed. Ottis now was a white-haired retired Church of God preacher, mild of manner compared with Ruth.

Ruth's fierce spirit, with the help of her Smith & Wesson and Bad Bill's lessons, saved Ottis' life and probably her own the night of August 6, 1976.

She and Ottis told us about that night. Three men had tried to rob them in their back yard on Van Dyke Place in Detroit as they were unlocking their back door after attending a Friday night church service. One of the men announced, "It's a holdup!"

As Ottis shouted from the porch, "Don't shoot," the holdup man shot him in the abdomen. Then the gunman shot Ruth under the heart, the bullet piercing her upper bowel.

The bullet split the zipper off Ruth's purse, knocking it from her hands onto the porch. Ottis instinctively leaped off the porch to try to take away the gunman's pistol. As Ottis landed in the yard, the gunman shot him again in the stomach.

From the porch, Ruth saw her critically-wounded husband lying in the grass beside the walkway, and saw the gunman walk toward him and raise the pistol in both hands to shoot him in the face. Ruth lunged for her purse lying on the floor and snatched out her Smith & Wesson.

"I just throwed that gun up and shot him right in the center," Ruth said. "I shot four times. I shot two of the guys."

The third robber dived head first over the back fence.

"Boy, he went out of there with his heels sticking up," Ruth said. "I don't think I hit him, though."

Ruth cackled as she told us about seeing the robber scamper away in fright. Ottis said Ruth told him later that the comical sight of the holdup man tumbling desperately over the back fence had tickled her, despite her gunshot wound, and that she was laughing as she fired at him.

"She had hollow points," Ottis said. "That really fixed that guy who was about to shoot me. She prayed for him."

Ruth said the gunman screamed and threw his arms in the air when she shot him.

"He was laying on the ground hollering," Ruth said, contempt in her voice. "I never did holler. I didn't feel any pain, except I felt it burn when the bullet went in and through my colon."

The two wounded gunmen made their way out of the yard

while Ruth went inside the house to phone police. She also spoke with contempt of police, for their refusal to chase down the wounded robbers.

"They were too big a coward to go through there and look for them," she said sarcastically. "They were afraid they'd get their hides busted."

A few days later, police found a man's body in a sewer in the Ellises' neighborhood. Ruth was convinced he was one of the men she shot.

Ottis was temporarily paralyzed and lost his spleen because of the bullets, which he still carries in his body. Emergency room doctors said he lost all life signs three times on the operating table that night.

"The doctors told Ruth I died three times," said the Church of God preacher. "I spent that time with the Lord. The Lord said to me, *Do you remember preaching, 'I am the light, and I am the resurrection. He who believeth in me shall not die.'? Do you believe that?* I said, 'Yes, I remember it, and I believe it. He said, *Walk out before me, and be perfect.* And here I am. Now I'm still telling him I can't walk before him and be perfect."

"I believe the Lord really whupped him," Ruth said.

After Ottis rose for the third time, he couldn't be convinced Ruth was not killed in the robbery.

Ruth said she told her doctor to take her to see Ottis. "I knew it would do him more good than anything in the world," she said.

Her doctor told her she was in no condition to go to her husband's room. Ruth said she told her doctor, "You might as well do it because I'm going to do it anyway."

So her doctor took her to Ottis' room.

"When he saw me, he started crying," Ruth recalled. "I told him, 'If you're going to cry, I'm leaving.'"

Ruth said she never had any pain from the gunshot wound.

The bullet flattened when it hit her purse zipper.

"The doctor said it saved my life."

She told us she wasn't surprised that she recovered long

before her husband because she had experienced a miracle recovery from illness two years before the shooting. She had cancer of the breast and throat, a blood-sugar problem, a bad heart and an enlarged liver, she said, and doctors told her there was nothing they could do for her.

Doctors told her, "We don't know where to start, you are so bad off," she said.

"I told them I might as well go home," she said, "and contact the doctor who heals it all. They said, 'Who's that?' I said, 'Doctor Jesus.'

"I went home and was healed instantly. God healed me that night. That was thirteen years ago. I just don't hear well. Maybe the Lord will heal that, one day."

Ruth and Ottis grew up in the Henderson Settlement area named for her grandfather. Both quit school after the eighth grade. Both had brothers named for Reverend Hiram Frakes, the Indiana preacher who settled there and built a high school and started a church.

Ottis went to work beside his father in the nearby Chenoa, Kentucky, coal mines when he was fifteen years old and later followed his father into the pulpit.

Ruth was sixteen years old when Ottis asked Bad Bill for her hand. Ottis was twenty-one and had been married before.

"I was a little bit scared to ask him to let Ruth marry me," Ottis said. "Ruth was his pick."

Ottis and Ruth had lived in Detroit since 1952. Ottis pastored churches in rundown Detroit neighborhoods populated by Hungarians and Hispanics. He retired after he was shot in Detroit. His last church before he retired was the Dearborn Avenue Church of God in the Delray section of southwest Detroit.

Ruth opened the East Side Thrift Store, a used clothing shop on Mack Avenue in one of Detroit's toughest inner-city sections. Robbers held up Ruth's store three times during the nineteen years she ran it, but she ran one of them off and shot another. She suffered a bad cut on her hand when she grabbed the blade of a knife that a woman robber held at her throat.

"I said, 'Lord, don't let her cut my neck,'" Ruth said, "and I grabbed the knife blade and the girl let go of the knife and ran. What about that!"

After another holdup, the robber ran out of Ruth's store and fled down Mack Avenue. Ruth stepped out onto the sidewalk and calmly shot him.

"He was running as hard as he could go," she said, laughing scornfully. "They said, 'You got him.' I said, 'That's what I was trying to do, shoot him in the leg.'"

Police followed the trail of blood to a garage, arrested the wounded robber and recovered Ruth's money.

"I'm not afraid of the devil or man," Ruth told us as we sat talking in their living room cluttered with framed photographs of children and grandchildren. "I'm only afraid of the Lord. You have to look out for yourself. Nobody else is going to do it."

She said she carries her gun when she leaves home.

"She loves her gun," Ottis said.

We asked Ruth to describe Bad Bill Henderson.

"Do you want to see a picture of him?" she asked.

When we told her we did, she popped up from the couch and went into the dining room. She returned with a tinted photograph in an oval shaped wood frame painted gold. The picture showed a handsome, smiling, middle-aged man in profile. He had on a wide-brimmed brown felt hat with a high crown and a brown suit coat over blue overalls and a blue work shirt. It was the pose of a confident man, and the smile was genuine, not one struck for the photographer.

"He was a good father," Ruth said, looking at the photograph. "He was the greatest dad in the world. He never whupped a girl he had in his life."

Bad Bill had the reputation for making the best whiskey around Cumberland Gap. Starting around age eight or nine, Ruth served as his official moonshine taster.

"She would mix it up and sup it till she would go home drunk," Ottis told us.

"Poppy would have me mixing it till I got drunk," Ruth confirmed. "He said it was good for me anyhow. He said it was good for anybody with asthma. See, I was born with a bad heart and asthma. He never would let me be whupped."

She said her father took her everywhere, including his stills.

"I'd ride astraddle poppy's neck," she said.

As quality control officer at Bad Bill's distillery, Ruth became an expert on moonshine and told us she could still make it if she had to.

"The first that runs off is pure alcohol," she explained. "You can't taste it hardly. It'll burn the fire out of you. It gets weaker the longer it runs."

Ruth told us her job was to mix the strong stuff with the weak, tasting it frequently until she determined it met her father's exacting standards for his straight corn whiskey.

Ottis said Bad Bill loved to sit by the fire and tell stories. Ottis recalled nodding off to sleep listening to his father-in-law's stories by the fireside. Ruth had heard the stories from the time she was a little girl.

"Her father killed thirteen or fourteen men," Ottis told us.

"No," Ruth said, "he killed seventeen. He killed six in Chicago one time."

"That's hard for me to believe," Ottis said.

"It ain't hard for me to believe," Ruth said. "He had the .22 bullet in his shoulder. You could feel it any time you wanted to."

Ruth said the Chicago killings came about when an acquaintance of Bad Bill's in Cumberland Gap lost $1,000 in a con game in the Windy City.

"It was either Jim Boy or Cisco Hamblen," she told us.

She said a rumor had flashed through Cumberland Gap that you could double your money quickly at a given address in Chicago and that Hamblen had taken $1,000 and returned with $2,000, but he found it was counterfeit.

Ruth said Bad Bill told Hamblen, "Give me $1,000. I'll get your money back."

She said her father went to Chicago and was wounded in a shootout with the con men but that he killed six of them. He came back to Kentucky with Hamblen's $2,000 and an extra

$1,000 of the con men's money—genuine, this time—for himself, she said.

When Bad Bill was en route home on a bus, he noticed a man had followed him from Chicago, Ruth told us.

"He told the man, 'You've followed me far enough. Me or you had better get off this bus.' The man got off at the next stop."

Ruth said, "I've heard him tell that story many times."

"So have I," said the skeptical Ottis.

Ruth said Joe Massus killed Bad Bill's brother, Green Henderson, and that Bad Bill killed Massus.

"He killed papa's brother and rolled him down the steps of a hotel in Middlesboro," she said.

Bad Bill and his brother-in-law, Johnny Frazier, tracked Massus down.

"They run him across two mountains," Ruth told us. "Papa said, 'You'd better pray and get right with the Lord, because I'm going to kill you.' When they caught him, he had Uncle Green's gold and silver, his money. Uncle Johnny said papa set him up on a stump and said, 'Now, I'm going to give you time to pray. You can pray, but I'm going to kill you. You killed my brother.' Uncle Johnny said he blew his brains out with a forty-five."

Ruth and Ottis told a different version of one of Bad Bill's killings than we had heard from an old family adversary, Wiley Maiden. They said Bill, then a deputy sheriff in Pruden, Tennessee, arrested an Italian coal miner. But instead of killing him to avoid a long hike over two mountains to the Tazewell jail, as Wiley Maiden claimed, Bad Bill shot the coal miner in self-defense, Ruth and Ottis told us. They said the prisoner hit Bill on the head with a stick, then jumped on his back and tried to choke him. Bill managed to reach around his body with his pistol and shoot the Italian, who was still on his back, Ottis said.

"He hit my daddy in the head with a stick," Ruth said. "He had a pump knot on his head till the day he died."

While he was still deputy sheriff in Tennessee, Bad Bill also killed a man in Morgan Hollow, they told us.

"He was a guy that tore up stumps all the time," Ruth said.

"Tore up stumps?"

"Tore up people's houses, that sort of thing. They couldn't arrest him. They asked poppy if he'd come over there and try to arrest him. He said, 'I'll come over there and arrest him or kill him one.' He killed him."

Ottis said the man got the drop on Bad Bill, who said to him, "Cy, let's be friends."

"As Cy put his gun away, he pulled his'n out and it was a'smoking," Ottis said.

Ruth was enjoying the old tales. She started laughing as she related how her father killed peg-legged Charles Sessions in the Quarterhouse battle, a story Bad Bill had told her many times.

"He'd tell that story and laugh," she said. "He said when he shot him, he spun on that leg. He used that guy's leg for toothpicks. He sawed that fellow's leg up and used it for toothpicks."

Ottis obviously felt uncomfortable about his wife laughing as she told the gory tale.

"See," he said, "she's turned out a whole lot like him. That bothers me."

We asked Ottis why there were so many killings in the Cumberland Gap area where they both grew up.

"To me, when I lived down there, I didn't realize there *was* much," he replied.

Ruth told us how the family managed to pull off Bad Bill's fake funeral to keep him from going to prison for killing the Mayhan boys. She said it probably happened before she was born.

"Mommy always told us about that," Ruth said. "They were aiming to send him to the penitentiary. He went off and sent back a casket with his name on it. They buried poppy."

She cackled.

"Yeah, they had a funeral," she said, "but they didn't open up the casket. They said he died a natural death, that there was some kind of disease he had and they were afraid somebody would catch it."

When Bill Henderson married Lou Alice Partin, both already had children. Bad Bill had four by a previous marriage.

Lou Alice, twenty years younger than Bill, had a son named Marion Overton who came to live in the household. Bill and Lou Alice had eight children of their own.

Ruth, their third child, was Bad Bill's favorite. Lou Alice doted on Marion and was protective of him. A rivalry developed between the two children.

Ottis and Ruth told us about several heated disputes between Marion Overton and Bad Bill going back to Ruth's childhood.

When she was twelve years old, Ruth said, Marion threatened to kill her father with a knife.

"I said, 'If you pull a knife on poppy I'll shoot you.' He ran like a turkey from me."

In another altercation between Marion and Bad Bill, Ottis said, Ruth chased her step-brother with a double-bladed axe.

After Ottis married Ruth, he too became involved in disputes with Marion.

Bad Bill and Lou Alice owned adjoining tracts of land. They lived on the property Bill owned. After he grew up, Marion moved into the house on Lou Alice's property.

The final dispute between Bad Bill and his step-son came about when Lou Alice deeded the property that was in her name to Marion. He had it surveyed to establish the boundary line.

"Lou Alice had willed it to Marion, had made him a deed and signed it," Ottis said, "and Marion wanted Bill Henderson to sign it. And he wouldn't sign it. He said, 'No, Marion, I can't afford to sign this for the whole thing. It wouldn't do the other kids right.'"

Marion drew a knife and grabbed Bad Bill. Bill's oldest son, Dorsey, and nephew, Lester Bennett, chased Marion off with an axe, Ottis said.

Despite Marion's effort to establish the boundary line between the two farms, a dispute developed over some fallen chestnut trees, valuable for making rails for fences. The trees lay on a hillside not far from Marion's house.

On a Thursday morning, a few weeks after Bad Bill refused to sign Marion's deed, Bill, Ottis and several other men in the family set out with axes and cross-cut saws to split the chestnut trees into rails.

"Marion saw us coming with those saws and axes," Ottis recalled. "He said, 'Don't stick an ax in those trees.' I was the one that answered. I got mad. I hollered at Marion. Marion cussed me out. He said, 'Come on down here. I've got yours down here.' I said, 'Okay, I'm a'coming.' I jumped that rail fence."

Ottis said he was unarmed but Marion had a gun. As Ottis jumped the fence and started down the hill, he said, he saw Ruth running toward him.

"I met her out there," Ottis said. "She had a rifle in her hand."

When Ruth gave him the rifle, Marion fled, Ottis said.

He laughed as he recalled the sight. "Marion was running with his shirt tail sticking out."

"His shirt tail was in the air," Ruth chuckled.

Ottis said Marion took his gun in the house and came back out as if nothing had happened, then walked away over the ridge.

"Old man Henderson said, 'Don't do anything. Let him go.'" Ottis recalled.

"He was working for peace all the time," Ruth said.

But Ottis said he and Lester Bennett, both carrying guns, tried to track Marion down. After awhile, deputy sheriff Jim Frazier intercepted them and turned them back. Ottis said the deputy told them that Marion's mother had sent for him.

Ottis told us Lou Alice feared he and Lester Bennett would kill her son. Ottis and Marion had been schoolmates and friends. But Ottis said Marion had told Jim Frazier, "I know Ellis. Old Man Henderson's going to cause him to turn against me."

Feelings were still running high the following Saturday, two days after the ruckus over the chestnut trees. That morning, Ottis said, Lou Alice expressed concern about having a gun around the house. Ottis said she told Bad Bill, "Will, I wish you'd take that old gun out and put it away. Why don't you take it out to the crib and lock it up?"

"He took the gun away," Ottis said. "That was the only gun on the place."

On a slope, about sixty yards from the house, Ottis was plowing to put in a potato patch and saw Bad Bill leave the house and head for the barn, carrying the rifle in one hand and a walking cane in the other. Bill's twelve-year-old son Edward was with him. It was 9:30 in the morning.

Bad Bill and Edward were at the barn shoveling manure to spread on the potato patch, and Ottis was still plowing, when Marion walked down to the barn and started cursing the old man. Ottis said he decided he would try to make his way past them and get Bad Bill's rifle out of the barn.

"My heart was a'beating," Ottis recalled. "I walked on by Marion. I didn't say anything. I thought I would walk in the barn and get the gun and make the old man feel more comfortable."

Ruth watched from the house.

"If I'd had a gun," she told us, "I could have killed Marion as Ottis walked past him."

Ottis said, "I looked around in the barn. I couldn't see no gun nowhere. I knew we were stuck, the way he was cussing the old man. I believe he was scared. He was just stuttering when he was talking to him."

Unable to find the rifle, Ottis went outside.

"Marion stepped back even with me," Ottis said. "He was laying it on the old man, just cussing him. Marion said to me, 'I'll shoot your heart out,' with a curse word. He pulled his thirty-eight out of his overalls and said, 'I'm going to shoot your heart out.' *Pow!* He like to have done it. I felt that bullet roll out my britches leg. It went clear through me."

Then Marion shot Bad Bill in the chest and headed for the house to hunt down Ruth.

"Marion hated her," Ottis said. "He went in at the front door moving the beds, looking for her."

Ruth said she left by the back door and went around the side of the house to the barn, where her father was still standing.

"Poppy was heart shot," Ruth said. "He was shot bad. He

was standing with his hands up against the barn logs. I laid him down before he died. Poppy said, 'Lord have mercy on Marion. Forgive him for what he's done. I have.'"

After Marion fled, Dorsey Henderson and Lester Bennett shot the lock off the corn crib in the barn and found Bad Bill's rifle with the notches in the stock. They grabbed it and headed out to find Marion. He eluded them. Nearly a year later, law officers walked in on him at a house near Middlesboro and found him oiling his .38 special.

Hiram Frakes preached Bad Bill's funeral at the graveside in Henderson Grove cemetery.

"I remember one thing that Reverend Frakes said," Ruth told us. "He said, 'It don't take a brave man to kill you. It takes a coward.'"

The killing of Bad Bill affected members of his family in different ways. Ruth remained bitter into her old age. Edward hated guns. Ottis ended up feeling sorry for Marion Overton.

Marion lost the farm his mother gave him, deeding it to his lawyer to pay for his defense. He served eight years of a life sentence. A handsome ladies' man in his youth, he ended up a pitiful figure, destitute and living in state institutions.

When Marion's father died, Ottis preached the funeral. After the service, Ottis said, he left the pulpit and walked up to Marion. Ottis put out his hand, and Marion didn't quite know whether to accept it.

"I took his hand," Ottis recalled, "and said, 'Come on up, Marion, let me pray for you.' But Marion just stood there and didn't say anything."

Fifty-five years after the shootings in the barnyard, when we talked to Ottis in Detroit, he told us, "I'm sorry for Marion in a way. He'll be before a just God, the same as I will. I hope he repented."

Ruth said she had a vision on the Thursday before her father's death.

"I saw it before it happened," she told us.

"She cried and tried to get her daddy to leave," Ottis confirmed.

"I tried to get my daddy to leave and go to Ohio. I saw it on Thursday night. They told me I had a dream. I said, 'No, I didn't either.' Neither one of them would listen to me. I told them it would happen at 9:30 Saturday morning."

Ruth said she also had a premonition the night before she and Ottis were shot at their back door. This time, she acted on it. She said she normally didn't carry her gun, but she put it in her purse before they left for church that night.

"Ottis didn't even know I had my gun," she said.

Ottis said his wife was convinced Bad Bill Henderson went to Heaven. We asked her why she believed that.

"Because he quit all that before he died," she said. "I've heard him pray, and I've heard him testify. He died a Christian."

She told us about a dream she had about her father.

"I dreamed my daddy was in a big field, and I thought that field was full of thousands of little kids," she said. "Poppy loved kids. They were climbing all over him."

As we were leaving, Ruth told us, "We feel like we've known you all our lives. If you're Christians, pray for us. If you're not, pray for yourselves."

VII

Voting 'em Right in the Carolinas

SOUTH CAROLINIANS have always been obsessed with local control. They fired the first shots of the Civil War to take control of federal property in Charleston Harbor.

In later years, the citizens refused to grant the governor enough executive power to manage the state's affairs.

That power came to rest with legislators from the rural county of Barnwell. The Barnwell Ring had sound reasons for investing state powers in its local control. Along with the honor of the thing, it was enormously profitable for the legislators and their voters back home.

Another rule of local control turned South Carolina political campaigns into carnivals. Candidates had to make joint appearances in each of the state's counties. The voters were entertained more than enlightened.

Across the border in North Carolina, politics was less entertaining and no more enlightening. North Carolina produced no Cotton Ed Smith, no Old Gene, no Folsom. But back up in the Blue Ridges, a shrewd political operator proved "thar's gold in them thar hills" if you vote 'em right.

25

The Barnwell Ring

SOLOMON BLATT WAS A short man, bald as a basketball, with a face like a snapping turtle.

More than any other man, including governors, he ran state government in South Carolina for thirty-three years as Democratic speaker of the state House of Representatives.

We met Blatt in May 1978 at his law office next to the Family Dollar Store in Barnwell, a sleepy little town built around a courthouse square, just east of the Atomic Energy Commission's Savannah River Plant. He was eighty-two years old, and although he remained in the Legislature he had retired as speaker. Republicans controlled the governor's office in Columbia.

But it didn't take us long to learn that Blatt had retained his clout in Columbia and that he was vigorous enough to chug-a-lug a tea glass of bourbon.

"I'll tell you what I'll do," Blatt told us. "I've got three friends of mine that I'm going to take to a fish supper. If you'll come along, we'll have some fish. We'll have some liquor. I'm not going anywhere without liquor."

The three friends turned out to be the Republican chairman of the Alcoholic Beverage Control Commission, a top aide to Republican Governor James Edwards and an influential Democratic lawyer from Columbia.

Blatt had summoned them to Barnwell to get Floyd Atkinson a job as a state liquor inspector. On paper, Floyd's qualifications fell a little short. The job called for a high school diploma. Floyd only finished the fourth grade.

"He's a really skilled roofer, and he was a liquor head, but he's a fine fellow," Blatt told us.

Before we went to the fish fry, Blatt took us to his house to have a drink with ABC Commission Chairman Ken Powell, governor's aide John LaFitte and lawyer Bobby Kneece, who had served under Speaker Blatt as chairman of the House Judiciary Committee.

Blatt filled a tea glass almost to the top with Old Crow and drank it straight down. He sensed our astonishment and said, "If you're going to drink it, don't mess with it."

At the fish fry, we witnessed probably the most elaborate job interview in the South Carolina Lowcountry that year. Employees at the state Wildlife Resources Department's regional headquarters in Barnwell, assisted by Floyd Atkinson, were frying up heaping platters of golden catfish and corn dodgers, and a huge cauldron of delicious-smelling catfish stew was bubbling over a fire. The regional headquarters was built with state money that Blatt put into an appropriations bill.

"Every time I feel like we need some fish and stew, I just call some of the boys and they get the fish," Blatt told us.

LaFitte told us he learned the hard way how Blatt practiced power politics in Columbia. LaFitte was a freshman legislator from Richland County, one of South Carolina's most urban counties that includes the state Capitol and state university.

"We've got at least three farmers in the whole county," Lafitte said. "I went in the speaker's office to see Mister Blatt, and he said, 'What's your committee preference?' I said, 'Well, I'd like to get on the Ways and Means Committee.' He said, 'Bullshit. Agriculture is fascinating.' Bam!"

"I made a farmer out of him," said Blatt. He appointed the city boy to the House Agriculture and Conservation Committee.

"He didn't know a damn thing about farming," Blatt said, "and he didn't know a damn thing about anything else. I thought maybe he could take care of these farmers. He turned out to be a damn sorry member of that committee."

Blatt told us he assigned his worst enemies in the House to the State House and Grounds Committee and that its membership was rather large.

"That was a shithouse committee if there ever was one," LaFitte said.

"I loaded it up," Blatt said. "It took a ten-ton truck to haul that crowd to a committee meeting."

As a zealous junior Republican member of a judicial screening committee headed by Blatt, LaFitte made the mistake of asking the state police to run a drunk driving check on a candidate for a judgeship.

"Mister Blatt said, 'What the hell do you want that for?'" LaFitte told us. "I said, 'If a man's going to be a judge, one DUI won't be so bad, but if he's had three or four, we might want to look at him.' After the meeting, Mister Blatt asked me to come over to the hotel for a drink. After about three drinks, he said, 'All right, you goddamn Republican. Go get in your car and drive home. I've got the Highway Patrol down there.'"

LaFitte said he believed Blatt. So he went downstairs and drank coffee until he sobered up.

Blatt laughed, and told LaFitte, "Goddamn, I broke you from sucking eggs."

A lot of people urged him to run for governor, Blatt told us, but he thought he couldn't get elected because he was Jewish. Besides, he wasn't the kind of politician who would want to take the reduction in power. In South Carolina, the Legislature was far more powerful than the governor, and Blatt and another Barnwell lawyer, state Senator Edgar Brown, dominated the Legislature for three decades.

In the late 1930s, Barnwell County politicians had a lock on state government. Blatt was speaker of the House and appointed all the committees. Brown was president pro tempore of the Senate and chairman of the Finance Committee. Winchester Smith of Williston, also in Barnwell County, was chairman of both the House Ways and Means Committee and the state Democratic Party. And J. Emile Harley of Barnwell was governor.

Blatt came from tough stock. His father, Nathan Blatt, couldn't speak English when he came to Charleston, South Carolina, shortly before the turn of the century, leaving behind a wife and young son in Russia. He became a peddler.

"He walked with a hundred and fifty pounds on his back from Charleston to Augusta, and he always came through Blackville over in the county, ten miles from Barnwell," Blatt told us as we sat in his law office. "He told me time and again people wouldn't let him in their homes. So in the wintertime, he had to sit up all night.

"But he continued to peddle until he saved enough money to send for my mother and brother. Then he opened a store in Blackville that wasn't much bigger than this room. He had a little fireplace in the back, and he cooked his own meals. He slept on the counter he had there. People over in Blackville used to tell me that the days my father made nothing, he wouldn't eat. Neighbors felt sorry for him, and they would bring him something to eat."

Sol Blatt was born February 27, 1896, in Blackville, from where he went off to the University of South Carolina and earned a law degree. He started practicing law in Barnwell on June 20, 1917, with Harley, the future governor.

"I made fifty dollars the first six months," Blatt recalled.

He got to know Edgar Brown and thought he had Brown's support in his first race for the Legislature. But he said Brown double-crossed him and he lost.

It was the only election he ever lost. He was elected to the House in 1932. When we interviewed him, Blatt was in his forty-sixth year in the House. For thirty-three of those he was speaker.

Strom Thurmond got elected governor in 1946 running against the bosses of the Barnwell Ring, as he labelled Blatt and Brown. Thurmond later got elected to the United States Senate and switched to the Republican Party. Blatt was supporting Thurmond for re-election when we were there.

Sol Blatt, Jr. was a U.S. District Court judge in Charleston. Senator Thurmond had recommended his appointment.

Blatt and Brown didn't always get along, but they joined forces when it was necessary. One such time came in a drunk driving case.

Brown was a notorious driver. Barnwell businessman Calhoun Lemon told us people hid their cars to keep Brown from hitting them. Lemon said Brown had an old, battered, white Lincoln he referred to as his cross-country car and a shiny new black one that he called his parade car. Brown, in his eighties and retired from the Senate, died in the white Lincoln when it collided with another car at a Barnwell intersection.

"Edgar was coming home from Columbia one weekend," Blatt told us. "He had been drinking pretty good before he left. An old fellow by the name of Brodie who lived over at Springfield, about twenty-five miles from here, was driving an old pickup truck that was worth about a dollar and a half. He couldn't go over about ten miles an hour in the damn thing.

"Edgar is coming up in back of him and run right square into the back of the truck, straight roads, hit him, knocked him out of the damn truck, broke his leg. The poor fellow was out there on the ground, couldn't move, and Edgar got out of his car and went up to him and said, 'You're in bad shape. You need a little something. I'll go get it.'

"He went and got his bottle of liquor out of his car and poured a hell of a big drink down him, and in a few minutes he poured another one and another one, and by the third drink, the fellow didn't know whether he had a broke leg, broke neck or whether he was flying or an angel or what. So Edgar sent for the highway patrolman, and when he comes to investigate, Edgar tells him, 'He's drunk. Smell his breath.'"

Blatt said the truck driver sued Brown, who hired Blatt as his lawyer.

"The accident happened right near Robert Cave's little store," Blatt said. "Robert saw it and gave the other side a statement. I told the other lawyer, 'It's Edgar Brown's word against this fellow Brodie.' His lawyer said, 'Oh, no, we got a witness.' They said it was Robert.

"So I rode out to see Robert, and I asked him, 'Did you know that was Edgar Brown driving that car and that I'm representing him?' And he said, 'No, I didn't know that.' I said, 'Well, are you going to testify now?' He said, 'I didn't see a damn thing. Looked like to me the other fellow was drunk.'"

26

Cotton Ed, Machine Gun Olin and Bacon Brown

GOVERNOR OLIN Johnston couldn't stop the Barnwell Ring with machine guns.

He found this out after he got elected governor in 1934 on an anti-highway ticket and tried to fire the state's chief highway commissioner, a powerful politician named Ben Sawyer who had the backing of Edgar Brown and Sol Blatt.

In the Depression, South Carolina was so broke it had been paying its teachers in scrip and couldn't pay faculty members at the University of South Carolina at all for two months. But Sawyer's Highway Department was rolling in money, thanks to a $65 million bond issue pushed through by Edgar Brown, who had friends and business associates in the road contracting business back home in Barnwell County.

"The Highway Department was trying to pave every goddamn track in the state," said Dr. Daniel Hollis, University of South Carolina history professor. Hollis told us how Sawyer retained the financing for the Highway Department while the rest of the state was broke.

"He would go to Senator Brown and say, 'Now, senator, what roads do you want paved in the next couple of years?' Brown would say, 'Well, Ben, I would like this road out of Elko paved.' The Highway Department takes care of that. 'And I'd like to get so and so a job.' They take care of that.

"When the appropriations come up in the Senate, Brown is right there to take care of it, and Blatt's doing that in the House, and they just had locks on everything."

When Johnston took office as governor in 1935, he set out to keep his campaign promise to curb highway spending. He fired Ben Sawyer and the chief engineer and several other top members of the Highway Department staff, but they refused to leave.

On October 28, 1935, Johnston called out the National Guard, which forcibly evicted Sawyer and the other officials, took over the Highway Department and set up machine guns in the yard in front of the Highway Department building. The governor declared the Highway Department to be in a state of insurrection, but the courts ruled he had overstepped the law. By February 1936, Sawyer had resumed control of the Highway Department.

The Barnwell Ring wasn't through. Johnston had promised voters that he would reduce the price of auto license plates to $3. Brown and Blatt let him keep that campaign promise for a price.

In his biography of Edgar Brown, *The Bishop from Barnwell*, William D. Workman, Sr. quoted Brown: "Eventually, we determined that we had to put Johnston out of control of the Highway Department if we were going to make any progress. So we took his $3 highway tag bill which he had passed in the House, and added to it an amendment taking away the governor's power to appoint the highway commissioners. We forced him to sign that bill, putting himself out of control over the highway commissioners. He cut his own throat, but he had promised the people a $3 tag and he stuck to it. That episode is one of the reasons the governor of South Carolina has less power today than he had before, and even before that he didn't have much."

Brown had two other nicknames besides the bishop from Barnwell: Satchel Edgar and Bacon Brown.

Hollis said that in 1932, the Democratic Party put the arm on road contractors for contributions and sent Brown to Montgomery, Alabama, to collect from a big asphalt company. Brown brought back $500 in a satchel and turned it over to a disappointed party treasurer, who was expecting considerably more.

"So a year or two later," Hollis told us, "one of the party bigwigs happened to run into the key man from the asphalt company, who asked, 'Did you get the contribution we gave Mister Brown last year?' The party official said, 'Well, yeah, just five hundred dollars.' The man said, 'Five hundred dollars? Hell, it was five thousand dollars!' And so he got the nickname of Satchel Edgar."

Powerful as he was in the Legislature, Brown could never get elected to statewide office. In 1938, he ran for the United States Senate on a promise to "Bring Home the Bacon" from Washington. It became his watchword. At rallies all over the state, he told voters, "Elect me, and I'll bring home the bacon."

His opponents were Olin Johnston and incumbent Ellison (Cotton Ed) Smith, who served in the Senate longer than anyone up to his time and was the leading champion of the South's cotton farmers. Cotton Ed wore a cotton boll in his lapel and plastered his clothing with cotton lint and rode to campaign rallies straddling a bale of cotton atop a wagon pulled by a pair of mules.

Gedney Howe, a Charleston lawyer, told us how Cotton Ed handled Machine Gun Olin and Satchel Edgar.

"They had this big rally," Howe said. "Everybody was there. Candidates for all kind of offices were up there, and they were speaking. All but Cotton Ed. He showed up about the time Johnston was in the middle of his speech, showed up as if he were the only real politician.

"Johnston was a pretty good speaker, and he was a demagogue, of course, giving Smith hell about his low wages and the fact that Roosevelt had come south to try to purge him. But he could make mistakes, like the time he stood in a semicircle of pretty girls from home visiting him in Washington and told a crowd, 'As I gaze at my rear I'm proud of South Carolina.'

"When Cotton Ed showed up, everybody started shouting and screaming, just about breaking up old Johnston's speech. But Johnston got through his speech, and then Brown got through his speech. Smith had these long moustaches and chewed tobacco. He was a typical old timer and really an orator. You don't realize that those fellows in their day were really great orators. They were really great actors. They would have been great anywhere, not getting into their philosophy.

"Smith had the polish and pause and timing of Jack Benny. And he was just as good in his time as Jack Benny was. Cotton Ed was an artist of timing. Smith started out in his normal way, and then he got around, and he looked over at Johnston and Brown and said, 'Would you look at these two things running against me, these two things that have been dragged out by the New Deal to run against me.'

"He said, 'Well, here's Oleander Johnston. Has he got his machine gun with him?' And from then on, for the course of his speech addressed to Johnston, Cotton Ed kept an imaginary gun trained on him. Then he said, 'Oleander Johnston. Brother Oleander. He's a fine looking figure of a man, but God was cruel to Olin. Forgot to give him a brain.' And Cotton Ed kept his gun on him. Of course it was devastating.

"Then he wheeled and he said, 'Now I want to turn my attention to the senator from Barnwell County, Bacon Brown. The one thing I want to let you all know, about one thing there can be no question, if you send him to Washington he will probably accumulate more bacon than any man that could be sent from any state in the union. So the fact that he tells you that if you send him to Washington he will acquire bacon, and that he will bring it home, with that I agree. I don't think there's any question about the fact. What I want to ask, and I know you want to ask right along with me, is *whose smokehouse is he going to put it in*?'

"That was the end of Brown."

27

Barrymores of The Branchheads

SOUTH CAROLINA politics was Southern vaudeville. In those days before television, it not only was a tradition, it was a Democratic Party rule that every statewide candidate had to speak in each of the state's forty-six counties. They did it together from the same platform. It was a traveling road show, and there were the quick and the dead. The long campaigns got tiring and boring to these bucolic Barrymores, and they had a thousand ways to spice things up.

"These fellows were famous for that," Gedney Howe told us. "You had Cole Blease, who pardoned everybody in the penitentiaries. A fellow accidentally bumped into Blease and said, 'Oh, pardon me, governor.' Blease told him, 'You'll have to see me at the office about that.' His name was Coleman Livingston Blease, a very handsome fellow and a race baiter.

"When he was running, they'd plant a man in the audience for these county meetings. People would turn out by the thousands. And Blease had a fellow in the audience who would get up at the right time and start yelling, 'Tell us about your pardoning record! Tell us about your pardoning record!' Blease would ignore him and go on with his speech. The fellow Blease had planted in the audience would start yelling again about the pardons, 'Tell us about your pardoning record!'

"Finally, Blease would stop. He was a magnificent looking fellow, and he'd put his hand up, and he'd say, 'Just a moment. Is there a stableman in the crowd?' He'd wait, and then he'd say, 'Is there a *stableman* in the audience?'

"Another fellow Blease had planted in the audience would come running in from the back of the hall shouting, 'Yes, sir, I'm a stableman, I'm a stableman.' And Blease would say, 'Fine. Would you be kind enough to let me have a bale of hay? I'll pay you immediately after this meeting. Right now, I've got a jackass over there I want to keep quiet until I can get through talking.'"

Candidates always had to be on the lookout that they didn't get trapped at their own game. Once, Cotton Ed Smith planted someone in Blease's crowd to taunt him repeatedly, "What have you ever done about the price of cotton?"

Blease ignored the heckler, who kept yelling, "What about the price of cotton?"

Finally, Blease lost his temper.

"I've never been able to do anything about the price of cotton," he said, "but if I had more jackasses like you I could lower the price of mules."

Looking for these South Carolina stories, we were lucky to find Dr. Daniel W. Hollis, a historian who had taught at the University of South Carolina in Columbia for thirty-one years and was an expert on politics of that era. He also had written a history of the university.

"For twenty or thirty years, these traveling shows made very good entertainment," he told us. "The farmers had laid the crops by, and there wasn't anything else to do, and they would come in to the towns to hear Pitchfork Ben Tillman or Cole Blease get up and raise hell with the aristocrats: *Down with the ruling classes*. They were great entertainers, because they had to be. Cotton Ed Smith was one.

"In 1914, Cole Blease was going for the Senate, after Cotton

Ed's seat. They were down in Orangeburg, and Blease had pardoned a notorious rapist-murderer in Orangeburg only two or three years before. The people down there were upset about it. When he was governor, he pardoned 1,727 inmates in the penitentiary and other correctional institutions, the chain gang and jails.

"World War I had broken out in Europe, so Blease is talking about the kaiser and the British blockade and the price of cotton, the banks, Woodrow Wilson. And this yahoo starts yelling at him, 'Hey, governor, how about all them men you done turned loose!' Blease interrupted his speech and said, 'Now, my friend, we're running for the United States Senate. We're not talking about local issues. We're talking about the price of cotton, the U.S. Senate, the banking laws, Woodrow Wilson and the farm program.'

"And so the man settled down, and a couple of minutes later he's back again: 'Governor, tell us about all them men!' And the crowd mumbled. And about that time, this string-tied, elegant looking gentleman on the front row gets to his feet and says, 'Governor Blease, I'm incensed at this rude treatment you're getting from an Orangeburg audience, and if you'll yield to me, sir, I'll dispense with this rabble.

"And Blease fell right into the trap Cotton Ed had set for him. He said, 'All right, sir, I'll yield.' And the man with the string tie got up in front of the audience and said, 'Now listen, you. Governor Cole L. Blease didn't turn those men loose. He threw open the gates of the penitentiary and said, 'Last one out's a son of a bitch.'"

Blease lost that race to Cotton Ed, but he got elected to the Senate in 1924, handing James Byrnes his only election defeat in South Carolina. Blease had lost in 1914 mainly because of his attacks against Woodrow Wilson, who was really popular in South Carolina. By ten years later, Blease's popularity had rebounded, and Byrnes was an aspiring young congressman from Aiken who would later become Franklin Roosevelt's secretary of state.

Byrnes grew up in the Catholic church in Charleston but

later switched to the Episcopal Church. Charleston's former mayor was a powerful politician named John P. Grace whose political machine had been known to vote the graveyards. About Byrnes' age, Grace was Irish, Catholic and proud of his heritage. He was irked that Byrnes had switched religions and was running as a Protestant.

"The 1924 election was coming down to the second primary between Byrnes and Blease," Hollis told us. "It was going to be extremely close. Byrnes had been running a series of advertisements, an extensive advertising campaign. And Blease didn't do any. There was not a newspaper ad, almost nothing for Blease.

"Byrnes had a big campaign staff and newspapers full of ads. One of them was an endorsement ad that said, 'We the ministers of Aiken County and the vestry of St. Thaddeus Episcopal Church endorse our fellow townsman, James F. Byrnes.'

"The ads said that Byrnes was a fine Christian fellow, and Mrs. Byrnes was a fine Christian at St. Thaddeus Church. They used the war ad: 'Cole Blease was against Woodrow Wilson. Byrnes was a patriot in 1918.' They did all that.

"Well, about three or four days before the final primary, a little five-inch ad appeared in the Charleston *Evening Post*, which had no circulation out of Charleston at that time. It said, 'We the former altar boys and acolytes at St. Paul's Roman Catholic Church endorse our former acolyte and altar boy James F. Byrnes for the U.S. Senate because of his fine Christian character. We knew him when he was a good Roman Catholic boy here in Charleston, and we rejoice in his rise to high station.'

"It was signed by a group of Irish people down in Charleston.

"Now, this little ad was John P. Grace's means of informing the Charleston faithful that here's a man who has left the Catholic Church. The Blease camp had been tipped off, and they immediately picked this up, printed it as a campaign pamphlet and put it in every Baptist and Methodist church pew in the Upcountry to show those Protestants that Jimmy Byrnes was once a Catholic. And so, Jimmy got ripped in Charleston, he got ripped in the Upcountry, and he lost by about three or four thousand votes."

Hollis told us about two South Carolina legislators known for their illiteracy. One of them was Josh Ashley, who represented Anderson County in the state House of Representatives for about twenty years. Hollis said someone asked Ashley, "What's the elevation of Anderson county?"

"Oh, it's Baptist by a big majority," he replied.

Another time, Hollis said, the House got into a big fight over raising the age of consent from twelve to fourteen.

"It was something very radical," Hollis said, "and Josh was listening to the debate, and my father, I think, was in the Legislature at the time. Josh jumped up and said, 'Mister speaker, I'm ag'in it. We done got too many laws on the books already. Up in Anderson County, we have a saying that if a gal is old enough she's big enough, and if she's big enough she's old enough.'"

Another of these representatives, Hollis said, was Quince Edward Britt from York County.

"Quincy, we called him," Hollis said. "He was a real clown, although he didn't quite realize how funny he was, but he was pretty well steeped in a lack of education. York County has a lot of textile workers, and Quincy was out there speaking to them. He told them, 'I want to tell you people out here at Aragon Mill number two, if I'm elected I'll give you the same kind of service I give the better class of folks who live uptown. I'll fight for you down under the doom of the Statehouse.'

"He was against the sales tax, but at the time, free school books for kids was a hot issue. So he went down to the Legislature and told them, 'We've got to do something to give school books to poor farm girls and boys and the children of these textile workers. And I've found a way to do it without all this cost. We'll just set up printing presses down in the penitentiary and print 'em off. They make license plates down there, so why not school books?'

"So he went on about this for some time on the floor of the

House, and finally a young lawyer, Tom Polk of Newberry, rose and said, 'Mister speaker, point of order. I have just one question for Mister Britt on this fine scheme. Copyright, Mister Britt. What about copyright? How are you going to handle the problem of copyright?'

"And Britt retorted, 'Copy right! Hell, that ain't no problem. We'll stand over 'em with a stick and make 'em copy right.'"

28

Zeno Ponder: "Don't Call the Roll Up Yonder"

DAVID COOPER, A friend of ours who was an old hand at North Carolina newspapering, told us about a Democratic overlord in Madison County who "made Richard Daley of Chicago look like Bambi."

"They have a saying up there," Cooper told us, "Don't call the roll up yonder till you check with Zeno Ponder."

Ponder's mother had named him after a Baptist preacher, not the Greek philosopher. Zeno Ponder was Irish.

After World War II, Zeno returned home to the western Carolina mountains a Democrat in a county Republicans had controlled for 104 years. But we discovered that Zeno hadn't done bad for an old boy from the Smokies whose first job after the war had been teaching school for $300 a month.

His big brick house was at the end of a long driveway on a mountaintop outside Marshall, North Carolina. A Lincoln Continental was parked next to the house, and there was a pickup truck over by a big red barn. Miles of fences enclosed a pasture where herds of cattle grazed. Set amid fifteen large oak trees, Zeno's mansion commanded a sweeping view that was his as far as you could see. He owned eight hundred acres and leased eight hundred more.

Zeno was on the telephone to a favor-seeker when we arrived. He was a man of fifty-six, with a close-cropped moustache and gray sideburns reaching the bottom of his earlobes. In the room were a piano, a pool table, a bust of John F. Kennedy and autographed photographs of President Carter and his wife, Rosalyn.

Another photograph, of North Carolina Attorney General Rufus Edmisten, an investigator for Senator Sam Ervin's Watergate Committee, was inscribed, "To my friend Zeno, whose hard work and dedication led to my election as attorney general, my sincere thanks, Rufus."

Before he hung up the phone and turned to greet us, Zeno told his caller, "Let me check into it and see what I can get done. It just takes time to turn them around."

He explained, "That was Turner Stevens, a friend who's been a long-time state transportation employee, and he wants to get his boy on the state transportation payroll. But the department says it can't have a father and son on the same payroll."

We asked him if Stevens was somebody checking with him before they called the roll up yonder.

"I'm chairman of the Democratic Party, and as chairman of the party my recommendations carry more weight than just any John Doe," Zeno said.

He confessed that he'd had a little trouble with the law along the way, but said he beat the indictment.

The first bold move of Zeno and his brother, E.Y. Ponder, came in 1952, when they decided to take over Madison County's chief power base, the sheriff's office. They ran E.Y., who was eleven years older than Zeno, for sheriff.

"I was vote registrar for the Marshall precinct," Zeno told us. "We carried it for the first time in history. The vote was 604 to 602. I was there at the counting. That was more excitement. Every deputy, everyone who had ever been deputized, had a pistol or two pistols. Hell, you couldn't have collected them in the back of that pickup truck out there. There were all kinds of threats that we wouldn't live through the night and that kind of bullshit."

The count gave the sheriff's office to E.Y.

"The Republican sheriff, Hubert Davis, refused to vacate the office and held the jail with machine guns and tommy guns for two months," Zeno told us. "We had them whipped, and we knew we did. We'd drive down there to the jail late at night and throw out a string of firecrackers, and they would start passing out pistols like passing out apples at Christmastime. They'd man those windows and get ready for battle, and we'd go driving off. We kept this up for two or three weeks."

On another front, the Ponders were fighting in court. A local court ordered the sheriff's salary of $200 a month to be paid to E.Y. Ponder, even though the Republicans still held the jail.

The Democrats finally got control of the jail after the North Carolina Supreme Court ruled that E.Y. had gotten the most votes for sheriff. The opinion was written by Sam Ervin, who was from nearby Morganton. Ervin later was elected to the United States Senate from North Carolina and was chairman of the Senate Watergate Committee that investigated President Nixon shortly before his resignation.

Zeno said Ervin's opinion stated: "The only criticism I might offer is he and his friends may have jumped before they were spurred."

The next time Ervin's name was on the ballot in Madison County, Zeno told us, he got ninety-six percent of the vote. He never did worse than seventy-five percent after that.

One-sided votes were not uncommon in Madison County, Zeno said.

"I supported Kerr Scott for governor," Zeno said. "After the votes were counted, Kerr got twenty-eight hundred in the primary, and his opponent, Charlie Johnson, got a hundred and eighty. The county Democratic Party chairman, Fred Freeman, asked Scott, 'Governor, how did you like that vote?' Kerr never would look at you. He'd look down at the ground. He'd look through these real long eyebrows, and he finally said, 'If it had been any more, it would have been unethical.'"

As we talked in Zeno's spacious den, his friend Marge served us strong rum punch.

"Zeno was in Leningrad last year," she told us.

We asked him what he was doing in Russia. Before he could answer, Marge said, "Trying to be czar, what do you think?"

"Didn't get enough votes," Zeno said. "Couldn't get up with their system of counting."

Zeno's system of counting brought him to the attention of the Republican Eisenhower administration shortly after the Democrats consolidated their power in Madison County in the mid–1950s. The United States district attorney for western North Carolina, an Eisenhower appointee, got grand jury indictments against Zeno, E.Y. and eight other Democrats.

"He was Jim Bailey," Zeno said. "He indicted ten of us, and the charge was for conspiring to dilute the effect of the Republican ballots in the ballot box. That was the specific charge. It was under an old Civil War statute that read something like this: If a person had voted and had voted legally, and somebody comes along and adds in votes, that dilutes their effect.

"What he was really trying to prove was that we had stuffed the ballot box, that we had put votes in that hadn't been voted legally. I was chairman of the board of elections. If I had not been indicted, I would have been insulted. I felt I had done more than anybody else, and to have been left out, hell, that would have been like not being invited to your own Christmas party."

"So ten of you were indicted?"

"Ten of the best," Zeno replied. "E.Y., my brother, was one of them. He didn't do much, but he did enough to deserve an indictment. The ten of us were exonerated by a jury fourteen minutes after the jury got the case, after about a two-week trial. It was nothing but a political lawsuit."

Zeno said he had another problem with election officials in 1960. That time, it was with North Carolina Democrats, when he made his only race for elective office.

"I ran for the state Senate and won by about five hundred votes, but Terry Sanford got mad as hell at me and he showed me a thing or two," Zeno said.

Sanford had been elected North Carolina's governor in the 1960 election.

"Sanford sent his Board of Elections up here and threw out about twenty boxes and declared Clyde Norton the winner," Zeno said.

"Why did he throw the voting boxes out?"

"As far as I'm concerned, he could have found more reasons to throw out boxes Clyde had carried," Zeno said. "Over in Guntertown, a box was supposed to have had—it wasn't disputed, really—some twenty-seven votes more than there were names in the phone book."

Another time, when the FBI was investigating vote fraud in Madison County, the agents ran into Jackie Chandler, Zeno told us.

"You have to see him to appreciate it," Zeno said. "Little Jackie Chandler, who weighs three hundred pounds, and he's about five-six. He walks on his heels, and on the sides of them, slew footed. He will turn a shoe over thirty minutes after he gets out of the store. He went to school, I think, maybe part of two years. He didn't learn to read nothing.

"But there are some things he did learn. He can drive a car anywhere in the United States. He goes to Detroit about every week and brings back a carrier-load of cars, buys them for this nephew of mine, and they trade them. They make good money.

"During this particular election, he had come or sent, or some way obtained, directly or indirectly, some sixty absentee voter applications out of my office. They were applications for ballots for Aunt Susie, or Uncle John, or so and so. It's all as legal as can be. But he got a *tree-mendous* number. I believe it was sixty-something, maybe sixty-five. And he couldn't sign a thing. He'd make a mark. I'd sign his name, and he'd make a mark by it.

"Well, this actually happened right down there in Marshall, across from the electric co-op. Two of these FBI men were interrogating him about his ballots. They had an application blank filled in with the name of the person, his township, his precinct, and the reason why he needed an absentee ballot, sickness or whatever, and the name of the fellow who issued the ballot, the signature. They said to Jackie, 'Mister Chandler, is this an application that you made out?'

"Jackie spun around on his heel, grinning, and said, 'All I know is we beat hell out of 'em.' The FBI agents asked him about fifteen questions and got the same thing each time. He'd whirl around on that damn heel and say, 'All I know is we beat hell out of 'em.'

"The FBI agents walked directly across the street and asked Mister Doug Robinson—he was manager of the electric co-op and a Democrat—and said, 'Mister Robinson, do you know Jackie Chandler?' And he said, 'Yes, I know him.' And they said, 'Is that Jackie Chandler over there?' And Doug said, 'Yeah. Yeah, that's him.' They said, 'Isn't he a little off?' Doug said, 'They tell me he is.' They never did go back and talk to Jackie."

We asked him if he had any other operatives like Jackie Chandler.

"Oh, hell yes," Zeno replied. "I issued twenty-four hundred absentee ballots that year out of nine thousand votes in the county. They said it was an excessive number. I said, 'Goddamit, we had five hundred we missed.'"

VIII

VIII

Brotherhood of The Press

AFTER WORLD WAR II, a cadre of newspapermen rose in the South to chronicle and interpret the race issue in the region.

A courageous, hell-raising, God-fearing bunch, they were bound together by a common cause and a lot of drinking.

These reporters and editors fit E.M. Forster's definition of an aristocracy:

"They represent the true human tradition, the one permanent victory of our queer race over cruelty and chaos. Thousands of them perish in obscurity, a few are great names. They are sensitive for others as well as for themselves, they are considerate without being fussy, their pluck is not swankiness but the power to endure, and they can take a joke."

Five of these aristocrats were Johnny Popham, *The New York Times*' roving reporter and later editor of *The Chattanooga Times*; Ralph McGill, editor and publisher of *The Atlanta Constitution*; Bill Baggs, editor of the *Miami News*; Bill Emerson, Atlanta bureau chief for *Newsweek*; and Harry Ashmore, editor of the *Arkansas Gazette*.

They were talented and fearless. McGill and Ashmore won Pulitzer Prizes. But all of them were in the forefront of writing about the civil rights movement in the South. Together, they dodged the bottles and brickbats, literally and figuratively. Together, they shared the good times.

McGill, with his Presbyterian sense of guilt and great heart, was the conscience and father confessor of the group, Baggs the free spirit, Emerson the antic wild man, Ashmore the raconteur. And little Johnny Popham was simply the best reporter covering the biggest story in the nation, and nobody knew that better than his confreres.

29

A Pecker Man in the Country

"WRITING editorials," said Harry Ashmore, "is like pissing in a blue serge suit. It gives a momentary feeling of warmth, but nobody notices."

When we talked with him in Little Rock, Arkansas, in April 1978, Ashmore was no longer writing editorials and had switched to a gray suit. He was then an associate of the Center for the Study of Democratic Institutions in Santa Barbara, California.

One of the nation's best-known liberal newspaper editors, Ashmore wrote speeches for Adlai Stevenson and advised him on civil rights when he ran for president in 1956. Two years later, Ashmore won his Pulitzer writing about the integration of Little Rock's Central High School for the *Gazette*.

Ashmore's main concern at that time was Arkansas, and most of his reporter and editor friends were busy covering what was happening in their states. Working for national publications, John Popham and Bill Emerson ranged farther afield.

But all of them accumulated a wealth of political information, lore, rumor, gossip, scandal and wild tales. They shared it. And as we ranged over their old territory, the three who survive—Ralph McGill and Bill Baggs are dead—generously shared some of the stories with us.

Popham, especially, was wired to what was happening. In the late 1940s and early 1950s, he had been the only national reporter assigned to cover the South. He drove his Green Hornet 50,000 miles a year.

From wherever he happened to be, Popham would report in from time to time to Ashmore and McGill and his other friends.

Ashmore told us about a time when Popham was covering the last U.S. Senate campaign of Alben Barkley in Kentucky. Barkley, from Paducah, had represented Kentucky in the House of Representatives or Senate from 1913 to 1949, when he became Harry Truman's vice president. After Truman left office in 1953, Barkley was a white-haired old man. His wife had died.

But he married a younger woman and ran for his old Senate seat and won. Ashmore said he was in his office in Little Rock and Popham called him from Kentucky.

"I said, 'How is the Barkley campaign going? How is the old man doing?'" Ashmore recalled. "Popham said, 'Oh, yeah, the campaign's over. Old Man Barkley is in, ain't no question about that. There ain't but one issue that they raise up here. That's age. They keep talking about the old man being too old. But hell, he's got the answer for that.'

"I said, 'What does he do?'

"Popham said, 'Well, he comes to this little old town, gets the tobacco hall down there, and they get the mayor to introduce him. They get in there, all of them in the hall, and the mayor comes out with old Alben and says, *Ladies and gentlemen! I want to present to you a man who is old enough to know what to do and young enough to do it well!*

"'At that point, that young wife of Alben's comes out of the wings and sashays across the stage with her ass a'bobbin' and they just go crazy. They yell and throw those wool hats in the air. Lord, they love a pecker man in the country.'"

We lucked into our interview with Ashmore at his old paper, the *Arkansas Gazette*, where he was visiting his old friend and publisher, Hugh Patterson. As a reporter, editor and think-tank member, Ashmore had spent his life among politicians. That's where he began, as part of a courthouse gang in his native Greenville, South Carolina.

"When I was growing up, my immediate family wasn't active in politics, but all my cousins were," Ashmore told us. "Hell, they were a courthouse ring. When I started to work on the *Greenville Piedmont*, the paper there, my cousin John Ashmore was county supervisor, and Bob Ashmore, who later went to Congress, was the prosecuting attorney, and Morris Ashmore was the tax collector, and I was covering the courthouse.

"Somebody was running against old John. He was absolutely unbeatable as long as he lived because he had all the patronage and he took care of everybody in the county. This character running against old John Ashmore was saying: 'We have a terrible way here. Morris Ashmore takes the money in, John Ashmore spends it, Bob Ashmore won't prosecute, and Harry Ashmore won't write about it.'"

Ashmore said he was sitting in the supervisor's office in the courthouse talking to his uncle one day and said to him, "John, you're the patriarch of this family as far as I'm concerned, and you've got to know everybody. I can't figure out who in the hell in this county I'm really kin to."

He said John told him, "Son, the way I look at it, you're kin to everybody in this county, white or black, one way or another."

Born July 28, 1916, Ashmore grew up hearing stories about politics and Civil War veterans.

"There was a tradition in Greenville, and I think this was something common across the South, where they reserved the office of coroner for a cripple," Ashmore told us. "It was just traditional for somebody who was handicapped to be elected coroner. And that gave rise to a story I later heard. They had a joint primary, and all the candidates had to speak from the same platform. In the county, they went from town to town, and in the state races they went from county to county. It was a goddamn circus with all of them up there speaking one after the other in rotation.

"This was a meeting somewhere in Greenville County not too long after the Civil War. They called out the candidates for coroner, and the first one stood up with his left arm off at the shoulder, wearing his old Confederate uniform, with the sleeve tucked up, and he told them about how he had lost his saber arm at Shiloh.

"And the next one came out on crutches, wearing his old Confederate uniform and his leg gone. He told them how the Yankees shot it off with a minnie ball in the Wilderness. The third one came out and was practically a paraplegic, and he told them about the terrible time they had in the Tennessee campaign around Lookout Mountain.

"The fourth one came up, and he wasn't even a Confederate veteran. He said, 'Ladies and gentlemen, if I had known that physical disability was a qualification for the office of coroner, all I can say to you is I'm the worst ruptured son of a bitch in Greenville County."

He told us another Civil War story he heard as a boy about Major General John H. Morgan of Kentucky, leader of Morgan's Raiders in the Confederate Army, and his famous mare, Bess.

"Up in Kentucky, some years after the war," Ashmore said, "they decided to erect a statue to the memory of the general. They raised money and got a famous sculptor and created a double life-sized statue of General Morgan on a rearing charger. And they brought it down and erected it, put a shroud on it. Come the dedication day, they had all the old veterans from Morgan's Raiders, had all the old Confederate boys sitting down on the front row.

"Then the governor got up to speak. He made a splendid oration, and it came the time and he jerked the cord, and the shroud fell away from the statue. There was a moment of silence, and one of the old Raiders said, 'God Almighty, they done put balls on old Bess.'"

Ashmore told us he left South Carolina to serve in the Army in World War II, and was a lieutenant colonel in Europe. He took a job with the *Charlotte News* as an associate editor when he returned, then moved to the *Gazette* in September 1947 as executive editor in time to cover the school integration story.

"After we came back from the war, we were all not the same," Ashmore said. "A whole generation had been scattered around the world, and when we came back I had the sense, I began to realize that race was going to be the issue of my time in the South. As a newspaper editor I was going to have to face it. By the time I got out here to Little Rock, I had a strong sense that this goddamn thing was coming pretty fast, and we'd better get ready for it. I found that Hugh Patterson had the same feeling."

Before the Supreme Court's 1954 school desegregation decision, Ashmore got a grant from the Ford Foundation and took a leave from his job to write a book.

"Sometime in the middle of this leave," Ashmore said, "I ran into one of the politicians at the Statehouse, and he said, 'What the hell have you been doing?' I said, 'I'm studying and writing a book.' He said, 'What's the book going to be called?' I said, 'The book is going to be called, *The Negro and the Schools*.' He said, 'Son, sounds to me like you've got yourself in the position of a man running for son of a bitch with no opposition.'"

Like many liberal Southern editors, Ashmore often clashed with conservative state politicians who had a fondness for high living at taxpayers' expense.

"Right after I came here in 1947," Ashmore said, "there was a great fellow named Harold Hollingsworth, a senior member of the House. Harold was chairman of what was called the Efficiency Committee of the House of Representatives. Between sessions, it approved all expenses of the Legislature. They decided they were going to have vote tabulators.

"So the Efficiency Committee started traveling to all the states that had one. The whole committee. And each member had to take a secretary, traveled on the state expense account. To Minnesota and every damn place in the country to look at these voting machines. There was only one company that made them, and there wasn't much to look at. So we were conducting a great, vigorous editorial campaign denouncing this boondoggling. Hollingsworth told our Statehouse guy that they were going down to Havana to inspect the voting machines in the Cuban Parliament."

Ashmore explained that this was in the days before the Cuban revolution ended Havana's extravagant nightlife.

"So somebody here said, 'Check into that.' And we queried AP in Havana, and AP reported back that there were no vote tabulating machines in Havana in the Cuban National Parliament. Our Statehouse man went back to Hollingsworth and confronted him with this revelation that there were no voting machines down there. Harold said, 'Hell, we're going anyway. You can't believe a word them goddamn spics say.'"

When Ashmore was at the *Gazette*, one of the most powerful politicians in Little Rock was Pulaski County judge Arch Campbell.

"His job was running the county," Ashmore told us. "He had been a great drunk. He was an AA in the years I knew him, and I don't think he touched anything at all. But he used to talk about the days when he was really hitting the stuff. There used to be a bar on Market Street called Briels. It had a bar about ninety feet long, literally.

"Arch said that in his drinking days, one morning about ten o'clock, he was coming down Market Street in terrible shape, in bad need of a drink. But he had only thirty-five cents. He came to Briels and looked in there, and the bartender was back there setting things up. So Arch bent his knees so his chin was just above the bar, and he went down the bar to where the bartender was standing.

"The bartender looked up, and Arch ordered a gin fizz, the specialty of the house. The bartender turned around with his back to the bar and put the gin in the cream and broke the egg and started shaking it up and turned around. Meanwhile, Arch had stood up to his normal height. The bartender poured this foaming gin fizz, looked at Arch, then up and down the bar and said, 'Where's that little short son of a bitch who ordered the gin fizz?'

"Arch said, 'I don't know, but I'll tell you what I'll do. It's going flat on you anyway. I'll give you thirty-five cents for it.'"

Ashmore collected political campaign stories from across the South.

"In Greenville," he told us, "old man Tom Henderson was pretty much the county boss and of course was a cousin of the Ashmores. Cole Blease was running in the first primary against a man named Manning. Tom Henderson and the Ashmore family were backing Manning, but he was eliminated in the first primary. In the runoff, Tom Henderson called in everybody and told them they were going for Cole Blease.

"One of them said, 'Goddamn, Mister Tom, last week you said Cole Blease was the worst son of a bitch in South Carolina.' Tom Henderson told him, 'I said that, and he is. But he's our son of a bitch now.'

"You'll hear a lot of variations of that story, but it's the truth."

Ashmore told us a story he picked up when he was working for the *Charlotte News* concerning the re-election campaign of United States Senator Bob Reynolds.

"His opponent was a congressman from the Charlotte district, Cameron Morrison," Ashmore told us. "Morrison was very wealthy, and he had married a very wealthy woman and lived in grand style. Bob Reynolds' device was this fellow had been in Congress and lived at the Mayflower Hotel, had an apartment in the Mayflower Hotel in Washington.

"So Bob would get up with a menu from the Mayflower, and he would start off, 'Let me tell you what old Cameron Morrison eats for breakfast. Here's the menu. He lives there at the Mayflower Hotel.'

"Then he started reading off every item and the price. And he said, 'Looky here, caviar! Cameron, he eats that. You know what that is, folks. That's them red Russian fish eggs. North Carolina hen eggs ain't good enough for Cam Morrison, no sir.'

"He read off every price on the whole breakfast menu, and it came to something like $42.75. Reynolds would exclaim, 'Forty-two dollars and seventy-five cents for breakfast every morning, folks. Most of you don't make that much money in a month.' Which was the God's truth, too. That was old Bob. He won. He was a piss-cutter."

Ashmore had been in Arkansas about a year when Henry Wallace came to Little Rock in 1948. Wallace was running on the Progressive Party ticket for president and couldn't get a place to speak because he insisted that his audience be racially integrated. A radio station owned by the *Gazette* gave him half an hour for an interview by Ashmore.

"By the time they arrived here, they had this entourage of correspondents, and there were blacks with them," Ashmore said. "The Communists were in that thing, you know. By the time they got here, Wallace was in a nervous state. His men had been threatened, and he'd had eggs thrown at him. Across the street from the paper at the time was a Federal Reserve branch bank. We were up on the third floor, and I was looking down when they came up with Wallace. They had a black funeral home limousine, a big old long Cadillac. That was their official car.

"The police had motorcycles outriding, moving around. They were worried about trouble. The black limousine pulled up, and they all piled out and went across the street into the Federal Reserve bank, and the guards were in there—it's a wonder somebody didn't get shot—for they came charging in there like a flying wedge with Wallace. The guards came up with sawed-off shotguns. That shook them up a little. They turned around and came back over here and came up to the radio station.

"I met him, and we went on the air live. We agreed to do half an hour, but did forty-five minutes. We talked about hybrid corn and things like that. And he left with all the correspondents. I went to the window to see them depart. They came down in the flying wedge, they all rushed out and jumped into the big old funeral home Cadillac, and the motorcycles took off with the sirens screaming. The Cadillac didn't move. The next thing I saw, they all piled out, including Wallace, to push it off.

The driver had been sitting out there listening on the radio and had run the battery down.

"The escort was five blocks down the street, but they got it moving and went across the river to North Little Rock to a meeting in the Tobacco Workers Hall, which was the most left-wing union we had. When they got through, they were going to Memphis.

"We had people covering it, and Larry Obsitnik was over there. He was a *Gazette* photographer, and that was the end of the assignment for him. After the meeting, he strolled out of Tobacco Workers Hall and was going to his car over there. He looked around. The entourage had taken off, and they were headed for Memphis, sirens and state troopers up front.

"Larry took a look at this very familiar figure standing there. He took another look, and it was Henry Wallace. They had gone off and left him. Larry put old Henry in his car and went all the way to Brinkley before he could overtake them. Wallace had all these handlers around him, maybe a dozen. There were a dozen or sixteen national correspondents with him. It was a great sight.

During the Central High crisis in Little Rock in 1957, out-of-state newsmen flooded into the city to cover the story.

"They came in here for weeks and weeks," Ashmore said. "I'd go over to the Little Rock Club for lunch, and I'd wind up with eight or ten of them, drinking with both hands, eating lunch. It was genuinely a club, and they couldn't pay for anything. I had to sign the checks, which the paper was paying for.

"Hell, this had been going on for a month or two months, and I suddenly realized when the bill came in from the club it wasn't any higher than it usually was.

"All the attendants at the Little Rock Club were black, including Herbert Douglas, who was the chief bartender. I went over to see Herbert and said, 'I just noticed this bill from the club isn't running any higher than it usually does. I think I know what's happening. I've been bringing all these goddamned newspapermen over here, and you've been writing it off. Y'all can't do that.'

"He said, 'Nah, it ain't hurting the club any. The club is collecting.' I said, 'What do you mean, the club is collecting?' He said, 'We just lay it off on the segs.'

"They had all these goddamn drinks I was signing for, and they had all these drunken segs around. The attendants would add some on this one's bill and some on that one's.

"Herbert ran the Little Rock Club. Of course they had a white manager. It was quite a protected place, since all the gentry was there, so Herbert ran a financial operation on the side. If you wanted to place a few thousand on a horse race, Herbert could accommodate you. Or if you needed a check cashed, you never bothered to go to the cashier. You just wrote the check and gave it to Herbert, and he peeled off whatever you needed. It was marvelous. They called him the Herbert National Bank.

"The day of the Supreme Court school integration decision, Bob Downey, a Little Rock lawyer and one of the public service commissioners, went in there. The decision had been announced on the radio.

"Bob got over about the time the club opened, and Herbert was behind the bar. He said, 'Mister Downey, I just heard this thing on the radio. Give me your opinion. What does this mean, this Brown thing, this Supreme Court decision on Brown?' Bob said, 'Herbert, you black son of a bitch, it means I've got just as much right behind that bar as you have.'"

Ashmore told us of covering a national political convention with Bill Baggs, his friend from the *Miami News*.

"He got the idea that the best credentials to have were those of a chaplain, so he got chaplain's credentials," Ashmore said.

Baggs also put on a priest's raiment.

"We were out covering some demonstration, and Baggs got pushed up against a wall by the crowd," Ashmore said. "Baggs was a big, tall guy with a Georgia Cracker face. And there was a woman in the demonstration pushed up against him, and she looked up and said, 'Father, are you going to pray for us?' Baggs said, 'Yes, madam, and it's going to be a piss-cutter.'"

Most of the out-of-state reporters had never covered the

South and were intimidated by the prospect of facing the angry white mobs.

"Bill Emerson was with *Newsweek* through most of the trouble," Ashmore said. "He is a wild man. He's from Georgia, and he has the most imagination of anyone I've ever known. And all these waves of reporters started coming down, particularly the *Time-Life* people, suave, with their Brooks Brothers suits, didn't know where the hell they were.

"So Emerson would instruct the newcomers in the techniques of covering riots. He told them, 'The main thing to do when you go into one of these towns, take your coat off and turn it inside out, so the lining will stick out. Then you've got to learn how to take notes inside your pocket, and never show a pencil or piece of paper. Before you get all the way into town, rent a hound dog. There'll be one around. Just rent it. Get it going on ahead of you, and keep your head down, and kick the dog every now and then and say, *Get along, motherfucker, get along.*'"

We also looked up Emerson. He was teaching at the University of South Carolina and trying to get a book publishing company off the ground when we interviewed him at his home in Columbia.

"All hell broke loose in Nashville," Emerson told us. "I was walking along through a raging mob in front of the school, and there was this goddamned man with a kind of a sign with a misquote of Ecclesiastes, and it was Reverend Stroud. And Reverend Stroud was haranguing the cops. Stroud was saying, 'Throw your badges away, throw your badges away, you men of God, just don't bow down to these idiot sons of Ham. They got to be put down.'

"He was talking about putting the blacks down, and haranguing the cops. He was a really good demagogue. Naturally, I was attracted to him. I hate bad demagogues. So I got close to him, and talked to him, and he told me where his church was. I said, 'I'm going to want to come by and see you.' He said, 'Good boy, good boy.'

"He was muscular, had great wrists from dunking fat ladies in swift streams, you know. It made massive arms on him. He was a fierce, large man, really fierce, raising hell. So I went back to the hotel, and Murray Kempton."

Kempton was a *New York Post* columnist who once defined editorial writers as "the ones who come out of the woods after the battle and shoot the wounded." Emerson told us that John Popham had saved Kempton's life at an earlier demonstration in McComb, Mississippi.

"How did Popham save him?"

"He was wearing pink walking shorts," Emerson said. "Popham barely saved him from being beaten to death. Murray was wearing these pink walking shorts, and two or three rednecks wanted to take him away for a picnic. They hadn't seen anything that sweet since they'd been to the whorehouse in Memphis two years before.

"Popham hustled him off the streets, grabbed him by the ass and turkey walked him right off the streets into a building somewhere and said, 'We're going to have to find something more conventional for you to wear. These people do not understand your raiment.'

"So in Nashville, Murray came to see me and said, 'Can I go with you to see Reverend Stroud?' Reluctantly, I said, 'Yeah, you can go.' When we got in the church, the reverend was on the phone, in a little dusty study up above his church. He was saying, 'No, no, I don't hate Governor Clement. No, no, no, I don't hate these niggers. No, no, no, I understand theologically. I have a theological concept of all this.'

"Murray Kempton's eyes were bugging out. And Reverend Stroud finally put down the phone and came out and said, 'Who is this fellow?' I said, 'This is Murray Kempton from the *New York Post*.' And he said, 'God, poor damn Yankees. Bill, I'm sorry you brought him, but he's here. First, let us pray.'

"His arm shot out, and he caught Murray Kempton in his great goddamned hand, caught my hand, all three of us, our knees hit the floor, and little spurs of God shot up from the floor. And he said, 'Dear God, forgive this poor simple-minded Yankee here. Doesn't know what he's doing. God, you know I don't hate those niggers, and I don't hate Governor Clement, and I just don't hate.'

"He prayed on, and on, and on, and Murray is over there twitching like a hooked trout. He had not prayed in that sort of embrace before. Murray—it radicalized him, traumatized the hell out of him. He wrote a column later saying, 'Emerson and I are bound together through all eternity by this marvelous, horrible, wonderful prayer.'"

In this period, wherever news was breaking in the South, there was Johnny Popham. Reporters coming new to a story sought out Pop first. He was easy to spot. He was the little man with his hat pushed back on his head who was always where the action was. Pop served as interpreter for his press brethren.

Popham never won a Pulitzer Prize, but his reporting was the most important coming out of the South during this entire period. Popham's brothers in that special fraternity knew it and honored him for it. After the civil rights movement ended, they established a tradition of holding a Popham Seminar every year or so that attracted the best minds of the South to drink, tell stories and exchange ideas. It was the perfect tribute for Popham. He liked nothing better than talking.

It was a hard-drinking fraternity except for Popham.

We found Popham in his *Chattanooga Times* office, although he supposedly was retired.

"I didn't drink for eighteen years," Popham told us. "I had an ulcer. They said I could take a drink or two, but to see that it was well diluted with water. I don't call that drinking. To me, the only way to drink is to be convivial and have several hours."

But when Ralph McGill died, Popham and all his old friends in the press gathered in Atlanta to bury him. Popham took his first drink after eighteen years when they got back from the cemetery.

"I felt convivial, and I felt very upset about McGill," Popham told us. "I missed him a lot. It was time to have a drink."

Popham's tumble from the wagon surprised Ashmore.

"I suddenly looked up," he told us, "and there was Popham

with a double bourbon. I said, 'What are you doing? Are you going to drink that?' He said, 'Yes.' I said, 'It may make you garrulous.' He's been hitting it up pretty good ever since."

When Popham retired, the old friends gathered again, including Ashmore and Emerson.

"Emerson was a great drinking man," Ashmore told us. "He was all liver. At Popham's retirement party, Emerson said, 'The little son of a bitch! Look at him. He saved up his liver for the golden years.'"

30

"God, You Love the Rogues"

JOHNNY POPHAM CLOSED out his newspaper career as an editor, but he had the heart and soul of a reporter.

"One is full of fun and joy, and the other is a goddamn headache," Popham told us in the Virginia Tidewater accent he never lost in his years in China, New York City and Chattanooga, Tennessee.

"Of course when the day is over, as an editor you have so many things to take home and still fuss around with," Popham said. "And the reporter is standing in the door beckoning, saying, *C'mon, Pop, a bunch of us are going up the street for a drink, and we want you to come with us.* Tempting little bastard. You know you can't get through with what you've got to do. And you know damn well if it involves employee relations, when you come back the next day and you make a mistake, that's going to be the first son of a bitch who's going to be after you about it."

We interviewed Popham in his cluttered *Chattanooga Times* office in late April 1978. He was a small, courtly man wearing a tweed coat, khaki pants, tie, white shirt and narrow-brim hat that he kept on while we talked. He had retired as editor several years earlier but told us he still came to his office every day.

Popham was born in Fredericksburg, Virginia, and spent much of his boyhood there before going to China with his family to live in Tientsin and Peking. The son of a career Marine Corps officer, he returned to China as a Marine Corps officer himself in World War II. He grew up a Catholic, his mother's religion, studied law at Fordham University and went to work for *The New York Times* before he graduated.

As a young reporter, Popham covered Murder Incorporated and other New York crime stories, as well as the disappearance of Judge Crater and the Lindberg kidnaping case. He helped found the American Newspaper Guild and walked the picket line.

In 1947, the *Times* made him the first national reporter to cover the South full time. Popham was based in Chattanooga, where the Ochs family founded the *Chattanooga Times* before going to New York and launching *The New York Times*. Refusing to ride in airplanes, Popham drove his car 50,000 miles a year and rode trains to cover the South for thirteen years.

"The South is not monolithic," Popham told us. "There are hundreds of Souths. They are no different from people in other parts of the country. Sometimes they function a little different in the myth-making process. They're very good at it. They are masters. That's a protective device, too, as well as selling you a bill of goods, protective, I guess, in the Faulknerian sense against the agony of despair and the dark night of the soul. I think of a courageous people. If you look at them over a long period of time, with a sense of guilt that race gave them over the years, a sensitive people."

He told us he left *The New York Times* to spend more time with his family. He became managing editor, then editor, of the *Chattanooga Times*.

While we were in his office, Popham got a telephone call from a young woman attending Harvard University, who was writing a thesis about how he covered the South. She told him that she had read all of his stories and wanted to interview him. He agreed to an appointment.

"My wife said, 'You never come home as long there's some son of a bitch to talk to,'" Popham told us. "That's the heart of the business. That's why I did well in the newspaper business. Every day I was working, every hour of the day. You're no stronger than the goddamn information that you get.

"When I first came South, I might cover a speaker at a black college. Hell, they all got Ph.D's. They got them at Ohio State and places like that. I'd write the story for what it was worth and take it to Western Union, and they would say, 'Come on back.' I'd go on back, and around the punch bowl we'd get to talking, and you can imagine what the black man's reaction was. Nobody ever treated them with that courtesy before.

"I stayed with them, and a little later on, a history teacher or English teacher would say, 'Mister Popham, we're going to have a few drinks over at my house later tonight. Would you come over?' I'd say, 'Why certainly.' Ten or eleven or twelve o'clock that night, I can tell you exactly what is in the heart and soul of an educated black man in the South at that moment better than any man in America because I paid that damn price that night.

"From then on, that black man will tell me anything I want to know because I stayed in his house until midnight, maybe two o'clock in the morning. And I wrote honest about it. The second time I go to his house, I take a box of candy for his wife, I bring something for the kids."

Popham saw himself as the only link between the black communities in the South and the outside world. Soon, leaders of the NAACP and other civil rights organizations coming into the South began making Chattanooga their first stop so they could be briefed by Popham. This worked two ways. Popham picked up advance information on the emerging civil rights story, and very little happened that he wasn't the first newsman there.

He also worked the other side of the street.

"Talk to *anybody*, goddammit," Popham said. "Love 'em all."

Popham knew the segregation governors right down to the brand of whiskey they drank. He told us about a time when Georgia's Governor Marvin Griffin was host of the Southern Governors Conference at Sea Island.

"As soon as I arrived, he sent for me," Popham told us, "and said, 'Now, Johnny, goddamn, you know them all here. You're the one we count on. I want you to get me a list. I want you to tap these prohibitionists. Give me a list of all them who drink whiskey. I want to have a bottle in every bed.'"

Popham told us about a time Griffin hailed him in downtown Atlanta and yelled across the street, "Johnny! Johnny! When you coming to see my new Capitol office? Why, it's just as plush as a Persian whorehouse."

From the civil rights leaders, Popham could find out where the action was going to occur next, and he could get the segregation governors to help him cover it.

"I know something is coming up in a town," he told us. "It's a development. I call the governor. I'd say, 'Bill, who do you know down there in that town? Who's your friend? Who's your wheel?' You know, in every little town it was a pharmacist or seed and feed man or some goddamn thing like that. I'd say, 'Tell them I'm coming to town.' The governor would say, 'Oh hell, Johnny, glad to, glad to.'

"The governor would call the fellow and tell him, 'Johnny Popham of the *Times* is coming to town. He's a good friend of ours.' I'd go into the town and get a hotel room, and I couldn't be in the place before the phone would ring. It would be the fellow the governor had called, and he would say, 'I'd like for you to have breakfast with me, Mister Popham.' I'd say, 'I'll be downstairs.'

"I'd eat breakfast, all that kind of stuff, and let people around town see me with Mister Jones. And he'd say, 'This is Mister Popham of *The New York Times*.' And somebody would say, 'We're having a little party at the country club tonight. Like to have you go out there.' And I'd say, 'I'd be delighted.' I'd go out there, and I've got pretty good background, too, in my family. My wife has cousins all over the goddamned South, and I come from four straight generations of Marine officers. I've got something tied everywhere.

"I would play that ballgame a little bit, and by the time that goddamned town blows up, and they're cussing those goddamned Yankee press, this and that, but everybody says, 'He's all right. Mister Popham is a friend of Mister Jones.' I last three days longer than anybody in the fucking town. During those three days, other reporters would ask, 'Pop, how come they don't bother you?' I'd say, 'I'm Mister Jones' cousin.'"

While Popham did more than any other reporter to keep the civil rights movement in the news columns during those early, tough years, Ralph McGill in Atlanta gave the movement its strongest voice on the editorial pages of the South. They were fast friends.

More than any journalist, McGill was despised by the segregationists, who called him "Rastus McGill," a traitor to the South and a Communist. They fired shots into his house, called him at all hours and promised to kill him. In reality, he was a devoted Southerner. McGill was born on a Tennessee hay farm between Soddy and Daisy, thirty miles east of Chattanooga, and attended McCallie Preparatory School in Chattanooga and Vanderbilt University in Nashville, where he played guard on the football team. He joined the Marine Corps in World War I, and anti-war critics of the 1960s and 1970s accused him of wearing his leggings patriotically through the Vietnam protests. He grew up a church-going Presbyterian with a sense of Calvinist guilt.

When the abuse rained down on him, McGill found a cocoon of care in the small fraternity of Southern journalists. As they did with Popham, they gave McGill a special place.

That didn't mean they weren't irreverent about him.

"McGill used to have the worst hangovers of anyone I've ever known," Harry Ashmore had told us in Little Rock. "God, he suffered. I traveled with him a lot. And he'd wake up in the morning and he'd sit there moaning and groaning and he'd say, 'God, I know I've got to pay the piper, but why does the son of a bitch charge me time-and-a-half?' Oh, he would suffer. He said the Hound of Heaven was chasing him and breathing on his neck. He felt guilty all the time."

Popham told us of being in Los Angeles with McGill, Ashmore and Bill Baggs.

"McGill got loaded," Popham said. "Oh, God, he got blind. Baggs finally brought him home about three o'clock in the morning, struggling with him in the elevator. A horrible sight. McGill looked like a beached whale when he got drunk, floundering all over the place. We all stayed at the same hotel. The next morning, we went to breakfast. McGill was hung over and red-eyed. Baggs hadn't shaved and was pissed as hell at having gone to all that goddamn trouble. Finally, we all got on the elevator going down. A lot of people were going down for breakfast. We wore name tags. This fellow was looking at the name tags, and he said, 'Oh, Ralph McGill! Are you carried in Los Angeles?' Baggs said, 'Only at three o'clock in the morning.'"

When we talked with Bill Emerson in Columbia, he remembered McGill as "a very complex man."

"I was devoted to him," Emerson said. "He was reflexively brave beyond belief, a great, stout-hearted person. He went through abuse that would have scared the ordinary person to death. He never even allowed a police guard on the place."

Emerson said he was at McGill's home one night when McGill received a call from someone who said he was from the "Confederate underground."

"The caller," Emerson said, "told McGill, 'We're going to kill your goddamn nigger-loving ass.' McGill said into the phone, 'General Lee, my God, it's nice of you to call. Passing through? I know how busy you are. No, General Lee, don't protest. I really want you to know how I appreciate your calling.'

"This cat went absolutely wild on the phone. When an obscene call would come in to McGill, and nobody was around, he would injure the person's central nervous system. He could be more creatively, electrically obscene than the obscene caller. He could maim the person's psyche. He attacked, struck back.

"But McGill could be wild, frantic. He would get drunk and

raise hell, pull the plug on swimming pools, swing on chandeliers. There would be places he couldn't go back to."

Popham told us, "That was an awful hard life he had to live once he became the so-called conscience of the South. And he was sensitive. I'm sure it hurt like hell. He had his own private problems in life. His wife was ill a great deal. He had his own drinking problem, and he was a man in search of God, a worrier, with a great sense of guilt, you know. He couldn't find any happiness.

"He became an Episcopalian. He probably got enough liturgy, enough Thomistic conversation with a few able clergymen. When he had a chance to do good, he did it so wonderfully well, with such goodness of heart, that I couldn't fault him for anything.

"One year there, he was not allowed by his paper to write a single story on the race question. He couldn't have his column deal with the subject. So he took off. He roamed around the world a great deal, and filed from somewhere else. Mac had the exposure none of the rest of us had. Mac had the daily column. Mac had the honors. We would frequently feed Mac with information, understandings and discoveries we would make in shifting politics, race, so that Mac would be able to pass it on to outsiders. Most of them always came to Mac. That was the network we had.

"Mac had to live under the attacks more than any of us. I think drinking was the story of his life. He had a puritanical, Presbyterian guilt from Soddy and Daisy and McCallie School up in Tennessee. He was a damn good football player. He liked men. And he liked to go out and drink and enjoy the public. He used to write great columns about hound dogs. He liked to sit around the fire at night and drink. He liked the soldierly type.

"Yet at the same time he was a very sensitive, imaginative person. He loved ballet. Ballet was his greatest love. He would go a thousand miles, walking, to see a ballet performance. He was very sensitive to the poor and to the hurt. He turned to drink for his sorrows, I think, more than anything else. It was just out of his life of agony, his makeup, his chemistry, his hurt.

"I live with the same thing, too, but it doesn't bother me. I accept I'm guilty. Hell, there's no goddamn redemption for Pop. I quit worrying about that a long time ago."

Nobody ever enjoyed being a reporter more than Johnny Popham:

"I was a good reporter. I enjoyed the game. I enjoyed the convivial side of it. In this society we live in—I guess it's been true almost since the country was formed—a good reporter must always distinguish between the rogue and the criminal and love and enjoy the rogue. Particularly if you're reporting politics. The rogue's the guy who gets the information for you. He's got a foot in the other camp, he's playing a little bit, he's loose, he isn't quite bad. And your rule with him is, *Joe, I love you, I'm with you all the way. I'll take you right down until they close the gates at Sing Sing. When they do, you and I are through, goddammit, it's all over then.*"

Popham laughed.

"And you know, the guy inevitably has got a little touch of conscience, or he's got a sense of color, imagination. He loves to show what he knows. He wants to talk. Oh, God, you love the rogues. The rogues are what give you the goddamn tie to what's going on. The rogue says, *Come on, have a little drink, talk.*

"Do a little favor for him once in a while, something like his daughter's graduating at Lady of Perpetual Health School, and she's got her First Communion dress on. Get a picture of her in the paper. You've got the Kellys with you forever.

"And for God's sakes, have some of the poet in you, you know—*What rough beast its hour come round at last, slouches towards Bethlehem*—there's always some son of a bitch wants to be born somewhere, you know, for crookedness. Keep an eye on him."

Popham was having a good time, laughing uproariously.

"Keep your eye on him. Watch him. Find out what rogues are fucking with him. Move around. Reporting's a great business, huh? Huh? Figure out how to evaluate the rogue. It's wonderful. The people we're talking about in this business, for the most part, that's the way we lived. We have to carry a certain number of Hollywood columns, you know. There's no skill in a goddamn thing like that. Oh, God, Walter Winchell, he made millions. Anybody can do that. But there's nothing in the world like being a good reporter. And love those rogues. And that's what they don't teach them in those journalist schools at all, to love the rogues."

Index of Names